Palgrave Studies in Relational Sociology

Series editor
François Dépelteau
Laurentian University
Sudbury, Canada

In various disciplines such as archeology, psychology, psychoanalysis, international relations, and philosophy, we have seen the emergence of relational approaches or theories. This series seeks to further develop relational sociology through the publication of diverse theoretical and empirical research—including that which is critical of the relational approach. In this respect, the goal of the series is to explore the advantages and limits of relational sociology. The series welcomes contributions related to various thinkers, theories, and methods clearly associated with relational sociology (such as Bourdieu, critical realism, Deleuze, Dewey, Elias, Latour, Luhmann, Mead, network analysis, symbolic interactionism, Tarde, and Tilly). Multidisciplinary studies which are relevant to relational sociology are also welcome, as well as research on various empirical topics (such as education, family, music, health, social inequalities, international relations, feminism, ethnicity, environmental issues, politics, culture, violence, social movements, and terrorism). Relational sociology—and more specifically, this series—will contribute to change and support contemporary sociology by discussing fundamental principles and issues within a relational framework.

More information about this series at
http://www.springer.com/series/15100

Christian Papilloud

Sociology through Relation

Theoretical Assessments from the French Tradition

Christian Papilloud
Institut f. Soziologie
Halle-Wittenberg University
Halle, Sachsen-Anhalt, Germany

Palgrave Studies in Relational Sociology
ISBN 978-3-319-87943-7 ISBN 978-3-319-65073-9 (eBook)
https://doi.org/10.1007/978-3-319-65073-9

Printed on acid-free paper

This Palgrave Macmillan imprint is published by Springer Nature
The registered company is Springer International Publishing AG
The registered company address is: Gewerbestrasse 11, 6330 Cham, Switzerland

Acknowledgements

This book is an attempt to outline the structure of the theory underlying our work on the development of a relational scheme in sociology based on the example of key debates in the French tradition. We did not choose this starting point by chance, and we want to explain briefly why.

A relational perspective in sociology is a controversial matter for reasons internally and externally related to sociology. On the one hand, "relation" and a "relational perspective" are very concrete events that everybody intuitively figures out in his or her daily life, and that are taken for granted, so that one could wonder why they should need to be explained. On the other hand, in sociology, they tend to be understood as general expressions for other more concrete, well-established terms, such as "interaction" or "process", that are no less taken for granted. This makes it all the more difficult to show that, when we use the terms relation and relational perspective, we are not speaking only of an abstract theory with no practical consequences, and we are not merely reinventing the wheel, using new terms to speak of interpersonal interactions, of processes regulating social actions, or of similar functions holding together social elements like a type of glue. This might be a surprise to some, but in our discipline, this remains the common way to understand and use these terms. To go beyond this common understanding is a difficult task, and could perhaps be seen as a useless one. What would another understanding of relation, and moreover a theory of society through relation bring about? This book aims to give one or two answers to this question.

This book would not have been possible without the help of Thurid Chapman and Jennifer Plaul, who have provided important support by correcting the language, and by establishing the structure of the book. To both of you, my warm thanks.

Contents

CHAPTER 1

Introduction: Sociology Through Relation and Relational Sociology

A book about theories is often an ambivalent work because it has a seductive side, but also some rough edges. On the one hand, it is an invitation to walk through a vast landscape of authors, theories, and concepts fostering insights, leading us sometimes to reconsider our views on some specific object of investigation, and to debate them. On the other, however, there is often a high mountain on the horizon of this landscape that the reader has to climb in order to enjoy the view of that landscape. If we take the viewpoint of the reader, s/he would inevitably ask us: why should we travel with you, what would be the reward for our pain, what would we win in the end? These are legitimate questions, and one way to answer them is to entice our reader with what it feels like to reach the top, with what it looks like at the end of the walk. Therefore, let me give you a foretaste of what you will get at the end of this book. This book delivers an understanding of relation as a macro-phenomenon in society. It appears concretely as a configuration of institutions, organisations, social groups or similar non-personal actors (in this book, they are called "institutions", the reason for which will be explained later) and individual actors. This configuration involves reciprocity between non-personal and personal actors, which requires some explanation.

First, we speak of relation as a macro-phenomenon in order to say that it cannot be reduced to personal interaction(s) between individual actors, even if these interactions obviously contribute to the real existence of a relation. This leads us to our second point: relation

C. Papilloud, *Sociology through Relation*, Palgrave Studies in Relational Sociology, https://doi.org/10.1007/978-3-319-65073-9_1

is a configuration involving reciprocity between non-personal actors or institutions and personal or individual actors. By configuration, we do not mean a context of observable interactions between actors, but an embeddedness of these actors in a reciprocity from which they directly or indirectly benefit. We shall see later that this benefit is not the same for institutions and individual actors—for institutions, it opens new possibilities of expansion; for actors, it means new possible positions within society. In order to speak of the transition from one to another configuration of the relation, we use the expression "cycles of the relation", or "cyclical development of configurations of the relation".

Our third point regards reciprocity. We understand reciprocity as a special relationship that legitimates institutions and personal actors, and whose concrete manifestation is strongly conditioned by the expansion strategies of institutions on the one hand, and to a lesser degree by the personal actors on the other. This leads us to the final point of our explanation: relation is not the product of personal actors. In other words, we understand relation not in the context of a bottom-up perspective, but instead in the frame of a top-down approach. Relation depends on the interplay between the expansion strategies of institutions, which strongly conditions reciprocity between personal actors. Personal actors can also affect this reciprocity, but in order to do so, they must gain in legitimacy. This presupposes that they already have been embedded in a reciprocal relationship with an institution, which in turn presupposes a lot of work of gathering the support of other actors and everything that depends on them, as well as a social position enabling them to do this kind of work efficiently. In this sense, our concept of relation would enable us to understand how institutions have an impact on the life and social careers of personal actors, and how these personal actors can affect the expansion strategies of institutions by contributing to the meaning of reciprocity with the institution and, therefore, to the legitimating operations which these institutions produce. We call this sociological perspective *sociology through relation*.

In many respects, our contribution could be seen as a rehabilitation of reciprocity. This is only partly true, however. We shall see over the course of the book that reciprocity remains an interesting concept in order to describe the meeting point between corporate and individual actors or, more precisely, in order to describe how they meet when they meet. In this book, we provide a detailed analysis of what this "meeting" means. But for now, let us promote the view that reciprocity is only a special concrete relation, materialised in this special circumstance, and nothing else. Therefore, the sociology through relation that proposed here is not some sociology of reciprocity. On the one hand, this is consistent with the attempt to keep the "relation" as something that cannot be reduced to a special kind of relationship, like power relationships or personal interactions. On the other hand, this is also consistent with the opposite consideration that argues that "relation" is society in its most elementary expression. This ontological concept of relation will be discussed, both in this introductory chapter and later in the book. Let us say for now that, once we get rid of such an ontological framework and once we do not consider relation as another word for personal interaction(s), then we can take a lot more activities into account, and we can see how they contribute to the materialisation (or not) of this special configuration where a reciprocity occurs between institutions and personal actors that legitimate them and their activities.

However, it might be asked: is there a point in writing such a book? Relation is, as we know, a concept widely shared in sociology and the social sciences. It can be found in every kind of sociological theory, and one might think that for this reason, everything that we can say about relation has already been said. In this book, we certainly agree with the idea that relation is widely spread in sociology and the social sciences—and this is precisely the problem: if relation is everywhere, it hardly is at the centre of sociological theory. It has hardly been taken into account as the kernel of a corresponding theory, and it hardly leads to a sociological investigation of society through the analysis of this relation. Nevertheless, there have been, and there are, attempts to do so—we might think of relational sociologists, for example, who consider relation as more than interactions only, and who try to promote it to take the centre place in the sociological investigation. In our view, the works of these sociologists make an important contribution to rethinking the relation not only as one sociological concept among many, but as a new way to look at society. In this introduction, an example is used to describe such an attempt. This example enables us to better understand the contrast between a view on relation as a concept among many, and a view that puts relation at the centre of sociological theory. We are, however, not looking at all relational sociologists but will only investigate two debates between the network sociologists inspired by Harrison White, and their critics. Among the latter, we focus on the sociology of relation as conceived by Margaret Archer and Pierpaolo Donati, which criticises network sociology and some of its most important challengers.

This brings us to a second point: what do we mean when we are speaking of "a new way to look at society"? Do we mean that this new way is unprecedented in the sociological tradition? Certainly not. Even if it is hard to find authors whose aim is to deliver a sociology centred on relation, we nevertheless encounter intuitions and fragmented reflections which, once systematised, could lead to such a prospect. This book takes up these threads and proposes their systematisation based on the example of five key debates in the French sociological tradition. This analysis will provide a basis for a theory of relation that understands relation as a macro-phenomenon in society as described above.

* * *

To begin with, however, we have to explain the terminology that we use throughout this book. One of our colleagues once said that this part of the introduction is like mathematics, and this was not a compliment. To some extent, he is right, unfortunately. But explaining the special terms used in this book is unavoidable, if only to avoid misunderstandings.

First, we will not speak of "corporate actors", "organisations", "non-personal actors" but instead of "institutions". We suggest that a sociology through relation should pay attention to institutions—more precisely, to the context of inter-institutional space—in order to understand how these institutions and individual actors contribute to the manifestation of reciprocity, and what the consequences of their success or failure entail for both. We use the word "institution" in a global sense to refer to the non-personal actors who prompt the individual actors to live up to their specific principles, and who consecrate them at the numerous formal or informal stages of such an initiation. Thus, institutions can be social groups (families, associations, or clubs of any kind), public institutions, economic organisations, symbolic entities, and so on. Any sociologist reading these lines will probably ask what the difference between an institution and an organisation actually is. We do not see any fundamental difference between both concepts on the level of their definition. Both presuppose one or several groups of individual actors organised by legal rules and acting in public. With our concept of institution, we want to underline this very aspect of "legal rules" that determine their form and activities, and that is shared by the social groups referred to above.

Second, we have spoken of control, and we will have the opportunity to clarify what we mean by it. But let us say for now that control is neither limited to social control—the pressure to conformity exerted by a social group on individual actors—nor to surveillance. Control refers to a set of dispositions and practical, formal and informal deployments (rules, conventions, guidelines etc.), which contribute to the manifestation of reciprocity. What makes the reciprocity special is that it enables actors to maintain, obtain, and even produce a social position in the transition from one cycle to another of the relation. Therefore from a general viewpoint control is a relational orientation towards reciprocity given to various activities.

Third, we have said that a sociology through relation does not limit itself to existing or manifest social relationships. The actors, personal ones as well as institutions, invest time and effort in various activities that are not only social relationships, and that sometimes are far from being directly linked to social relationships. Nevertheless, such activities also have to be taken into account in order to understand how these actors bring at least some of these activities together, how they mobilise other actors and "mediations"—the word we shall use for material and immaterial things—in doing so, i.e. how they pass on a relational orientation or extend the configuration that the relation is to these other actors, mediations and activities, and how this could lead to a reciprocity with an institution. Extending the relation beyond manifest social relationships, personal networks or concrete interactions, is a good way to underline the amount of work that actors (individuals and institutions) have to perform in order to enter into a cycle of the relation. At the same time, this does not mean that every kind of activity is a relation, but that all activities more or less contribute to a cycle of the relation. We call this process a cycle because the starting and ending points are equally conditioned by the relation as a configuration, i.e. a perspective, an orientation that can be given to actors, mediations or activities, and that embed them in this configuration for a given time. The word "cycle" also assumes a dynamic view on relation, where institutions and personal actors transit from one to another configuration of the relation. Saying that, we assume a relativistic position in sociological theory, considering that the relational perspective is not only a useful tool for the sociologist in order to understand society through the relation, but also for the (personal and non-personal) actors who likewise use this perspective in order to make their everyday life more or less cohesive.

Finally, the same pedagogical intention led us to use another word that often appears in this book: the collective. This synthetic term has no other use than to designate the whole of possible actors in a society, which can be individual or corporate actors, as well as subjects and material or immaterial objects.

As our terminological explanations should now be complete, we can finally come to what is actually at the centre of this introduction, namely the view of the relation as the object *par excellence* in sociology. This is a shared statement in relational sociologies, and at the same time, it is a controversial one. Indeed, relational sociologists often diverge in the way they conceive of this object, and in what theoretical framework they see as most appropriate in order to support a sociology based on a relational scheme. In this introduction, we do not review all relational sociologists supporting theoretical considerations on the relation. Instead, we focus on two key debates that have given a valuable basis for sociologists discussing and working on this question of relation in a theoretical perspective. The first debate has been prompted by Harrison White and his network sociology, the second one by Margaret Archer and Pierpaolo Donati's views on society as relation.

The Relation as Interdependence of Actions

In the broad field of relational sociologies, those considering society as a network of social relationships or as a set of personal interactions generally face the difficulty underlined above, reducing the relation to particular kinds of manifest social relationships. These theories of network benefit from a certain popularity today, which is particularly related to the development of computer software for social sciences, allowing representations of society in the form of exchanges and interactions. In their more formal aspects, these theories use mathematics (in particular linear algebra) and statistics to develop methods and measures to understand the meaning of these exchanges and interactions, and the way in which they aggregate individuals and institutions.[1] The relation is a concept that network sociologists take as a starting point in order to rethink, on a more concrete basis, the concept of social structure. This link between relation and structure goes back to Harrison White, the founding father of network analysis.

White's starting point is his own frustration with quantitative sociology, which, in his opinion, is not able to adequately link the individual actor and social structure. He says that "the study of persons is not effectively joined to the analysis of social structure" (White 1970, 4), and on this basis, he develops his famous model of the "vacancy chain". This is a mathematical model among other "opportunity chains models" (ibid. 16, 245ff.) allowing us to explain the professional mobility of actors in the USA not based on employees or on their work, but on the transition from one job to another. White's key argument for such a perspective is to get rid of the concept of social structure—in the example of the "vacancy chains", this is the structure of occupational mobility—viewed as a set of positions occupied by individual actors, whereby these positions and actors are described by using a ready-made classification of occupations and several individual attributes (social, economic, demographic, for example). Rather than to assign *a priori* categories to the object of the sociological inquiry, the sociologist must start from the actors' manifest social relationships to their professional employment. He must examine how the structural properties of these relations highlight regularities that allow him to understand and explain a set of relations—a network—that provides a more realistic picture of the structure of occupational mobility at a given time.[2] For White, a manifest social relationship is, in its elementary form, a social relationship which exists concretely between two actors. This relationship is of a particular type (for example, friendship or membership) and, therefore, only makes sense when the actors have more or less the same understanding of what the relationship type means (cf. Schmitt and Fuhse 2015, 31–35). This basic conception of the social relationship as a dyadic concrete relation in a context of shared meanings is found today in almost all sociological works on formal networks. It stimulates various debates in sociology, some confined to the new quantitative methodologies that White has developed,[3] others specifically related to the relation. These latest debates are the ones in which are of interest in this introduction, and which bring us to the heart of the first controversy. This was initiated by Mustafa Emirbayer, a friend of White, who wondered about the way in which White sees the link between relation and culture in the framework of his network theory. Starting from a formal—mathematical—scheme of networks and social relationships, White more or less left aside the problem of culture, namely the sense of the relations for the actors involved in them which cannot be reduced to a concrete link between actors. Instead, White focuses on the structural properties of social relationships. White tried to correct this in his book *Identity and Control* (1992), where he proposes to view culture as a set of material and non-material resources that actors can mobilise in order to better control their actions (White 1992 (2008), 232–233; Bothner et al. 2004, 283). Culture becomes a system of meanings, which is nevertheless, even if not reduced to the system of manifest social relationships, interconnected with this latter system (White 1992 (2008), 376). However, what does this interconnection mean? This is the point underlined by Emirbayer when he says: "White is certainly correct in asserting that cultural (as well as political) discourses do inform—and are deeply embedded within—network patterns of social relationships...yet there is another—and itself no less critical—sense in which cultural discourses, narratives, and idioms are also analytically autonomous with respect to network patterns of social relationships" (Emirbayer and Goodwin 1994, 1438).

For Emirbayer, culture is not an integral part of social relationships. On the contrary, culture has an autonomous structure which differs from that of the networks of social relationships. Therefore, culture can influence these networks either in a compulsory way, by forcing their development in a particular direction or, on the contrary, by supporting their development.[4] In a similar sense, Abbott extends Emirbayer's critique when he speaks about the encoding of actors' practices and activities in line with the practices and activities of other actors in society, an encoding whose success or failure determines whether or not social relationships are built.[5] Following Abbott—and if we pay attention to these operations of encoding—we cannot say, like White, that social relationships and culture are interconnected. Moreover, we understand what it is that is still difficult about the concept of relation in White's network sociology, namely that relation as a concept or as an analytic tool in sociology depends on the theoretical framework of action used in order to conceptualise the relation itself. This is not surprising.[6]

Indeed, it must not be forgotten that White's network theory is in part a critique of the theory of action supported by American rational choice theories, a critique that, however, does not suppose a radical rejection either of the theoretical framework of the action, or of rational choice theories: "As causal guides, means-ends schema can lead afield, but the impetus to adopt rational choice theory is natural in a scientific frame" (White 1992 (2008), 136). This is why "Rational pursuits along means-ends chains remain important" (ibid.).[7] Nevertheless, the way in which the action is understood by rational choice theorists must be put into perspective:

> Ends, and means-ends chains, are perfectly sensible constructs, but they are only of tactical help in uncovering social action. That is the practical objection to rational action theory, and also to many other role theories. An actor's social existence comes to pass only through embeddings that specify ends as well as support identity, embeddings that are matters of friction and mismatch rather than of induction into roles. Rationality should be seen primarily as a by-product from reading larger-scale patterns. Recognising context is the crux. (ibid.)

This way of understanding action is no longer in accordance with the succession of means-ends chains but, as contexts of meanings, leads White to extend his critique towards the sociological concepts of social structure. On the one hand, and against the structuralists, a context of meanings is not "decisive by itself in isolation" (ibid. 137). On the other hand, taking the context of meanings into account indicates that White's network theory does not seek causalities but dependencies between the actions produced by actors in specific contexts of meanings that combine these actions. In White's terms:

> Ends are supplied stochastically by the shifting embeddings in which actors are caught up over time. These same embeddings also frame means-ends chains, which can be important in much the way presumed by rational choice theorists, although more care is needed in specifying the dual embeddings in physical and social space. But such chains are limited in scope by their embedding; they show dependencies, not causalities. (ibid.)

From this viewpoint, the social relationship as a manifest relationship is nothing else than the interdependence of actions which occur in a given context of meanings—in the most strictly Weberian sense of *Sinnzusammenhang*.[8] We also find a relativist use of the action's framework in Emirbayer and Mische, particularly in their idea of network sociology as highlighted in their common article about the concept of "agency", which heavily draws on George H. Mead's action theory, as well as on the phenomenological sociologies inspired by Alfred Schütz. For Emirbayer and Mische, "agency" is "the temporally constructed engagement by actors of different structural environments—the temporal-relational contexts of action—which, through the interplay of habit, imagination, and judgement, both reproduces and transforms those structures in interactive response to the problems posed by changing historical situations" (Emirbayer and Mische 1998, 970). Their concept of agency "is intrinsically social and relational" (ibid. 973) in the sense that it allows an understanding of how "actors have to mediate the structuring contexts within which action unfolds. We have referred to this perspective as relational pragmatics" (ibid. 1012).

According to Emirbayer, this concept of agency extends and clarifies his critique of White's network sociology. Yet, the links between social relationships and culture are not only explained by the way in which culture as a structure supports or forces these relationships. Such links are constantly mediated by actors, and it is at the level of these actors and their actions that the sociologist can see if culture supports or constrains social relationships. The actors produce these links in a dialogue with other actors (ibid. 974). They use habitual schemes of action to project themselves into the future, and to face the present. Regarding the relation, the idea remains that it is a formal context of typical links, i.e. of actions sharing common meanings resting on analogous cultural value. In other words, what Emirbayer and Mische emphasise and contribute with their concept of agency is less a concept of relation than attention to the time dimension of agency, which should explain why there is no direct link between actors and social structures, and why relation cannot be identified with personal interactions only. This rests on a general argument that Margaret Archer has made famous, saying, "structure and agency can only be linked by examining the interplay between them over time, and…without the proper incorporation of time the problem of structure and agency can never be satisfactorily resolved" (Archer 1995, 65).[9] This reference to Archer's agency and actionalist viewpoint is not trivial. It does not only point at an affinity of viewpoints between Archer and Emirbayer. It also accentuates that, for Emirbayer, relation actually means a formal link of interdependence between actions.[10] Thus, it is not surprising to read in Emirbayer's manifesto for a relational sociology that such a sociology should support a "relational point of view on social action" (Emirbayer 1997, 282).[11] Emirbayer certainly delivers a complete critique of White's network sociology, joining to some extent Abbott's consideration on encoding and, more generally, on the actors' strategies. Nevertheless, his relational sociology, as White's network sociology, depends on an underlying relativist theoretical framework of action from which Emirbayer deducts the relation, before putting the concept of relation aside, in order to promote the concept of "transaction" instead. As Emirbayer says, "In this point of view, which I shall also label 'relational,' the very terms or units involved in a transaction derive their meaning, significance, and identity from the (changing) functional roles they play within that transaction. The latter, seen as a dynamic, unfolding process, becomes the primary unit of analysis rather than the constituent elements themselves" (Emirbayer 1997, 287). The transaction, a concept that links up to the heritage of John Dewey and Arthur Bentley, is for Emirbayer similar to a "mutual commitment" (ibid. 310). Moreover, it has the advantage of putting agency, actors and their actions in the centre of relational sociology.[12] The transaction is a kind of dialogue, of negotiation, of "interplay", as Archer says, between individual actors and social structures, which conditions the orientation of the action and therefore the association between the action of one actor and the action of other actors, taking them up in the same context of meanings, i.e. in the same culture.

Nevertheless, these affinities between Emirbayer's relational manifesto and Archer's morphogenesis do not lead to a convergence of the two perspectives. Archer is rather close to another kind of relational sociology proposed by the Italian sociologists close to Pierpaolo Donati. Donati also sees the relation as the prior object in relational sociology, but he instead gives it an ontological status and a foundation in reciprocity.

The Relation as Reciprocity

In her article "Critical Realism and Relational Sociology" (2010), Archer details the convergence between her morphogenetic approach to society and Donati's relational sociology. She also explains why their concept of relation has nothing in common with that of White, network sociologists, and Emirbayer (Archer 2010, 199–207). For Archer, these sociologists conceive of the relation as a simple link "such as the statistical relations established between independent variables at the empirical level" (ibid. 202). According to Archer, the relation is much more than a link, and much more than a concrete interaction (ibid.). The relation is primarily characterised by reciprocity. It is an emerging phenomenon that cannot be reduced to interpersonal relationships, and it fits in a humanistic idea of society where social relations not only connect human beings, but express their desire to live together (ibid. 203–204).

Archer attributes this concept of relation to the Italian sociologist Donati, in particular to his *Teoria relazionale della società* (1991), in which Donati proposes to consider society from the viewpoint of social relationships, even to see society as relation.[13] For Donati, this first means to define the relation as the cardinal object of sociology, saying that:

> Social relation could not occur or exist without a minimum of gratuitousness (to enter into a social relation is, to some extent, already a form of gift). The analogy states that what is valid for the individual cell and for the entire psycho-physical body is also valid for individual social relations and for the entire society (understood as the whole set of particular relation systems). Therefore, the analogy holds true for generalised social relation, if and to the extent to which the relation is human. Social relation may occur without gratuitousness, but then—although it may be social—it is not human, it is something else (and it must be noted here that no value judgement is implied, but only a factual description) since it is mechanical, impersonal behaviour with no intentionality. (Donati 2003, 249)

Donati's relational sociology is motivated in the first place by a critique of Talcott Parsons' Adaptation, Goal Attainment, Integration, Latency (*AGIL*) scheme, which defines the structure of social action.[14]

Against Parsons' *AGIL* scheme, Donati opposes a structure of the relation as, first, a link between at least two individual actors. This is "the semantic of the religo (the operation of 'connecting')" (ibid. 256), which refers to "a significant symbolic purpose" (ibid. 255).

Second, relation is an "emerging effect" (ibid. 256), meaning that it "constitutes the subjects in relation" (ibid.). This allows Donati to conclude, "What is in play is pure giving of oneself to the Other. This is the source of society as relation" (ibid.). This pure and free gift is the "motor of reciprocation" (ibid. 257). The unilateral act of giving the gift—with the risk that the gift is given in pure loss—becomes the motivation of reciprocity which puts the relation in a dynamic exchange where the relation cannot be restricted to the pure donation but becomes something other than a gift like, for example, a relation of competition between actors. This is why Donati speaks of the internal structure of the relation, which is based on the coordination of four concepts—"value, norm, intention, means employed" (ibid.)—this coordination being what Donati calls the "reflexivity" of the relation (ibid.). A relation that comes from the act of free giving has to be contrasted in terms of its internal structure with other relations that are not motivated by the free gift. These are Hetero-nomy, Instrumental, Auto-nomy, Gratuitous (*ESAG*) relations, whose structure is made up of the coordination between autonomy and heteronomy on the one hand and disinterestedness and instrumentality on the other (ibid. 257–258). Therefore, the relation is still fundamentally motivated by an action, the free gift. But this action takes a particular meaning depending on the empirical contexts of its production (either the free gift is performed for itself—autonomy—or it is performed in order to acquire other relations—heteronomy), and to the corresponding meaning of these contexts (either the relation is purely disinterested, or it is performed to acquire other ones).

A first lesson that can be drawn from the double structure (internal and external) of the relation is that Donati shares with White and Emirbayer a relativist idea of action—here in the form of a free donation inspired by the gift, as conceptualised in Marcel Mauss' essay *The Gift* (1925). However, Donati does not support the contextual statement of White and Emirbayer, and he says instead that "society does not host relations, it is not a space-time where relations happen, it is relations" (Donati 2011, XV). In Donati's sociology, this statement—society is relation—is understood as an ontological view of social relations. Social relations are "a sui generis reality" (ibid. XVI) and, at the same time, the reality in which we live, a reality which is in itself not contingent. In his dialectical argument, Donati argues:

> To carry the relation to the level of a primary, general presupposition in the metaphysical environment of knowledge does not imply in any way assuming the absolute contingency of the social world. Similarly, it does not imply any accommodation to a type of ontology which denies the human being or social subject. On the contrary, it means assuming that the relation has its own non-contingent 'root', whilst it unfolds in contingency. (Donati 2011, 17)

This idea of a "non-contingent 'root'" is very important in Donati's argument because it means that the relation is a permanent link constituting the social as "the product of reciprocal actions of subjects-in-relation with each other" (ibid. 42, 62 and 122 for similar formulations).

Yet, let us observe that between Donati's first concept of the relation based on the act of free giving, and his later ontological perspective on the relation, there is a shift. Indeed, the relation no longer comes from the act of free giving, but rather from reciprocity, as Donati is freeing himself from a theoretical framework based on theories of action. In addition, the ontological perspective which supports this new foundation of the relation in reciprocity becomes a transcendental ontology in resonance with Archer's critical realism. Indeed, Archer and Donati share the idea that reciprocity produces some effects which do not only affect the actors in relation, but also lead to other relationships[15]—this is the complete scheme of the reflexivity of the relation.

This evolution of Donati's position can be better observed in the book that he and Archer wrote together on *The Relational Subject* (2015). Reciprocity is regarded as what "creates (activates and reactivates, generates and regenerates) a social relationship as such, for the super-functional value that it has" (Archer and Donati 2015, 249). The free gift is "different. It consists in recognizing the otherness of the alter, whose 'existence' as a subject is endowed with his or her own dignity…it is found inside the (limited or expanded) circuits of reciprocity. There it takes on the role of the 'motor' (initiator, activator) for exchange and social binding" (ibid. 250). However, this distinction lacks clarity because in the same paragraph the authors claim,:"Where there is no expectation of (direct or indirect, immediate or delayed) reciprocation, there you have a gift relationship" (ibid.). We therefore have to ask what it is that stabilises this transcendental ontology of the relation. Is it reciprocity, or is it the free gift?

For Archer and Donati, there is no need to ask such a question because "Reciprocity and free giving are two ways of acting united by the fact that they share a certain anti-individualism, a certain anti-utilitarianism, and a certain orientation to horizontality (that is, to a non-hierarchical reticular action)" (ibid.). If we leave aside the idea that reciprocity as well as the free gift suppose "horizontality" between actors but not hierarchy (we shall come back to this argument later), we nevertheless observe two difficulties with this argument.

The first one regards reciprocity and the free gift as two normative ways of acting, in the sense that to give a gift or to be in reciprocity with other actors presupposes an anti-utilitarian and anti-individualistic attitude on behalf of the actors. This seems to contradict the idea that the attribute of a relation that makes it a special relationship in respect to other ones, is not given *a priori*, but comes from the forms that the actors give to it—an idea elsewhere defended by Donati (2011, 44).[16]

The second difficulty comes from the fact that, by considering reciprocity and the free gift as two ways of acting, the relation is no longer the foundation of relational sociology—the framework of the action comes back to help to conceptualise the relation. If, as Archer and Donati propose, the relation should motivate an ontological perspective on society, then this ontology is ambiguous. Archer and Donati attempt to circumvent this ambiguity by proposing to give the relation another basis that is no longer the free gift or reciprocity but the distance between individual and corporate actors. As they say, "between two (or more) entities there is a certain distance which, at the same time, distinguishes and connects them" (Archer and Donati 2015, 37). However, the ambiguity remains since speaking of a distance whence the relation would emerge is actually saying that the relation emerges from a form of the relation that is this distance itself. This is not a dialectic argument, but it is based on the Greek etymology of the word "distance", which means "form". In this sense, the relation would be nothing more than the emergence of manifest social relationships from other/past manifest social relationships.

We have seen that this is the opinion more or less supported by White and Emirbayer, whom Archer and Donati vigorously reject. Indeed, in their opinion, these sociologists either do not propose a proper concept of relation, or they do not take social structures into account, other than those that manifest social relationships produce.[17] So, what is relation for Archer and Donati? Is it some metaphysical, extra-social entity, or the emergence of concrete relationships from other concrete relationships? To add to this ambiguity, Archer and Donati eventually take up the definition of the relation based on reciprocity. As they say, "If we conceptualise the social relation as reciprocal actions between Ego and Alter in a social context, the relation can be regarded either from the subjective side (of Ego and Alter, respectively) or as an objective reality existing between the two" (ibid. 26). How should we understand this succession of proposals, namely that reciprocity is at the base of the relation, that it starts with the interpersonal manifest social relationships between two actors, which is, however, a point of view that Archer and Donati themselves criticise?[18]

In *The Relational Subject*, the authors provide no analytical justification for these successive statements, but only a rhetorical one. Indeed, on the one hand, this idea of reciprocity allows Archer and Donati to contrast their views on the relation with the contributions of classical sociologists, and to mark their own difference to these sociologists. On the other hand, it allows Donati to maintain his double structure of the relation which assumes reference to a symbolic order, and which leads to the emergence of other relations, as well as to other actors in relation (ibid. 27–28). This rhetoric strengthens the link between the critical realism of Archer and the relational sociology of Donati where the double structure of the relation and its roots in reciprocity constitute the base of Archer's morphogenesis. The relation in the sense of Donati generates actors, societies and other relations (morphogenesis), leading to actions which can be reproduced (morphostasis), and between which causal links can be reconstructed. For Archer and Donati, this causality is inherent in the emerging character of the relation (in other words, at its reciprocal root), which generates actors, societies and relations in a context, i.e. in a frame or a specific structure.

This causality is not necessarily empirically given—for example, a child can learn from his parents, but what he has learned from them cannot be reduced to the behaviour of his parents towards him (ibid. 49, note 64). This causality does not only affect actors in relation, but also other relations that such a relation generates, and even wider contexts such as groups, institutions, organisations, societies, cultures emerging from them (ibid. 118).

As for the relation, this flexible concept of causality is similar to the way in which for example Emirbayer conceives the relation, namely less in terms of causal chains of actions than in terms of contexts of social relationships taking similar meanings. As we can see, despite the authors' effort to mark their difference, their concept of the relation not only converges on many points with the sociologies of White and Emirbayer. In addition, it highlights a difficulty similar to that faced by these sociologists—seeing the relation as the cardinal object in sociology—the "what"—instead of delivering a sociology of social phenomena through the relation—the "how" question.

As mentioned above, this is a difficulty because in saying "relation", we use a concept that has neither defined boundaries nor a specific conceptual content, but is rather a collective word (like society) that can depict various realities at various levels. It is certainly true that in saying "relation", relational sociologists want to escape the holistic and individualistic perspectives in sociology (Degenne and Forsé 1999, 4–5; Mische 2011, 83; Archer and Donati 2015, 277). Nevertheless, it is not sufficient, and our review of the positions taken by White, Emirbayer, or by Archer and Donati, shows this. White and Emirbayer do not escape the individualistic framework because their concept of the relation is anchored in the theoretical framework of action, and it supposes that at least two actors are acting in order to develop a manifest social relationship. Archer and Donati do not get out of the holistic framework because they think that relation is society, ultimately founded in reciprocity, and globally framed in an ontology. Today, like yesterday, we are then in a paradoxical situation where there are debates about an object—the relation—which tends to be substantiated in one way or another. In order to legitimate this substantiation, the authors often refer to the sociological tradition. Possibly the best example of such a reference concerns Georg Simmel.

Georg Simmel or How to Link Relation with Sociological Tradition

If there is a sociologist who has particularly been considered as the promoter of relation as a concept and a perspective in sociology, it is Georg Simmel. Let us first look at the way in which White and network sociologists inspired by him consider Simmel's contribution to the question of the relation.

It is interesting to note that Simmel, even if he is seen as the initiator of an understanding of society as a network of relations (White et al. 1976, 730; Breiger 1990, 453–476), is not necessarily strictly considered as the founder of this perspective, but rather as a sociologist who delivered key concepts that influenced such a perspective. Any such reference to Simmel must therefore be made with caution, even if these sociologists do not always avoid distorted judgements. For example, they often include Simmel in the great family of American interactionists (e.g. Grossetti and Bes 2003, 43), or they promote him to head of the German formal school and see in Leopold von Wiese the founder of the so-called Cologne School in German sociology (e.g. White et al. 1976, 730; Fuhse 2006, 245–263; Fuhse and Mützel 2011, 1068ff.). However, it has long been known that Simmel was never an interactionist (Levine et al. 1976, 813–845), that he did not propose a concept of relation (Becher 1971), that he was not the founder of a German formal school of sociology, and that von Wiese was neither his student, nor one of his followers, but instead one of his most determined critics (Wiese 1910, 882–907). Network sociologists are too optimistic by far in assigning interrelationalist attributes to Simmel and tend to recruit him to their cause too quickly. Let us take as an example the Simmelian concept of "circle" mentioned by these same sociologists in order to say that Simmel had some proto-concept of what we call today "a network".

The circle demonstrates how individual actors are embedded in many social groups within which they assume different roles. This observation is not entirely misleading. Actually, Simmel's concept of circle makes sense in network sociologies because it suggests that individual actors do not have to be seen as isolated, but instead as embedded in several social circles and, therefore, in relationships.

However, this is not exactly the contextual meaning of the "circle" emphasised by Simmel when looking at social circles. Instead, Simmel takes on the social Darwinism promoted in his time by Albert Schäffle (cf.

Dahme 1988, 4), according to which considering individual actors from the viewpoint of social circles allows us to better understand how they develop a personal life (Simmel 1890 (1989), 191). The social circle and, by extension, society (which Simmel uses as a pedagogical concept only, not as an analytical tool) provide individual actors with countless resources with which to develop their personalities. Because individual actors are embedded in groups, we can observe a great diversity of individual actors, as well as of social groups. This emphasis enables Simmel to underline two complementary aspects of social differentiation—a concept also coming from Darwinism—where the differentiation of social groups goes hand in hand with the differentiation of individual personalities, and vice versa (Simmel 1908 (1992), 485).

Social differentiation certainly links to a kind of relation *lato sensu*. But for Simmel, the social circle tells us, above all, about the complementarity between the two processes of differentiation. It refers to a broad and abstract context—therefore Simmel says "circle", and not "groups"—that exceeds by far the context of manifest social relationships between individual actors and social groups or personal networks. Moreover, for Simmel, these social circles develop concentrically. This is a point of detail, but its importance is generally missed: the more the group differs in time and space, the more its hierarchy becomes visible to the individual actors inside and outside the group. In other words, differentiation of social circles always supposes a hierarchical structuration of the social groups, which has consequences for the manifest social relationships between these actors and these groups. These nuances do not discredit the way in which network sociologists anchor their perspective in Simmel's sociological considerations. Nevertheless, they indicate that we must not try to look for something in Simmel's sociology that is not there, namely a concept of relation, or the idea that manifest social relationships are at the core of the sociological inquiry. Simmel does not promote a concept of relation in his sociology, and according to him, the core object of sociology is actually social forms—or in other words, the forms enabling the socialisation of actors in society. Yet, Simmel proposes something else in sociology that is related to a perspective on society through relation, for which he uses, among other concepts, the *Wechselwirkung* which Donati puts in the foreground in his relational sociology.

As Donati says, "Georg Simmel's 'relational turning-point' can be considered the very beginning of a proper relational theory in sociology" (Donati 2011, 6), an observation which is not self-evident. Which "relational theory" is he referring to? For Donati, this means above all that for Simmel, "As is well known, the fundamental theoretical category…was the social relation. According to him this category should be understood as interaction" (ibid.). Above, we have already seen the inadequacy of this kind of statement; therefore, we are not returning to it but are going beyond it.

> For Simmel, a phenomenon is social to the extent that it expresses a particular and sui generis character that is its 'constituent': namely, the fact of being an inter-relation, or inter-dependence, or better still a reciprocal effect or an 'effect of reciprocity'. All these terms are included in the concept of *Wechselwirkung*. For Simmel, the social phenomenon is neither ***a priori*** an emanation from a subject, nor a product of an abstract system. The social is the relational as such, that is, reciprocal action, inasmuch as it produces interaction, is incorporated and manifested in something that, even though non-observable, has its own solidity. Unfortunately, in Simmel this 'solidity' is not sufficiently well clarified. Instead, the category of *Wechselwirkung* becomes a metaphysical principle. (ibid.)

Donati clearly highlights one of the fundamental aspects of the meaning of *Wechselwirkung* in Simmel's works, which indeed evokes something like an effect of reciprocity.

But let us begin with the literal sense of the word *Wechselwirkung*. It means "effect" (*Wirkung*) which, in itself, becomes a cause producing an effect back in the original cause, i.e. cause and effect are switching places (*Wechsel*). All changes thus involved do not have to be understood as changes of roles only, but as global transformations at the levels of individual actors and of society, turning both of them towards each other. *Wechselwirkung* is, in this literal and general sense, a principle of non-indifference on the side of (personal and non-personal) actors, which describes how they turn towards each other, and which stems from a "general life energy" (e.g. Simmel 1908 (1992), 1992, 130–144). *Wechselwirkung* is, for Simmel, not a principle of interdependence or inter-relationship because, and this is an important point, Simmel's *Wechselwirkung* expresses changes that a possible reciprocity would bring about. These changes and this reciprocity are conditioned by a possible relationship, which, at the level of the *Wechselwirkung*, does not exist in reality as a manifest social relationship. What makes this relationship exist are social forms, or *Vergesellschaftungsformen*. What makes these social forms aggregate more actors, mediations, and activities in society is their circulation, which concretely happens in the exchange or *Tausch* of these forms in society.

Now, we better understand what Simmel's "'relational turning-point'" means, namely that the relation is not an empirical process, but an analytical perspective which claims to take into account *Wechselwirkungen*, *Vergesellschaftung* and exchange (*Tausch*) all together, in order to understand the aggregation (and disaggregation) of actors, mediations, and activities. These concepts give form to a cycle that does not begin with reciprocity as a concrete manifestation of the movement of (material and immaterial) mediations between (personal or non-personal) actors, but rather ends with reciprocity.

From this point of view, it is true—and Donati emphasises this—that the basis on which *Wechselwirkung* rests "is not sufficiently well clarified" (Donati 2011, 6). But this is not because it does not exist. It is because *Wechselwirkung* refers in its simplest expression to a "general energy of life" (Simmel 1995, 39–118), whose *Wechselwirkung* is only an abstract expression. This general energy of life is based on the dialectic of elective affinities between social actors, of attraction and repulsion, which never come to any sort of synthesis (Landmann 1987, 16).[19] Therefore, *Wechselwirkung* is, on the one hand, a first step in the concrete development of a manifest social relationship as Donati says (cf. also Utz and Krämer 1994, 21; Pyyhtinen 2010, 7, 75), and, on the other (and contrary to Donati's affirmation; cf. Donati 2011, 7) *Wechselwirkung* is not the relationship *in statu nascendi* in the form of "'events' or pure 'emergent phenomena'" (ibid.). This is simply because the dialectic of attraction–repulsion does not lead to the spontaneous generation of such concrete relationships. *Wechselwirkung* and, *a fortiori*, relation are not a kind of synthesis out of such a dialectic.

But why, we ask ourselves, is *Wechelwirkung* the one but not the other? Because, for Simmel, the relation is less an object than an orientation given from subjects and objects to other subjects and objects—be they human and non-human, or material and immaterial. It is a perspective that actors collectively develop with other actors, mediations, and activities in bringing them together in a specific configuration which concretely expresses this perspective. By doing so, they put them in contact, they mobilise them to bring about concrete relationships as we will say later in this book, and to eventually build a reciprocity together. This presupposes a lot of work at the level of socialisation and exchanges between these actors, mediations, and activities. For Simmel, this understanding of society not as relation, but through relation, is not only the analytical perspective that the sociologist takes in order to investigate social phenomena. It also is the practical perspective through which all (personal and non personal) actors live, do, feel, experience society. They extend this perspective to other actors, mediations and activities in order not only to live more, but also in order to do more than to only live in society—to develop a personality, as we mentioned in the context of the social circles above.

In passing, such considerations enable us to stress the differences between Simmel and von Wiese, the latter making the relation a reality while giving it a formal and an ontological status at the same time—a proposal which has much in common with the theoretical framework that Archer and Donati deliver. However, von Wiese develops his approach against Simmel, in the assumed sense of a formalist sociology which should ideally accurately record the original social forms of the relation present in every society and culture. This way of giving society an ontological origin reflected in the fundamental forms of the relation is a prospect that Simmel has never had, because such a prospect does not make sense in the framework of sociology through the relation. For Simmel, the aim is not to deliver a catalogue of the fundamental forms of the relation and neither is it to make the relation the essence of society.[20] These brief considerations do not make the task easier when it comes to building a theoretical framework able to do justice to a sociological perspective on social phenomena through the relation. But they at least highlight a number of difficulties, which need to be tackled.

First, what impairs this kind of perspective is the ongoing use of one or other theory of action that aims to deliver a concept of relation. We have particularly seen this in the case of White and Emirbayer, with the side effect that the relation is then more or less reduced to manifest social relationships. Even if this is less the case with Archer and Donati, who counterbalance the scheme of action (as the action of free giving) with reciprocity, they also have to deal with another side effect, which is to overextend the relation to society in the framework of an ontology.

Second, these difficulties can be traced back to using the sociological tradition in order to find support and legitimisation for the kind of relational sociology to promote. Using the example of Simmel, we have not only seen how both parties tend to take Simmel's relational perspective in support of their concept of the relation. We have also seen that their use of Simmel does not really take into account what Simmel intends with his triptych of *Wechselwirkung*, *Vergesellschaftung*, *Tausch*, which is not to define the relation, but to build a perspective allowing a description of social phenomena through relation. So, what is the point of delivering such a perspective?

For Simmel, the point is to understand cohesion—cohesion of a group of actors, as well as cohesion of historical tendencies, personal will, even life in the frame of his philosophy of life. Such cohesion refers to the way in which Simmel conceives *Wechselwirkung*, as a tool to describe a collection of opposite tendencies remaining together without leading to emergent phenomena, but building a social form. This social form is fundamentally a social distance that, at the same time, brings actors, mediations and their activities together. However, there is a difficulty—such a prospect is not a dominant topic in Simmel's works, and it is not limited to sociology. This is one of the main reasons why Simmel's relational perspective cannot be taken as a theory. Rather, Simmel provides useful insights pointing to the analytical context in which a sociology through relation can be useful, namely the problem of social cohesion. But Simmel does not address social cohesion as a problem, which, if we turn back to the sociologists so far discussed, remains critical when it comes to the social order and, in the end, to the society that the relation is supposedly bringing about. In this context, French sociologists are often seen as having delivered key insights—particularly the sociologists affiliated to Émile Durkheim. In this regard, Donati as well as White and Emirbayer stand out somewhat as Donati refers to Durkheim's nephew Marcel Mauss, and uses his essay on *The Gift* to promote his view on society as relation, while White and Emirbayer refer to Durkheim in support of their view on social structure (White et al. 1976, 1442), and agency (Emirbayer and Goodwin 1994, 1438–1439; Emirbayer 1996, 109–130). However, can French sociology reconcile the questions of relation and social cohesion? And, if so, would such reconciliation be restricted to Durkheim and Mauss, or would it go beyond them?

The Structure of the Book

It has already been stated that, in sociology and the social sciences, there are relatively few attempts to promote a theory centred on the relation. The French tradition is not an exception. However, there are specific debates about a relational perspective in the French tradition, which historically relate to the concept of solidarity and express an ideal of social cohesion through relationships between personal and non-personal actors. As is well known, solidarity is a cardinal concept in Durkheim's sociological work, but little is known about the controversies it generated, inside the Durkheim school at first, in respect to the purpose of a relational perspective in sociology. The most important of these controversies is without doubt the dispute between Durkheim and his challenger, Gaston Richard, who developed a sociology of solidarity and competed with Durkheim's sociological programme on solidarity. The book starts in this chapter with this debate and shows how it has been picked up and extended in four key successive debates in the French sociological tradition. The reconstruction of these debates enables us to systematise the most important milestones, which lead to six proposals for a theoretical framework in sociology that is able to analyse social phenomena through the relation.

In Chap. 2, on solidarity, we shall see that the comparison between Durkheim and Richard leads to a notion of resistance, at which we will take a closer look in our third chapter by comparing Richard (who offers the most extensive analysis of resistance available) and Durkheim's nephew, Marcel Mauss, who also takes this topic into account in the framework of his writings on sacrifice and magic.

Chapter 3 enables us to isolate the idea of contact (less a concept than a fact of observation), which allows Richard and Mauss to locate—in the contact between individuals and societies—the starting point of their sociological idea of resistance, as well as their sociological understanding of social phenomena through the relation. The contributions of those two authors experienced very different fates. Richard was to inspire a programme related to the sociology of law and of sociability disconnected from relational attempts in French sociology. Mauss was to gain more attention than Richard in France, particularly because of his famous essay, *The Gift*. We therefore return to Mauss' *Gift* in Chap. 4, and we compare Mauss to Pierre Bourdieu. Bourdieu is probably one of those French sociologists who emphasised the productivity of Mauss' *Gift* in sociology very early, offering at the same time, in his ethnology of the Kabyle society, a critique of Mauss, from which he builds his own relational framework in sociology.

This comparison allows us to highlight the way in which Mauss and Bourdieu, starting from "the gift", provide elements for understanding the social position of actors from a relational point of view. Mauss and Bourdieu put this question in the foreground of their concept of the gift, suggesting that the relational understanding of the social positions of actors in society should take into account the way in which these actors give a relational orientation to their activities, as well as to other actors and to the mediations of their exchanges. However, when it comes to the mediations of exchange, Mauss' concept of the gift lacks a systematic theoretical framework which would deepen the role of such mediations not only in the context of gift exchanges, but also in the case of other kinds of social relationships. Mauss certainly understands that the material and immaterial things that surround us contribute to a relational perspective on social phenomena, but he mostly excludes them from his theoretical considerations. By contrast, Bourdieu's sociology delivers a framework where "things" are present in the form of capitals that the actors possess, and that they use during their social career in order to affirm their social position in the context of struggles with other actors. In their relation to actors and their activities, these capitals are essential for highlighting the relational character of social reality, as Bourdieu says. This statement finds an echo in Bruno Latour's sociological investigations, for which these "things" are indispensable actants that have to be taken into account when it comes to a relational perspective in sociology, which, for Latour, actually means a sociology of associations.

In Chap. 5 we compare Bourdieu and Latour on the problem of these mediations and their contribution to a relational sociology. We shall see that for Bourdieu as well as for Latour, this attention to things allows them to highlight the way in which the relation is reduced to a power relationship in Bourdieu's sociology, whereas Latour rather speaks about concrete associations. Association is a concept for which Latour refers to Tarde in order to better distinguish himself and his sociological view from the Durkheimian sociologists and their affiliates, be it Bourdieu or Durkheim himself. Nevertheless, Latour is not so far away from Bourdieu, as we shall see, or from Durkheim. In order to address this last point, Chap. 6 compares Latour and Durkheim, beginning with the concept of association. This will lead us to examine Latour and Durkheim on the concept of control, which we shall discuss in relation to their view on institutions and, finally, on reciprocity.

These five chapters then allow us to formulate six proposals for a theoretical framework in sociology likely to take account of social phenomena through the relation. The book closes with a brief discussion of how these six proposals show similarities and differences as compared to the contributions from sociological theories discussed here in this introduction.

Notes

1. See for example Burt (1982) and Pattison (1993).
2. White has made this approach famous, using "blockmodels", which offer "a view of social structure obtained directly from aggregation of the relational data without imposing any *a priori* categories or attributes for actors" (White et al. 1976, 731). In more technical terms, blockmodels are a family of algorithms able to identify the structural similarities between different networks (White 1995, 710–711). White's blockmodels have been influenced by static physics, in particular by Ernst Ising's model used to describe ferromagnetism in crystals (Abbott 2001, 143 note 27).
3. About the school of relational sociology inspired by White, as well as the debates it has stimulated particularly in the field of quantitative methods, see Mische (2011, 80–97), and Schmitt and Fuhse (2015). On the resonance of White's work in Europe, see in particular Schmitt and Fuhse (2015), as well as the work of Michel Forsé, Alain Degenne and Michel Grossetti in France, which is close to White's work (for example Degenne and Forsé 1999; Bidart et al. 2011).
4. Emirbayer anchors his distinction between culture and relation in the work of Talcott Parsons, who sees culture as a system that is structurally different from the social system, and therefore from social relationships, even if, on an empirical level, the two structures seem to be always interrelated (Emirbayer and Goodwin 1994, 1438).
5. For a typical illustration of how Abbott uses his concept of encoding, cf. Abbott 1988. See also his summary in Abbott 2016.
6. Abbott similarly underlines this when he says that for White, as well as for his colleagues John Padgett and Christopher Ansell, the "direct focus is on action in structure" (Abbott 1997, 1167).
7. White also says it more directly: "Rational choice theory has suggested new phenomena, and the present task is to determine contexts in which it is likely to be productive" (White 1992 (2008), 15).
8. It is well known that, for Max Weber, action is a social action because it is a motivated action towards other actors, these motivations delivering the context of meanings shared by the actors for whom the action has the same or a similar sense (Weber 1922, 5). This concept of *Sinnzusammenhang* holds a very important place in the phenomenological sociology of Alfred Schütz, who proposes a critique of Weber's comprehensive sociology (Schütz 1932 (2004)). Keeping in mind White's evolution from network sociology to phenomenology, this parallel with Schütz is worth a note.
9. Emirbayer's critique of network theories in many respects takes advantage of Archer's morphogenesis perspective in sociology, for example regarding the "analytical dualism" (Archer 1995, 169) between social structures and

social actors that Emirbayer picks up and applies to the link between social relationships and culture (in particular, Emirbayer and Goodwin 1994, 1439 and 1444).

10. This concept of the relation as a formal link between actions is also found in Mische's work on the networks of young Brazilian activists (Mische 2007).
11. Emirbayer's tendency to put the concept of action into perspective and, at the same time, to keep it can also be found in Abbott's last book on the social process defined as "three kinds of relation: emotion, action, and meaning" (Abbott 2016, 286). The emotion as "immediate understanding of others and their particularity" (ibid.) is the starting point of the social process. Abbott also sums this up with the word "sympathy", a concept with which he refers to the ecological sociology of the Chicago School (Abbott 1997, 1149–1182), and which—beyond the Chicago School and the pragmatic tradition in American sociology—links back to Adam Smith and the utilitarian tradition in social philosophy. In Abbott's book, sympathy means that "we can envision action only with respect to other beings whom we understand…to be beings" (Abbott 2016, 287). Nevertheless, it is action that plays the central role in the development of the social process because, thanks to action towards other actors, emotions will be concrete. They do not remain at a stage of personal feelings, they lead to the production of meanings in public, in a sense near to what Weber understands when he defines social action. Thus, even if Abbott speaks of the social process as a set of three relations, these relations stem from the framework of action.
12. It has to be noted, however, that Dewey and Bentley do not assimilate transaction with interaction: "If inter-action is procedure such that its inter-acting constituents are set up in inquiry as separate 'facts,' each independent of the presence of the others, then Transaction is Fact such that no one of its constituents can be adequately specified as fact apart from the specification of other constituents of the full subject matter" (Dewey and Bentley 1948, 126). Even if not precisely defined, the transactional point of view links to a kind of relation between Ego and Alter which makes Ego and Alter who they are, and who they will be as long as they remain in relation. However, it has to be noted that Dewey and Bentley do not actually speak of a relation while specifying their concept of transaction, but of some sort of emerging effects of actions, showing that their concept of transaction also remains based on a framework of action. Currently, Dépelteau (2008, 51–73) and to some extend Crossley (2010) return to the concept of transaction in order to develop a pragmatic relational scheme in sociology.
13. Cf. Donati 2003, 255, and 300; cf. also Donati 2011, XV, and 71.

14. Donati says, "Parsons' 'general theory', failed precisely because it tried to unify 'action theory' and 'system theory' without having a generalized theory of social relations, i.e. without arriving at a 'relational theory' of society, freed from the assumptions of modernity" (Donati 2011, 1).
15. For Donati, this means that the relation is an emergent phenomenon where reciprocity produces relation, which produces other relations. Donati refers his understanding of the emergence of the relation back to Georg Simmel's concept of *Wechselwirkung* (Donati 2011, 88). However, these are problematic statements. This is discussed in greater depth later in the book.
16. This idea also seems to be problematic from an ethical point of view, since for Donati, the attribute of a relation would show us if we are facing a human relationship or not, and—this peculiar statement seems to us the most difficult one—what type of humanity we are speaking of regarding this or another form of relation. As he says, "It is the quality of the relation that expresses a social form, which decides the type and degree of humanity contained by that social form compared to another one" (Donati 2011, 44).
17. These critiques are expressed in rather direct terms (cf. Archer and Donati 2015, 19–25). They reappear more or less explicitly throughout their book.
18. For Archer and Donati, relational sociologists and affiliated ones like Dépelteau (2008, 51–73) or Crossley (2010) reduce the relation to an interaction between two actors, from which they deduct their concept of network. On the one hand, they do not take into consideration the *sui generis* character of the relation—its character of independent reality. On the other hand, they do not consider that actors and social structures constitute themselves mutually (Archer and Donati 2015, 80–81).
19. This dialectics without synthesis and without emergence is not a literary trick that Simmel would use to distinguish himself from the German intellectuals of the nineteenth century. After all, many of them use the term *Wechselwirkung* in a sense similar to Simmel's (Christian 1978, 110). It is more basically the application of the framework of Newtonian physics to the analysis of society, particularly the gravitation of the planets which was to be one of the main sources of inspiration for the German theorists of society and culture (among other subjects) in the nineteenth century (ibid.; cf. also Waszek 2002, 71–85).
20. On this point, it is useful to mention briefly the quarrel in which von Wiese opposed Georges Gurvitch. It shows both the difficulty that von Wiese had in convincing his interlocutors of the merits of his conception of the relation, as well as the sacrifices he was ready to make in order to see his sociological programme accepted by other sociologists, not only as one proposal among others, but as the *lingua franca* in sociology. This would not change Gurvitch's opinion of von Wiese's *Beziehungslehre,* which he

rejected also because Gurvitch was himself convinced that he was the only one able to bring about such a *lingua franca* in sociology (cf. Gurvitch 1952a, 94–104; also Gurvitch 1952b/1953, 98–105; Wiese 1951/1952, 365–374). Von Wiese was so confident in his own sociology that he was almost ready to throw his ontological concept of the relation overboard in order to win Gurvitch and other sociologists like Edward Ross and his sociology of the social process, for example, over to his cause (cf. Liebersohn 1982, 123–149).

CHAPTER 2

Solidarity: Émile Durkheim, Gaston Richard and Social Cohesion

Solidarity is the fundamental concept of Gaston Richard's sociology,[1] which he brought into the debates in social sciences at the end of the nineteenth and the beginning of the twentieth century. For Richard, solidarity requires individual responsibility. Both concepts—solidarity and responsibility—allowed him to work on the foundations of a history of law, and of a historical sociology that focused on the development of the idea of law in society.[2] Solidarity does not only mean that the actors are bound together in society because of the social relationships between them. Solidarity also refers to the detachment or the untying of actors, just as individual responsibility refers to transgressions as well as to rights and obligations. Richard's concept of solidarity links the collective to the individual on the one hand, commitment to detachment on the other, and he also linked order to the chaos that moral evil is spreading into society, which Richard, using a genetic method,[3] wanted to analyse from a historical perspective. This perspective, in his own view, distinguishes his sociological contribution from those of his predecessors and contemporaries, especially from that of Auguste Comte and later positivists, as well as from his young competitor Émile Durkheim. It leads to consider society from the viewpoint of relation.

Richard had no difficulty in pointing out his difference from Auguste Comte and the positivists on the problem of solidarity, in part because he did not feel any sympathy for Comte. This was shown, for instance, in 1902 on occasion of the planned inauguration of a statue of Auguste

C. Papilloud, *Sociology through Relation*, Palgrave Studies in Relational Sociology, https://doi.org/10.1007/978-3-319-65073-9_2

Comte under the supervision of Pierre Laffitte. Laffitte was the President of the 13 liquidators of Comte's estate, who had taken over as chief editor of the *Revue Occidentale*, and who was the Honorary President of the *Comité International de la Statue d'Auguste Comte*. The ceremony was supposed to have been attended by an international panel of academic and political celebrities forming the *Comité de patronage de la Statue d'Auguste Comte*, among them Durkheim and the German sociologist Ferdinand Tönnies. But not everything went according to plan. Right-wing extremist groups regarded Comte as one of their major thinkers and made an attempt to take over the event. In this difficult context, Henri Charriaut, the secretary of the editorial board of the daily *Le Siècle* newspaper, speaking in the defence of the positivists, pointed out that "nationalists and reactionary forces—but is this not a pleonasm?—have resolved to take over Auguste Comte, to make him a kind of saint philosopher for the believers, rejecting any secular and republican assertions or affirmations in his work. But the positivists will not allow this" (Charriaut 9 May 1902, 2). If it can be said that Comte, like Charriaut, was not a nationalist, making him the defender of republican values was far too exaggerated for Richard. In his response to Charriaut, he is rather clear about what he thinks of Comte:

> Auguste Comte has denied freedom of conscience in religion and freedom of thought in the sciences...Auguste Comte has been an implacable opponent of the parliamentary system...Auguste Comte was neither Republican, nor was he anticlerical. [John] Stuart Mill has clearly shown that he [Comte] aspired to nothing less than to be the High Priest and the Grand Inquisitor of the West, and in 1851, he offered Tzar Nicolas the presidency of his positivist church. Finally—a point which must concern you [Charriaut] especially—liberal economy has never had another opponent who has done more to discredit it, and who has formulated against it a regressive social 'static' borrowed from Bonald and de Maistre, intended to impose tradition on reason, feeling on intelligence. (Richard 18 May 1902, 3)

What Richard criticised in Comte most of all is that he had founded sociology on "altruistic utilitarianism", a social version of the "egoistic utilitarianism" inherited from Thomas Hobbes and Jeremy Bentham (Richard 1903a, 151, 205).[4] For Richard, Comte's utilitarianism was characterised by a theory stating that the actors mobilise resources for attaining not personal goals but collective ones. In a utilitarian framework, the difficulty then returns to reconcile individual choice and collective aspirations.

Comte solved this problem by speaking of duty, which would be the condition of individual freedom and individual choice (ibid. 193). If everyone is free to choose, such choice is affected by a sense of duty towards other actors, a sense of duty that becomes the root of law in society.[5] Comte attributed this sense of duty towards others to the maternal instinct that women communicate to men: "Only women can teach devotion to human society" (ibid. 205)—which, for Richard, was a paternalistic assertion coming "from the philosopher most hostile to the civil and political emancipation of women" (Richard 1909a, 309).[6] It was also important to Richard to show that Comte's conservative views on society resulted in "roughly equivalent concepts of social consensus, social organization, social solidarity" (Richard 1912a, 54). In this sense, Comte had certainly had a deep influence on the precursors of academic sociology. Comte's concept of solidarity is, however, somewhat clumsy since he made it out to be a kind of functional equivalent to the interdependence of actors. "Solidarity becomes either a fusion of interests, or a coalescence of activities. Comte recognizes two kinds of solidarity, one of family that is based on the union of warm feelings and on the fusion of feelings and interests, and the other, [solidarity] of cooperation, is based on the division of labour...when Comte uses this improper concept of solidarity, he talks about...the mutual dependency between the different forms of social activity, and as a consequence, between their agents...the agents are placed in a state of mutual dependency which imposes on them a certain community of destiny; this community of destiny is what Comte names solidarity" (ibid. 82–83). In his critique of Comte, Richard finds all the elements he needs in order to develop his own concept of solidarity in the field of sociology—and he is not the only one. Another French sociologist had also been paying attention to Comte's concept of solidarity: Émile Durkheim, whose aim is similar to Richard's.

Richard and Durkheim knew each other from their years at the *Ecole Normale Supérieure* and worked together in the context of Durkheim's periodical *L'Année sociologique*. They both shared a strong interest in the question of solidarity, and some commentators regard solidarity as the main source of their future conflict,[7] even their "radical opposition" (N.N. 1946, 96). However, Richard was not sparing with compliments on Durkheim's concept of solidarity, as for example at the end of his life, speaking of the book that Durkheim devoted to the problem, *The Division of Labour in Society* (1893), which he recalled as having been of "unquestionable value" (Richard 1943b, 237). Should this statement be understood as a late recognition by a sociologist who has been regarded as the "second Durkheim" (Pickering 1979, 164), and who could just as well have been the first if he had not been "wrongfully" banned from French sociology (Moreau 1944, 375)?

On this point and in the absence of evidence—such as letters between the two protagonists—speculation goes on. Richard, who was the sociologist of the province compared to the sociologist of the metropolis which Durkheim was to become, is said to have developed resentment against Durkheim (Beaulavon 1937, 335; Clark 1971, 32; König 1978, 322), a jealousy all the more misplaced because Richard had never produced a similar oeuvre (Nielsen 1987, 284) and because he never had played on the same level as Durkheim. The biography of Richard contains some elements supporting the above thesis of him being a "second" Durkheim, particularly when we focus on the years from 1902 to 1905, when Durkheim leaves Bordeaux in order to apply for the Educational Science Chair at the University of Sorbonne and to succeed Ferdinand Buisson, who was going to retire. Richard, who arrives at Bordeaux in October 1902 (Richard 1943a, 58), wonders if he would be able to fulfil his commitments and ambitions: "Would I be able to hold my rank, and to play my role at the side of this elite? Will I be able to do it especially as a sociologist? The difficulty was to take with me the college of the Protestant professors while being the successor of two sociologists [Alfred Espinas and Durkheim; CP] whose religious and even moral doctrines were incompatible and irreconcilable with theirs [the Protestant professors]" (Richard 1943a, 62).[8] Richard obtained the support of Louis Liard, then Director of French Higher Education (Richard 1943a, 56; Pickering 1975, 343), who recommended him as alternative to Durkheim for the Chair of Sociology at the University of Bordeaux, a decision not fully endorsed by Durkheim. Indeed, he would have preferred that Paul Lapie, freshly graduated (Fournier 2007, 521), would have taken up his teaching in Bordeaux.[9] As it turns out, Richard's employment was confirmed in 1905, but he was given the Chair of Philosophy, while Lapie, until then lecturer in History of Philosophy, received the Chair of Sociology. Faced with this uncomfortable situation, Richard and Lapie agreed to swap their chairs (Pickering 1979, 166 note 1), so that Richard finally obtained the Chair of Sociology at the University of Bordeaux, which he then renamed the Chair of Social Science (Pickering 1975, 343). Do we have to interpret this as a desire by Richard to make Durkheim forgotten? Or, on the contrary, is this a sign that Richard wanted to affiliate himself with Durkheim?

The second hypothesis is not only supported by literature (Pickering 1975, 344) but acquires some credibility through Richard himself. Indeed, in a text written in response to a critical review by Angelo Vaccaro, Richard stated: "Mr. Vaccaro knows to which sociological school I am belonging, it is the one of which Mr. Durkheim is the recognized leader" (Richard 1900, 519). Moreover, when Richard began to work at the University of Bordeaux, he expressed his desire to continue the work done by Durkheim: "I had the firm intention to reduce to a minimum the legitimate regrets that his departure from Bordeaux to Paris had visibly caused in his students and his audience" (Richard 1935, 20). Therefore, it is generally thought that despite some tension, Richard would not only appear to have been content with being the "second", but, moreover, would have been ready to recognise, and even to acknowledge the *leadership* of Durkheim in French sociology. However, this biographical testimony is misleading. Richard had never been a Durkheimian, and solidarity is the topic where we can see this best. Among the questions related to solidarity, one in particular was to stimulate the interest of both Richard and Durkheim: the corporation.

The Corporation

For the young Richard, who began his career with a reflection on the relationship between law and society, and for many thinkers, particularly in Germany and in Russia, whose ambition was to develop a sociology of law, there was no doubt that the law only existed on the basis of solidarity. Richard recalled at the end of his life that his doctoral thesis written in 1892 had already delivered the message that "law is a pacification of social relations, not the decomposition of solidarity to the benefit of egoistic claims" (Richard 1943a, 60).

Solidarity is the bedrock of law and forms the individual's character (Richard 1935, 27). The reason is that solidarity, a concept drawn from, but, despite the writings of Fustel de Coulanges, not limited to, moral theology (Richard 1892, 27),[10] refers to an idea of security "of a human being or a group of human beings responsible for the acts of another one" (ibid. 28–29). This idea of collective responsibility belongs to the realm of law, and Richard saw its modern expression in *De l'esprit des lois*[11] by Montesquieu, an author not unknown to Durkheim, who, in 1892, wrote his Latin doctoral thesis on Montesquieu (Durkheim 1892a, 405–463). Nevertheless, if Durkheim, like Richard, saw Montesquieu as a precursor of modern sociology and took his contribution to the concept of solidarity into account, then he did not do so in order to bind solidarity and law together. He did it with the purpose of reflecting on the individual's place in society. Montesquieu is helpful in suggesting that solidarity evolves over time, that it does not only come in different forms but also in different meanings because individuals have become more independent from each other. The reasons for this independence have to lie in the division and in the distribution of social functions between individuals. This is his well-known thesis of the division of labour that Durkheim was subsequently to develop.

Up to here, however, it is important to understand that Richard and Durkheim did not share the same views on solidarity. For Richard, solidarity takes place in the relationship between collective responsibility and the law. For Durkheim, instead, it lies between the distribution of social labour—including the collective effort it presupposes—and the social relationships between the actors, making them interdependent. In other words, that what Richard attributed to law Durkheim was attributing to labour. The groups of workers must not be seen as single groups of professionals—and thus the questions related to them cannot be limited to solely economic questions. They must also be seen as a "moral force capable of curbing individual egoism, nurturing among workers a more invigorated feeling of their common solidarity, and preventing the law of the strongest from being applied too brutally in industrial and commercial relationships" (Durkheim 1893b (2013), 14).

Despite this critical distinction, Richard and Durkheim shared a common interest in the question that is at the foreground of their understanding of solidarity, namely the question of the corporation, where they argue in a similar way. Richard saw the corporation as "an extension of the family" (Richard 1897, 100) just as did Durkheim, who said that "in one sense the corporation was heir to the family" (Durkheim 1893b (2013), 20). According to Richard, the corporation is governed by rules similar to those prevailing within the family, as for example the rules governing "brotherhood", "hierarchy" and "inheritance" (Richard 1897, 100). But, above all, what characterises the built of corporations is what Durkheim calls their "position outside society", or their situation "outside the official organization", when referring to Roman Antiquity (Durkheim 1893b (2013), 21; ibid. 31 note 25). This outside situation is seen by Richard, quoting Durkheim (Richard 1897, 163 note 1), as affirmation of an "individual capacity" or, which is for Richard the same, as the decline of "the role of heredity and constraint" (ibid. 163).[12] Corporations are the product of artisans who develop their activities at the periphery of agricultural and military occupations. They lead to the formation of a bourgeoisie that both authors recognise as the social group that most typically represents the corporation, which develops its activities in communities and in cities: "for a long time bourgeoisie and tradesmen formed a single body... Bourgeois and city-dweller were synonymous terms" (Durkheim 1893b (2013), 22). Richard shares his opinion: "If we consider the bourgeoisie at its beginnings, we see it coming from the guilds, and from the corporative regime" (Richard 1897, 162). This bourgeoisie "has been built in the cities; it corresponds to the reaction of urban populations against the preponderance of rich landowners" (ibid. 161). However, this type of corporation does not last. It is soon challenged by the emergence of small enterprises and by industrial activities. On this point, Richard and Durkheim differ.

According to Richard, the development of enterprises and industries that gradually replace such corporations is the logical result of an affirmation of individuality in society as a whole. "Humanity goes from the domestic workshop to the capitalist enterprise, as it goes from impersonal to personal art, from tradition to discussion, from subjection to things to reign over things, and, I would add, from the struggle between domestic societies to arbitration and cooperation between individuals" (ibid. 107). These words actually partly veil the implicit formulation of a law of history, of an irreversible and irrepressible trend that leads from the corporation to society,[13] a trend that Durkheim equally underlines: "the corporation, as it then was, could not adapt itself to this new form of industry...What remained was that the old-style corporation would have to change if it were to continue to play its part in the new conditions of economic life" (Durkheim 1893b (2013), 24).

Why is this transformation irrepressible? For Richard, it is because the exchanges between the social actors grow outside of the municipal boundaries, and are soon going to be internationalised, lowering at the same time the power of the political authority over the economy, and thus, on the professional groups.[14] To say it in a word, this is—Richard quoting here Henry Sumner Maine—"the transition from status to the contract" (Richard 1897, 101).

For Durkheim, if the conclusions are partly the same as Richard's, his reasoning is exactly the opposite. If there is an evolution from corporation to enterprise and industry, this is because the corporation lacks adaption to the transformations that have affected municipal life, particularly to the extension of economic activities beyond the community.[15] While Richard sees the corporations' progressing disappearance as a transformation of the form and meaning of solidarity, Durkheim perceives that there is a risk of solidarity being destroyed. This motivated Durkheim in his preface to the second edition of *The Division of Labour in Society* to speak in favour of the return of corporations in a form adapted to modern society: "Thus, since the market, from being municipal as it once was, has become national and international, the corporation should assume the same dimensions" (Durkheim 1893b (2013) 24). Because for Durkheim, there is little doubt that "the corporation will be called upon to become the foundation, or one of the essential foundations, of our political organization" (ibid. 26). And what is the reason? Because a historical analysis of the corporations indicates to what extent the actors living in societies driven by organic solidarity are now less attached to their territory, an attachment to territory that has been the basis of the almost familial solidarity that characterised the corporation, bringing together actors who know each other because they live side by side.[16] If these contacts disappear because their activities bring the actors out of their city and their community, then solidarity is challenged and, with it, the actors' reason to live, as Durkheim shows in his book *Suicide* (1897). "The general health of the social body is at stake" (ibid. 28), and even if the comeback of a form of corporation is not the unique instrument by which solidarity in modern society can be promoted, it is "the sine qua non of their effectiveness" (ibid.).[17]

The difference between Richard and Durkheim is also apparent when, in the transition from the corporation to enterprise/industry, it comes to the link between territory and state. Although their starting point is similar, they once more disagree on the conclusion. According to Durkheim, "the organizational framework of the professional group should always be related to that of economic life" (Durkheim 1893b (2013), 24), an assertion which finds its complementary formulation in Richard: "No one can deny that the ratio between the population and the territory has no impact on the division of labour, and then on the social structure" (Richard 1902a, 305). Similarly, both authors express a convergent view on the transition from family to corporation: "The mass of the population is no longer divided up according to blood relationships, whether real or fictitious, but according to land divisions" (Durkheim 1893b (2013), 145), while Richard says: "After having studied the social bounds which keep them [the actors; CP] together, we shall see how the social bond is strengthened by the physiological inheritance in the clan and the family, by the division of labour and the extended impact of the national territory on the divided labour in the state" (Richard 1903a, 371). Even this reference to the state is supported by Durkheim, who considers the state as the necessary actor required for regulating the society driven by organic solidarity. However, if the state is necessary, it is not sufficient for regulating economic life: "we do not mean that normally the state absorbs into itself all the regulatory organs of society of whatever kind, but only those that are of the same nature as its own, that is, those that govern life generally. As for those that control special functions, such as economic functions, they lie outside its zone of attraction" (Durkheim 1893a (1922), 174). This is why, according to Durkheim, there is a need to expand the corporation on the national level so that it can meet the challenges of occupational diversification and specialisation in agreement with the state. It is a conclusion that Richard underlines in his review of Durkheim's *Suicide* (Richard 1898b, 404), but he does not accept it. Three years earlier, Richard had strongly criticised the idea of restoring the corporation in modern societies. Such restoration would perpetuate the inheritance of habits from tradition, leading to more or less automatic behaviours. According to Richard, modern societies must be freed from corporations in order to be able to develop harmoniously, and not to be trapped in traditions: "The French Revolution, which destroyed the monarchy and the hereditary nobility did also destroy the corporation, an institution which might express the solidarity and cohesion of generations, but at the price of an unbearable automatism" (Richard 1895a, 499). It therefore seems that the demarcation line between Durkheim and Richard has been clearly established.

In summary, we can say that, on the one hand, we have Durkheim who thought that the territorial extension of the economic activity first, and the professional specialisation second, contribute to destroying the solidarity or social bond between the actors. It is as if both of them would secretly conspire against the actors' interdependence that Durkheim sees as the element that makes social life in modern societies possible. According to Durkheim, the territory—first in the form of the village and later the city—has facilitated the emergence of corporations as a means of maintaining social relationships that are no longer blood relationships only and are thus no longer supported solely by kinship. If this is the case, then, in modern societies, the corporation itself must become the means by which society is stabilised while taking the same rank as the state even if it must remain specialised in the defence of professional interests. This would mean that mechanical solidarity becomes entangled in organic solidarity, supporting Durkheim's hope that maybe "the day will come when the whole of our social and political organization will have an exclusively, or almost exclusively, professional basis" (Durkheim 1893b (2013), 148).

On the other hand, we have Richard, who thinks—similarly to Durkheim—that society evolves while at least partially maintaining the vestiges of the past. However, these vestiges, these traditions have to be criticised, or, at least, should be resisted in order to find alternate ways for developing society. It would therefore be illusory to believe that the future of society lies in the development of new corporations, even if they were as powerful as the state or a counter-power to it. However, a few years later, Richard writes:

> The excessive weakening of the professional society or corporation at the beginning of our contemporary times has left the defence of labour and of the person performing it to the state alone. The limitation of the state's intervention in the economic order can therefore not result in a restoration of professional ethics or in the formation of a kind of corporation better adapted than the former to the requirements of the division of labour. (Richard 1903a, 249–250)

If Durkheim seems coherent in extending his argument about solidarity to the questions of the corporations and the state, Richard's statement seems inconsistent with his observations on corporations. What does he mean when he talks about the "restoration of professional ethics"?

Profession

For Richard, professional ethics refers to the general question of collective responsibility in the context of the modern division of labour (Richard 1903a, 149), in particular to the question of the power of the state over the different secondary groups—among them the professional groups—as well as over the individuals. "Experience shows that the life of these communities is the main cure to use against excessive intervention by the state in the individual sphere of freedom" (ibid. 197). In contemporary societies, the secondary groups have a double function for the individual actors, and first of all for their own members.

On the one hand, they make them aware of their rights, and in the case of professional groups, make them aware of the rights related to their profession. On the other hand, these groups help their members by ensuring their individual freedom. In the world of the professions, this means the freedom of contract (related to the right to trade), to choose a profession (related to the right to work) and to possess goods (related to the rights to own and to consume goods) (ibid. 222). This is why Richard considered that organisation of professional groups was necessary to any society, and that nothing in society could stop it.[18] Nevertheless, in contemporary societies, a professional group is not identical to the corporation, or to put it in the terms of Richard, it does "not lead to the egoistic fulfilment of the corporation's particular interests" (ibid. 226). The professional group is itself a means for employees to attain their professional goals under conditions that meet their own requirements. One of the most important of these requirements is that the employees are entitled to develop their potential in their professional activity, which, moreover, could be a "temporary" one—Richard does not exclude that, in modern societies, employees change their job several times (Richard 1903b, 61), something which would be impossible in a corporate regime. In addition, in contemporary societies where the state exerts legislative power, the political influence of these professional groups remains limited. The state "takes over and assumes the authority formerly exerted by domestic societies, local societies, professional societies, and, finally, religious societies…the individual only obeys the laws of the state. They can contract and form associations, and if they [the associations] could help him [the individual] in attaining his goals, they should have no jurisdiction over him" (ibid. 66). The restoration of professional ethics is therefore not a restoration of the corporation because professional ethics does not have the attributes usually associated with the corporation. The professional group does not continue the system of hereditary careers. As it defends the rights of the patrons as well as of the employees, it contributes to a weakening of the hierarchy between masters and workers found in the corporation. Moreover, if the professional groups stand against the power of the state to unilaterally legislate every aspect of labour, they are nevertheless subject to the state's legislative power. This situation has the advantage of providing guaranties to the members of the professional group, who can rely on the state if they consider their interests harmed by the professional group to which they belong.

Finally, because these professional groups do not have any power other than defending the professional interests of their members, they remain fundamentally anchored in local contexts, even if they have national representatives: "All coal miners of England, all the wine growers or fishermen of France could form a national professional society, but it will always have its roots in the ground; it will always be a local society. As a result, it will get an irreducible professional character, and it will develop its own way to feel the social needs, to plan the social prospects, and to react onto society" (Richard 1903c, 377). On this point, Richard cannot differ more from Durkheim who, on the contrary, speaks of the obsolescence of the corporate anchor in local territory, this all the more as the division of labour is progressing, which would justify, in Durkheim's view, extending the corporation at least on a national level in order to stabilise solidarity. As there is as yet no such extension in contemporary society, we cannot speak, according to Durkheim, of professional ethics, of its corresponding groups and rights:

> the professional group no more exists than does a professional ethic. Since the eighteenth century when, not without reason, the ancient corporations were dissolved, hardly more than fragmentary and incomplete attempts have been made to reconstitute them on a different basis…it [the corporation; CP] must become, or rather become once more, a well-defined, organized group—in short, a public institution. (Durkheim 1893b (2013), 11–12)[19]

To foster the emergence of these modern corporations, it will therefore be necessary to first make sure that they will be attached to the state, which will give professional ethics a real anchor in "common morality" (cf. Durkheim 1890–1900 (1958), 28–41).

Thus, Durkheim does not see these new corporations only as a necessary counterweight to the legislative action of the state but they provide a double benefit to the actors by recognising their rights and their freedom. He also sees them as an extension of the functions of the state, which, through the corporations, binds the individual actors together and ensures a kind of social cohesion in the division of labour. Therefore, it becomes obvious that for Durkheim, the question of "whether or not individuals should be bound to membership…is only of limited interest" (ibid. 39) since the individual actors join the corporations spontaneously. "In fact, from the day when the guild system was set up, it would be such a handicap for the individual to remain aloof that he would join of his own accord, without any need of coercion. Once constituted, a collective force draws into its orbit those who are unattached: any who remain outside are unable to hold their ground" (ibid.).

For Richard, this explanation rests on the spontaneity of the relation between individual actors and new corporations. However, "Is this spontaneity, the condition of normal society, a fact and a general fact, or is it the character of the most frequent social type? Neither, nor. It is nowhere to be found" (Richard 1911a, 396). For Durkheim, spontaneity, i.e. "the absence not simply of any deliberate, formal type of violence, but of anything that may hamper, even indirectly, the free unfolding of the social force each individual contains within himself" (Durkheim 1893b (2013), 295), remains indeed an ideal—even if Durkheim wants the ideal to come about because this would strengthen solidarity between the functions of society, and thus, between the different professions emerging through the division of labour. Therefore, the question of interest for Durkheim is how to get closer to this ideal, to this "perfect spontaneity" as he calls it (ibid. 296). And he answers: By promoting "equality in the external conditions of struggle" (ibid. 297) or, in other words, in ensuring that the social actors are not unequally favoured by qualities coming from the context, as for example favourable geographical environments, or any favourable economic or social heritage.[20] By removing these external sources of inequality, "social inequalities express precisely natural inequalities" (ibid. 295). Thus, spontaneity becomes perfect, because "If nothing hampers or unduly favours rivals disputing the tasks they perform, inevitably only those most fitted for each type of activity will succeed in obtaining it. The sole factor then determining how labour is divided is the diversity of abilities. Usually, this allocation is made according to aptitude, since there is no reason for it to happen otherwise. Thus a harmony is automatically created between the constitution of each individual and his condition" (ibid. 294).

It is now easier to understand what disturbs Richard in this idea of "perfect spontaneity". In appearance, such spontaneity seems to fit Richard's discourse, especially his critique of tradition, which tends to imprison the individual's originality in an automatism of habits. Spontaneity would allow insistence on the importance of individual resources for organic solidarity to develop harmoniously. In Richard's view, such harmonious development would change the structure of society by restricting the harmful effects of society's hierarchical stratification, even by making this hierarchy obsolete.[21] Nevertheless, if Richard does not agree with Durkheim on his idea of spontaneity, it is because Durkheim's spontaneous act of choosing a profession presupposes a dutifulness towards the collective strength inherent in the individual and perceived by the individual as part of his social environment. Or in other words, Durkheim's spontaneity eliminates the relation between the individual actors and the professional groups. Therefore, it eliminates any questions and doubts about such collective strength. If, according to Richard, we would apply Durkheim's reasoning to practice, this would mean that, once attached to a profession that reflects and suits his skills, the individual would no longer question his own professional commitment. He would then only play his professional role, occupying his function.

The same reasoning applies to the professional groups, which, following Durkheim, must bind themselves as groups as well as they have to bind themselves to the state, so that solidarity can be ensured in modern society. However, for Richard, any relation of this kind inevitably produces reactions and conflicts either between individuals, or between the professional groups and the state. To take these reactions and conflicts into account is of the utmost importance—not because they would destroy solidarity, but because they allow it to improve and cause the conditions of such improvement to be incorporated in codified law.[22] Richard mentions the example of the development of trade unions, which, far from diminishing the need of struggle, fight for the workers' "subjective rights", this all the more so as the professions are gaining in importance as instances of the individual actors' legitimisation in society (Richard 1912b, 225–247). And there is more. What the trade unions also highlight is the fact that the professional groups are, at the same time, interest groups that compete against each other, and whose objective is to ensure the maintenance of their interests in one way or another, not only in relation to the state but also in relation to their members. In these conditions, the question arises: how does one understand what Durkheim means when he speaks of intra-professional solidarity—between individuals of the same professional group—and inter-professional solidarity between the professional groups as such (Richard 1943a, 341)? For Richard, this is a problem that Durkheim fails to solve other than by making organic solidarity the equivalent of social and political justice. As such, organic solidarity becomes the unsurpassable horizon of society's development because Durkheim sees individual freedom and the freedom of the professional groups as conditions favouring ideal social harmony.

However, Richard has not always been that critical of Durkheim. For example in his book on socialism, Richard recognises that "M. Émile

Durkheim's *The Division of Labour in Society* completely does justice to this opposition between the person and the division of labour. It is precisely when there is cooperation, and a specific cooperation, that society feels its dependency on personal activity" (Richard 1897, 72). In the context of this discussion on the division of labour, Richard's sentence is important because Richard seems to suggest that Durkheim's reasoning is correct i.e. that, in order for modern society to develop, the individuals must cooperate with each other not only for their own benefit, but also in order to serve that ideal that exceeds them: society. Has Richard exaggerated his critique of Durkheim, in particular of Durkheim's concept of the relationships between individuals, professional groups, and organic solidarity? Or is he simply unable to criticise Durkheim, and consequently swaps Durkheim's concept of solidarity for his own? In order to answer these questions, we must address another important topic that, in the theories of both authors, plays a critical role for the concept of solidarity: cooperation.

Cooperation is the blind spot in the debate between Richard and Durkheim on solidarity, and it leads to two questions. First, how, in practice, does the relation of the individual to the social group occur as described in the discussion on organic solidarity? Durkheim uses an idea (spontaneity) rather than an argument, which Richard criticises as we have seen. Such spontaneity is nowhere to be found because no one can take it for granted that the individual actors will simply accept professional constraints. This even more so as they are not of vital necessity but rather, as Durkheim and Richard both show, correspond to the extension of domestic occupations outside the family, an extension which increases over time, and which is controlled by institutions. Second, if we consider Durkheim's and Richard's discourse regarding the replacement of the ancient corporations, the proliferation of professional specialities, the emergence of professional groups defending the specific interests of their profession, then we arrive at the question of how all these actors are going to cooperate with one another. Richard and Durkheim answer similarly: by contract. The starting point of the two authors is identical. It is the critique of Jean-Jacques Rousseau's social contract.

Cooperation

Richard and Durkheim are very critical of Rousseau's social contract theory.

> The idea of the social contract is not only in disagreement with any experience (and even with the historic law regarding the transition from the state to the contract); it also is contradictory...a contract assumes an existing power, at least a spiritual one, which sanctions. However, a priori, from the idea of two or several pure freedoms, only a restricting convention can be inferred which, however, does not provide any guaranty. A treaty of peace is not a treaty of alliance. (Richard 1892, XVII)

Durkheim argues similarly:

> The conception of the social contract is today therefore very difficult to defend, because it bears no relation to the facts. The observer, so to speak, does not encounter it on his way. Not only are there no societies that have had such an origin, but none present a structure bears the slightest trace of a contractual organisation. Thus it is neither a fact derived from history nor a trend that emerges from historical development. (Durkheim 1892b (1966), 156, 1893b (2013), 159)

If Richard and Durkheim find that Rousseau's social contract is too abstract to correspond to any social reality whatsoever, they also say that the contract, taken more generally, is not at the origin of society. According to Richard, any contract presupposes society: "The real contract, the source of a specific obligation, is only conceivable in a social state which has been already built, with a criminal law regularly applied and usually respected" (Richard 1892, 142). Similarly, Durkheim states, "The contract is not, as Rousseau believed, at the origin of society, but at its height" (Durkheim 1886 (1975), 40), the word "height" being understood as the horizon of the historical development of societies. Therefore, the question for Richard as well as for Durkheim is to assign a specific place to the contract within their sociological theory. If the contract is a social fact, where is it coming from? In this regard, the young Durkheim remains affected by his critical reading of the Göttingen jurist, Rudolf von Jhering, who believes that both the contract and the law originate from "the threats... organized and concentrated in the hands of the state. They support the built of law. Where there are not present, there is no law, and it is all the more inconsistent that it is less well organized" (Durkheim 1887, 293). According to Jhering, the contract develops along the model of the treaty—"the first form of law" (ibid. 294)—of which Durkheim retains its main function, namely to limit the use of threats. Why does Jhering say that the contract is used to limit threats? "In the material world and also among primitive human beings, when two forces are in struggle, the conflict only stops when one of both has been annihilated. But men have soon understood that it was far more economical not to eliminate the opponent party" (ibid. 293). The contract would therefore only be a set of legal measures limiting the struggles between individual actors.

In his *The Division of Labour in Society*, Durkheim takes the exact opposite view to Jhering by joining the question of the contract's origin and his discourse on cooperation: "The contract is indeed the supreme legal expression of cooperation" (Durkheim 1893b (2013), 97). To cooperate means "to share with one another a common task" (ibid.) and it represents the matrix of the division of labour.[23] Durkheim goes even further by saying that the composite division of labour—the functional specialisation—is the "form of cooperation…that the contract by far the most usually expresses" (ibid.). Richard gives apparently an analogical wording, since he says that "the common mean to build cooperation is the contract" (Richard 1912a, 82). However, the contract always assumes a set of compulsory measures, not general but criminal ones. For this reason, Richard links the contract to criminal law: "[if] contractual law is one aspect or a transformation of criminal law or the law of coercion, this is because between the contract and the constraint, there is more than verbal analogy and an identity of roots (*contrahere*): There is a real analogy and an identity of origins" (Richard 1892, 135). A similar idea is found in Durkheim, who does not ignore the importance of criminal law, which, according to him, was likely to summarise each kind of legal measure in ancient societies.[24] Thus, there is a link between criminal law and contract, contractual law only appearing while criminal law loses "its relative importance" and gaining in relevance while the division of labour leads to functional specialisation (Durkheim 1893b (2013), 112). However, for Richard, criminal law does not summarise all the law. Moreover, it cannot be understood without considering its relation to the treaty—the principle that, according to Richard, founds modern international law. Indeed, for Richard, penalties or sanctions are only conceivable and justified under the supposition that the belligerents, in a given time, can build mutual non-criminal social relationships in the future. This is the basic assumption of all treaties concluded between any actors (Richard 1892, 126). As in the case of Durkheim, Richard also sees that criminal law "rests on the idea of expiation" (ibid.), an idea that will lead Durkheim to seek the origin of criminal law in religion.[25] However for Richard, expiation does not exhaust the meaning of criminal law, because from the viewpoint of criminal law, the offender, the criminal, the enemy is only temporarily so. Therefore, if criminal law punishes, then not to eliminate the offenders, which would be a kind of sanction that would rather be emblematic of private vengeance (ibid. 127). Instead, criminal law punishes in order to protect solidarity. On the one hand, it gives the victims a promise that there will be reparation for crimes, and, on the other, it gives the offenders the opportunity to repair their wrongdoing and to provide compensation for the damage they inflicted before reentering society as a whole. It is the most important point in Richard's discourse on criminal law that it is not limited to the punishment of individuals but must also give warranties that these individuals can continue to enter into the relation with the whole society, with the collective. For Durkheim, the same argument, which states that criminal law does not mean private vengeance, leads to a different conclusion.[26]

Criminal law punishes to protect solidarity in the sense that it contributes to the conservation of the unity of society. This sanction has much more power in societies driven by mechanical solidarity where social similarities between individual actors, and therefore their social cohesion, is stronger. For Durkheim, however, criminal law has not, as for Richard, the character of repayment—nor the character of distribution in the sense that, by punishing, criminal law removes the actor (culprit) from one configuration of the relation (of his normal every-day environment) to another (e.g. prison), and therefore redistributes the actors in terms of these configurations. Durkheim attributes to criminal law a protective role. It protects individuals and societies against the weakening of the collective consciousness that the crime directly undermines: "If it is society alone that exerts repression, it is because it is harmed even when the harm done is to individuals, and it is the attack upon society that is repressed by punishment" (Durkheim 1893b (2013), 71).

It can therefore be observed that although they appear to agree on these issues, Richard and Durkheim do, in fact, differ. For Richard, the two aspects of criminal law—punishment and compensation—ensure the ongoing development of solidarity not by eliminating the offence and the offender, but by punishing the offender, as well as by releasing the offender back into the cycles of relation within society. For Durkheim, criminal law is based on the punishment of offences and offenders in order to protect society, meaning that the offender cannot take back his old place in society but is instead put outside of it. We can draw two conclusions from the relation between contract and cooperation.

On the one hand, for Richard, the contract—in its various forms—has always been part of the life of societies. For Durkheim, it can only appear when society loses its power over the individual actors. This can be seen in the idea that in a society driven by organic solidarity, criminal law is the subject to specific applications. It sets the tone for other rights evolving around it, but not originating directly from it, in all areas of social life.

On the other hand, Richard believes that the contract protects solidarity, which he understands as the inner property of manifest social relationships between actors, as well as between actors and social institutions. He sees the contract and criminal law as guarantors of cooperation which, in itself, spreads the relational perspective to other actors and thus to all of society, while Durkheim sees criminal law and contract as the conditions of cooperation brought about by reproducing social groups. For Richard, even if cooperation in the ancient Greek or Roman societies was not as intense as it is in capitalist societies, it was nevertheless existent. Cooperation rests on a given inequality between individuals, as well as between individuals and society. "[S]ocial cooperation requires heterogeneous units" (Richard 1911b, 309) says Richard who, critically referring to Herbert Spencer and Durkheim's division of labour,[27] observes that cooperation is all the more successful when it is *wanted*, or in other words, if there is a will to cooperate.[28] This will is not, as in Spencer or Durkheim, a way to oppose a mechanical step in favour of an organic one in the evolution of societies. Richard does not say that society forces cooperation from the individuals. Nor does he say that in an individualised society driven by organic solidarity, cooperation would only depend on individual initiatives. The actor's will indicates the presence of the rule in his consciousness, particularly of the legal rule that "by itself, does not constrain the cooperators. It is a rule, which is as external as personal. For it to be observed, there must be a force, a power. There must be a state, or in place of the state the corporation, the local community, the religious or the domestic community" (Richard 1912a, 144). In other words, cooperation presupposes the existence of various institutions that control respect for the rules—and therefore the execution of contracts. The more cooperation extends, the more these institutions differentiate without disappearing.

There is, therefore, a "correspondence between the extension of circles of cooperation, and the differentiation in the community" (ibid. 267), which means that there is something organic in mechanical solidarity and vice versa. For Richard, this above all means that cooperation and communities will support each other benefiting solidarity within society and sustaining a relational perspective. In Richard's framework, the division of labour does not appear to weaken solidarity. It appears to be a means for fostering the reciprocal influence between individuals and institutions to the benefit of cooperation, which Richard sees as the motor driving the active adaption of actors to their society. "Knowing the laws of social cooperation enables us human beings to complete this cooperation" (Richard 1925b, 350), and there is no need to look for any transcendent entity outside such cooperation. It represents the collective goal to whose development the actors, through their activities, their effort and their work, contribute. Seemingly, we are very far away from Durkheim's division of labour. But is this really the case? Let us look at Richard's arguments.

Firstly, cooperation is possible only because the individuals are different from one another—this is the argument of complementarity that we also find in Durkheim.

Secondly, cooperation can only be established by contract—this is the argument of warranty of cooperation that Durkheim also underlines.

Thirdly, the latter assumes the persistence of institutions, which diversified according to the evolution of the forms of cooperation—this is the argument that Durkheim uses when he speaks of ensuring that the contracts are performed. In other words, there is cooperation only if there is a constant mobilisation of a collective force stabilising a form of cooperation that is capable of channelling the differentiation of individual actors.

Is Richard tacitly assuming what Durkheim explicitly affirms, namely the eternal collective force that transcends the individuals, and that pushes them to planning and producing activities together? For example, let us take a closer look at the mutual relationships that Richard sees between the individual actors, as well as between them and what he calls the "communities".

While cooperation—particularly in modern society—returns to the professional groups, communities are a first step in the formation of social groups where social actors will be educated in order to prepare cooperation.

> Both of them [cooperation and community; CP] take advantage of the automatism of habits; thus, both of them create social needs which, once existing, become the stimulants of individual conduct and seem to be its very nature. The division of labour mostly rests on professional habits, which must be inculcated in early years. It is therefore always under the

> influence of that education that individuals have been given. But education is the work of communities. (Richard 1912a, 313)

This sentence would not be so surprising if we did not know that it is exactly this "automatism of habits" that Richard criticises. Because behind the automatism of habits is the idea of the individual actors' automatic adaption to society, which Richard rejects.

Therefore, if Richard's arguments about the contract and cooperation seem to diverge—at least in terms of their form—from Durkheim's, it must be noted that, regarding their content, Richard does not really break with Durkheim's discourse on solidarity. Thus, does Richard really deliver a different or an original explanation of the relation in the context of the transition from the domestic to industrial society or from segmented to functional differentiation? To be able to answer this question, we have to compare the works of both authors in respect to the concept that is needed to link contract to cooperation, i.e. the concept of obligation.

Obligation

The concept of obligation evokes an idea of duty in Durkheim as well as in Richard. Although their views are close on many points, on obligation they do not converge. Durkheim understands obligation and duty as two inseparable elements,[29] since obligation is directly linked to rules: "The obligation is the characteristic of the rules which command so that they must be obeyed only to be obeyed" (Durkheim 1893c (1975), 305). This is the "sign of a pressure" (ibid.) that subjects the individual to the "authority" (ibid. 307). For this subjection or obedience to be possible, it must be "founded in the nature of the individual" (ibid.), which, in itself, is founded in society (ibid. 308). Because the individual is a member of a social group and, beyond, of a society, subjection or obedience to the rules constitute an intrinsic part of the individual's identity. This leads Durkheim to say, "Law and morality represent the totality of bonds that bind us to one another and to society…Man is only a moral being because he lives in society, since morality consists in solidarity with the group, and varies according to that solidarity" (Durkheim 1893b (2013), 310–311).

This interdependency between obligation and duty leads to a more general interdependency between law and morality, where "sometimes moral rules become legal ones, and sometimes legal rules become moral ones" (Durkheim 1893c (1975), 123). Reading the work of German thinkers,

Durkheim became more and more convinced that there is a close relationship between law and morality.[30] From Albert Schaeffle and Jhering, Durkheim picks up the idea that "law and morality are…the conditions of common life; therefore, people are building them, so to speak, and they determine them while living" (Durkheim 1885a, 94). Law and morals have an "empirical and organic character" (Durkheim 1887 (1975), 283), which leads Durkheim in *The Division of Labour in Society* to insist on the fact that obligation and duty must not be taken in a general or abstract sense. Instead, we need to analyse specific empirical obligations and duties (Durkheim 1893c (1975), 182–183). From Ludwig Gumplowicz, Gustav Schmoller and Gerhard Wagner, Durkheim takes the idea that this interdependency between law and morals[31] does not rule out that law and morals have each a specific function. "In the same way that morality connects each individual to a social unit, law stabilizes the relationships between these units, and it rules their cooperation" (Durkheim 1885b, 631). This functional difference between morality and law grows over time, even if for Durkheim—who relies here on Wilhelm Wundt—morality and law remain closely connected to the same traditions and customs which, in the absence of differentiated morality and a differentiated law, determine the rules and exert sanctions "with great power of constraint. Their authority has not, as it is today, something which is a little unclear; it is very clear because it is the only authority, and any deviation from the customs is falling under strict penalty" (Durkheim 1887 (1975), 306).

The last element complements the overall scheme that Durkheim uses in his division of labour. The common source of obligation and duty is obedience/subjection to the rules, which symbolises the individuals' affiliation to society. In modern times, this affiliation means two things, namely the social cohesion supported by morality, and the legal regulation of such social cohesion, which is the purpose of law. If morality dominates law in those societies that are driven by mechanical solidarity, law dominates morality in societies that are driven by organic solidarity. Therefore, what is at stake in mechanical solidarity is social cohesion, and the systems of sanctions in such societies punish violations of cohesion. In societies driven by organic solidarity, it is all about justice and any violation of justice is punished by law. In those societies where social cohesion has dissipated because of specialisation leading to division of labour, the sanctions coming from morality are too vague to be effectively applied to particular cases. Moreover, if they were applied, they would generate injustice, which would undermine social cohesion even more.

The interdependency between obligation and duty is present in every kind of society, i.e. in societies driven by mechanical solidarity as well as in those driven by organic solidarity. However, the scope of their application changes. Obligation and duty pose a moral challenge—social cohesion—that is a priority only in societies driven by mechanical solidarity. In societies driven by organic solidarity, obligation and duty are connected to law and justice, which explains why cooperation is based on contracts, and not on customs, for example. This does not mean that customs have ceased to make sense in modern societies. But the sanctions attached to them would then punish a violation of cohesion rather than an injustice, which, however, is required in order to ensure equal treatment of the parties under contract.

Richard argues differently. He does not use the words obligation and duty in a strict sense, sometimes putting obligation on the side of morals, sometimes on the side of law, and doing the same with duty. Nevertheless, he mainly describes obligation as "a painful effort of the will to curb natural propensities, an effort which is necessary in order for the norm to be respected" (Richard 1903a, 116), which puts obligation rather on the side of morality. As for duty, it is "the fundamental norm, the norm used as a criterion to all others…the equivalent of a set of functional norms of which it expresses their unity and harmony" (ibid.), which places duty rather on the side of the law.[32] The expression "functional norms" refers to the idea of "social function",[33] and obligation is the effort of the individual to go beyond the private sphere in order to fulfil a social function, therefore to carry out his duty, going from what morality recommends to what law requires. Richard shares two similarities with Durkheim, which, however, lead to two corresponding differences.

First, there is, for Richard too, some "constraint" or pressure on individuality (ibid.), exerted namely by "our reasoning will over our likings" (ibid.), which is based on the individual's resistance towards himself and towards society.

Second, Richard, like Durkheim, does not champion a strict separation between morality and law. Moreover, Richard criticises the liberal view of a strict distinction between law and morality. He argues that law and morality have their own specific characteristics, so that they cannot be reduced to one another. For Richard, "The specificity of morality and law does in no way confirm the ordinary thesis that morality is autonomous. It does not allow the conclusion that any branch of morality could be developed outside the scope of social authority" (Richard 1894a, 499, 1903c,

399). There is no independence between morality and law, and no strict opposition between them because "the moral agent is a sociable being, subject to legal norms as well as to duties, seeking to subject the rules of law to the criterion of morality" (Richard 1903c, 123).

One would be tempted to see here the same tendency one sees in Durkheim when he affiliates law and morality, duty and obligation. However, Richard says, "consciousness of the obligation reaches its strongest intensity when duty is a formal and an indeterminate notion" (Richard 1903a, 119). This formal and indeterminate notion of duty returns to the *idea* of law, which, according to Richard, lies at the root of morality and law. This idea of law "transforms physical need into moral obligation" (Richard 1892, 182). It leads to "the subsequent emergence of a moral and a legal consciousness" (ibid. 73). The idea of law is at the bottom of the individual's resistance towards his own propensities and of that discipline that Richard sees as necessary in order for the individual to ensure his own preservation. At the same time, resistance and discipline are for Richard the symbols of the individuals' social nature and of their affiliation to society. Therefore, the constraint that expresses the ideas of obligation and duty is not that of a rule that applies to individuals. It is, instead, that of the individuals' double relationship to the rule in the sense that obedience to the rule goes hand in hand with criticism of that very rule. Without this, every compulsory or naive obedience to the rule would condemn the individual actor to merely repeat tradition, and would thus stop the development of society.

The legal rule is therefore, first, the symbol of society's power over the individual in that it tells the individual what he must do to make life with others possible. Second, it is also the symbol of society's debt towards the individual. This means that society suspends the rule's prescriptive character in order to protect the individual not only against complete subjection to the rules, but also against any potentially criminal character the rule may have. For Richard, the application of the legal rule becomes criminal if the rule is applied in a unilateral and compulsory way. It becomes criminal if the individual is deprived of the right to question that rule and, thus, to contribute to its interpretation. The legal rule then becomes "violence" which destroys the individual's "social feelings" and the possibility for individuals to live together (Richard 1892, 158–159). This is why, Richard says, "customs are present in history as duties that fortify collective habits", these customs being "licenses that the common consciousness… allows to itself, they are indulgences regarding one or several passions"

(Richard 1925b, 235). In morals as in law, rules are powerful not only because they have to be obeyed, but also because they allow indulgence. At the same time, this is the condition of the transition not from morality to law, but from authoritarian morality and authoritarian law to rational morality and rational law (Richard 1903a, 249).

Thus, both morality and law contribute to the improvement of the individual's consciousness. It also leads to an increase in social consciousness that brings individuals closer together and facilitates their harmonious development (ibid. 272).[34] Therefore, morals as well as law contribute to establishing "between the individual and society a relation of reciprocal purpose" (Richard 1903a, 249), where the individuals and society do not find their respective ends in themselves, but between them. It is in this sense that Richard sees morality and law as complementary in any society, regardless of their history.

What eventually distinguishes morality and law from one other is the evidence on which law depends, and which is not mandatory in morals (ibid. 400). The methodical examination of such evidence marks the boundaries between morality and law. These boundaries are not hermetical, however. The contract is a good example for the permeable nature of these boundaries as it involves both law and morality because it presupposes legal rules as well as moral obligations. Yet, the cooperation governed by the contract is driven by the contract's clauses, so that Richard says, "contractual justice becomes [in law; CP] the real approximation of the reciprocal assistance" between actors (ibid. 231). Indeed, contractual justice is close to morality but at the same time separate from it because contractual justice depends on the legal clauses of the contract, which have to be respected by the contracting actors. For Richard, this does not mean that law would be superior to morals. On the contrary, the development of law is part of the development of morality and moral law, just as the contract contributes to the improvement of cooperation between actors.

According to Richard, one of the most representative symbols of morality's improvement is the universal right to education, which was implemented in France in 1881 by a legal framework (the so-called Jules Ferry Act). The laws on education offer one of the best examples of what society can expect from legal proceedings—from the context in which evidence is discussed—, namely an important step "not only in the moral education of a society, but also in its intellectual education" (Richard 1894a, 496). If "morals are and always will be the whole of habits inherited by education" (ibid. 500; also Richard 1903a, 396), then the law contributes to the actors' education by setting it on a legal basis. Using the example of the Ferry Act, Richard says that law extends the right to education to everyone, and it creates an obligation for parents to send their children to school. In this sense, the law contributes to the improvement of morals in society, to the individual's awareness of everyone's responsibility towards society, as well as to a collective awareness of society's responsibility towards its individual actors.

Thus, there is an important difference in how Durkheim and Richard see the link between contract and cooperation. According to Durkheim, if the transition from mechanical to organic solidarity means progress of the division of labour, this progress then does not lead to further improvement of either the individual or society. For Durkheim, speaking about improvement means to give the investigation of social facts a moral direction that this kind of investigation is not supposed to have because it should be scientific. In respect to the example of economic development, Durkheim thus says, "Far from it assisting the progress of morality, it is in the great industrial centres that crime and suicide are most frequent" (Durkheim 1893b (2013), 42). The same applies to human dignity, a notion that Durkheim criticises but that, for Richard, is of great importance.

Indeed, Richard sees human dignity as "an ideal character, a possible one, virtual in the real human being that a sustained effort may gradually separate from nature" (Richard 1903a, 160)—in other words, human dignity has its roots in morality. Durkheim does not agree with Richard, and argues:

> As all the other beliefs and practices assume less and less religious a character, the individual becomes the object of a sort of religion. We carry on the worship of the dignity of the human person, which, like all strong acts of worship, has already acquired its superstitions. If you like, therefore it is indeed a common faith. Yet, first of all, it is only possible because of the collapse of other faiths and consequently it cannot engender the same results as that multiplicity of extinct beliefs. There is no compensation. (Durkheim 1893b (2013), 134)

Behind the "dignity of the human person", there is the potentially dangerous cult of the individual. This leads Durkheim to relativise and even deny the idea (which had been so important to Richard) of a reciprocity of purposes between society and individuals. "In vain is it maintained that the collective consciousness is growing and becoming stronger with that of individuals. We have just proved that these two factors vary in inverse proportion to each other" (ibid.). If there is no improvement and no reciprocity of purposes, no relational perspective between them, then how can Durkheim legitimise his argument on the division of labour, which, according to him, would evolve in the transition from mechanical to organic solidarity? Durkheim's answer lies in the fact that "the more we evolve, the more societies develop a profound feeling of themselves and their unity" (ibid.). This is all the more so as the cult of individuality supposes dissent, whereby one of the forms of such dissent is, *par excellence*, "reflective thinking" (ibid. 128), which for Durkheim refers to any kind of intellectual activity. Certainly, Durkheim conceives dissidents as necessary elements that are not only useful but are indispensable for morality and law to develop because any form of conflict exerts a structuring influence. While dissidents weaken the common consciousness, they make that it evolves, and they give it the opportunity to manifest its repressive power, which ensures further development of organic solidarity. Yet, if this kind of evolution is progress, it is functional progress that corresponds to the functional specialisation in organic solidarity and does not improve the relation between social actors. This relation cannot be improved but only be preserved. The contract as well as cooperation are typical means for such preservation. This is why the contract and cooperation are the best examples of Durkheim's notion of progress without improvement.

For Richard, the idea of progress without improvement causes Durkheim to misunderstand solidarity. "For Durkheim, society to which crime is indirectly useful is society considered in its becoming, in the totality of its development. And it is here that the contradiction within the system breaks out. In order for the roots of this future society to be preserved and to be saved from any rigidity that would weaken it, society has to produce criminals who avert society's rigor and anger by drawing them onto themselves" (Richard 1930, 115), thus presenting themselves as "easy targets". According to Richard, what Durkheim's solidarity presupposes is therefore that dissent—whatever its forms may be—must be punished (cf. also Richard 1934, 14–16). However, if contemporary societies must do everything possible to punish dissent, as Durkheim thinks, then, Richard argues, they are no different from societies driven by mechanical solidarity. The latter too presuppose punishment of dissent, and, in a broader sense, punishment of any deviation from the life of the social group that the group perceives as potentially harmful to itself. Richard is at the opposite end of that view. Solidarity is not evolving only in terms of its forms but also in terms of its structure. According to Richard, this means a transformation on the way to a reciprocity between individual actors and between them and their society. This is consistent with the distinction that Richard makes between social and moral solidarity. Moral solidarity "is the collective responsibility of a debt" (Richard 1905, 442). The collective nature of such responsibility is the "moral" attribute of solidarity. Speaking of moral solidarity—and not only, like Durkheim, of social solidarity—, Richard means that such a solidarity evolves in relation to the support it receives from individual actors in society. Moral solidarity is therefore linked to the transformations of the collective character in the history of societies. It is linked to the structural changes affecting the formation and development of manifest social relationships in everyday life and, even deeper, the actors' orientation towards each other, on the things embedded in their activities, and on these activities themselves. Social solidarity is "a solidarity of facts or, to say it better, a repercussion of each class of social phenomena on the other" (Richard 1910b, 49). It refers to the forms of social organisation in history, thus to the empirical manifestations of moral solidarity (cf. Richard 1910a, 103–106).

These two forms of solidarity do therefore not describe two different stages in the evolution of societies like Durkheim's mechanic and organic solidarities. Moral solidarity expresses a general trend in the development of societies, and social solidarity expresses the manifestation of this general trend in practice. Moral solidarity as this general trend is "the widening of personal responsibility" (Richard 1903, 136)—a consequence of the individual's moral will and of their willingness to improve themselves. This individual willingness, however, poses a problem.

Indeed, this widening of personal responsibility, which grows in time, tends, in fact, to make the individual responsible for anything and everything. Therefore, what are the practical forms that carry and, at the same time, limit this widening of personal responsibility? Or, in other words, how does a relation between moral and social solidarity come about? This is the question at the heart of Richard's work on solidarity. Contract and cooperation preserve individuals as well as societies from the consequences of this widening of personal responsibility. If such widening were not controlled, it would destroy them both. If there is therefore progress and improvement for Richard and if these are the two values of moral solidarity, then their price is the empirical adjustment of such widening of personal responsibility. This supposes the reorganisation of society's institutions in order to improve the individual's and society's practical life, which Richard conceives as qualitative improvement. According to Richard, this is what solidarity is about: its evolution means then that individual actors and society reinforce their reciprocal contributions to their mutual benefit. This implies that individuals and society do not only collaborate in terms of their emancipation, they together also build moral and legal institutions that are able to frame and to support such emancipation.

Conclusion

Richard's solidarity refers to a set of elements that are the most important tools of his sociology. We have seen that Richard does not agree with Durkheim's programme or his views on solidarity. Nor does he agree with his views on the specific questions that are related to it, namely the questions of corporation, profession, cooperation and contracts. What may characterise the differences between both authors on all these questions best is their view on obligation. Durkheim associates obligation with the compulsory power of social rules. Richard sees, in contrast, obligation as a combination of prescriptions and indulgences. In this chapter, we have observed that these two views on obligation and social rules stem from the authors' opposite convictions about how individual actors and society are related. For Durkheim, society transcends individuals and penetrates them at the same time. It is their collective consciousness that is reproduced by cooperation and contracts, as well as by punishing dissent that weakens solidarity. For Richard, solidarity is threatened by itself only. Failure of solidarity—never excluded—does not mean that dissension has won the collective consciousness over. It only means that there is a problem with the social organisation of society, as well as a problem with the control thereof. This problem arises when either society or individual actors fail to support the relational orientation that they give to their activities, i.e. when they fail to extend the relation to the collective that they form. The improvement of which Richard speaks is certainly different from Durkheim's progress without improvement, but it is not the same as the old philosophical concept of "happiness". "The idea of duty does not depend on any idea of happiness because we cannot be forced to continue or to achieve a prospect of which we only have an unclear notion. However, all notions of moral good are undetermined; indeed, they either mean perfection, or happiness, and both of them contain an idea of infinity or totality that can only be conceived negatively" (Richard 1903a, 94).

Happiness—similar to the moral ideals that we have found in Richard's observations on moral solidarity—leads to a correspondence that Richard hopes to see achieved between moral and social solidarity, a correspondence that is nevertheless subject to history as well as to the actors' practical life. This is why, in society, such correspondence can never be fully achieved. Moreover, if the ideal of happiness or any other such ultimate goal suggests that improvement of individual and social life is always possible, it does not protect the actors or society from regression, which too is possible at any time. In Richard's work, history and genetic sociology always take precedence over moralism but not over his conviction that society cannot be reduced to an impersonal force that threatens and punishes individual actors, not even if society itself would be threatened by its own actors. There is resistance by the individual actors towards their society as well as vice versa; there is resistance by society towards its actors. This resistance has no reason for being other than for the preservation of both actors and society. This is why, according to Richard, resistance—as much as the relation itself—is of first importance.

This fundamental ambivalence of solidarity, which acts both as a bridge and as a boundary between people, is ultimately what which was to give Richard the impression that he had been the only one who had delivered a fundamental critique of Durkheim's solidarity in sociology—a critique that he repeated and increasingly underlined over time without ever changing it. One of Richard's strongest criticisms concerns Durkheim's structural scheme of solidarity where solidarity appears to be a uniform structure applied to all social facts in order to give sociology its scientific foundation. If Richard shares the view that solidarity is *par excellence* the object of sociology, then Durkheimian sociology, according to him, pays no tribute to its scientific examination, and thus weakens sociology as a scientific discipline. Durkheim knew Richard's criticism, but pretended not to understand it.[35] For example, on occasion of his review of Richard's article *Sur lois de la solidarité morale*—an article in which Richard attacks Durkheim's understanding of solidarity—Durkheim confessed that he would "not know what is the concept which is referred to" (Durkheim 1907a (1975), 339). In fact, Durkheim thought that Richard remained extremely vague and general and that he did not understand what he, Durkheim, wanted to say (Durkheim 1913, 1–3).

Durkheim's opinion is shared by some Durkheimians such as Dominique Parodi, for whom Richard has been confused up to the point that he is no longer able to distinguish sociology from history. According to Parodi, Richard takes everything as history, so that "there is no longer any point of speaking of science, explanation, or rules" (Parodi 1902–1903, 165). Later on, Parodi criticises Richard's understanding of solidarity, which should be rather understood as "the determined and invariable influence that should be attributed to authority, to the example or to passion, to the fixed components of our nature" (ibid.). Paul Lapie, another Durkheimian, also criticises the kind of sociology Richard wanted to promote. According to Lapie, Durkheim's effort had been specifically aimed at building sociology as a science of social *facts*, and not as a moral discourse on *ideas*—which, for Lapie, is exactly the kind of discourse that Richard seemed to want. Lapie, instead, objects to the idea of changing the course taken by Durkheim and does not see why sociology should become a science of ideas—or a "science of beings", as Lapie says (Lapie 1903–1904, 171–175)—and thus a pale imitation of a social philosophy that would be neither new, nor scientifically useful. These disagreements between Richard and the members of the Durkheim School, of whom he was still a member, reinforced the tensions between Richard and Durkheim, so that Richard finally left the team of *L'Année sociologique* in 1907. Essertier speaks of a "sensational rupture" (Essertier 1930a, 244) that showed deep resentment against Durkheim, his solidarity, and sociology as a science. Richard's resentment turned into anger in 1911, when Richard published four articles against Durkheim (cf. Richard 1911a, 395–399, 1911c, 331–332, 1911d, 356–359, 1911e, 431–436). Although his anger lessened over time, Richard did not change his opposition to Durkheim or his notion of solidarity. According to Richard, Durkheim wants to make believe that sociology is an empirical science. But, in truth, he "make[s] sociology a moral science by transforming the social threats into a principle of obligation for consciousness" (Richard 1935, 20) while seeking at the same time to "claim the monopoly of sociological research" only for himself (Richard 1943b, xi). In Richard's view, his words are not an expression of his resentment against Durkheim but of "the need to free myself from the spirit of a school" (Richard 1935, 17). This claim of independence is certainly a bit exaggerated—after all, Richard has collaborated with Durkheim from the beginning of *L'Année sociologique* in 1896 until 1907. Nevertheless, Richard's claims will be regularly quoted by his supporters (cf. for example Ouy 1926, 229–233; also Beaulavon 1937, 335) in order to polarise Richard's and Durkheim's position on solidarity, as if they were not reconcilable.

Indeed, there are differences between Richard and Durkheim when it comes to their concept of solidarity and their understanding of solidarity in history and in contemporary societies, as we have seen. But there is also a common concern shared by both Richard and Durkheim regarding the question underlying solidarity, namely the question of social cohesion. How should this question be addressed? Should we consider with Durkheim that social cohesion leads to an examination of the role of the corporations and their controlling power over the individual actors? Or should we think with Richard that social cohesion leads to an investigation of the meaning, the structure and the function of the relation between individual actors and society itself, and of the other elements related to that relation, such as the activities of individual actors on and with the objects of exchange, the role of institutions or social organisations, and the role of ideas, symbols, and beliefs?

Richard is not the only one who thinks that solidarity and social cohesion have to be investigated based on an examination of the relation itself. In the Durkheim school, too, we can observe such an attempt. It is expressed in Marcel Mauss' work on sacrifice, magic, and the gift. As Mauss is Durkheim's nephew and his faithful collaborator at *L'Année sociologique*, it is then tempting to extend our comparison between Durkheim and Richard to Mauss and Richard. This would enable us to examine, on the example of the controversies between Durkheim and Richard, whether we are going to find analogous dissimilarities and conflicts between Richard and Mauss or, on the contrary, similarities. This shall be the subject matter of our next chapter.

Notes

1. Richard says at the end of his life, "I was more known…as a sociologist and theorist of solidarity" (Richard 1943a, 88). For him, sociology is "the methodical knowledge of solidarity" (ibid. 53). Cf. also Pickering (1975, 347).
2. This describes Richard's research programme which he reformulates at the end of his career as follows, "I had to seek, better than in my juvenile essay on the origin of the idea of law, the conditions of a harmony between cooperation and legal order, which itself is based on the harmony of active solidarity and the responsibility of the members of society" (Richard 1935, 14).

3. Richard defines his genetic method as the study of the structure and the modifications of the rules observable in social groups (Richard 1898a, 392–394).
4. Richard attributes this distinction between altruistic and egoistic utilitarianism to Wilhelm Wundt (Richard 1903a, 151).
5. Richard mentions the difficulty of such a link between duty and law in Comte's sociology, "When Comte, in his *Discours sur l'ensemble du positivism,* says that everyone has the right to do his duty only, he and the sociologists with him have been led either to deny any compulsory duty or to consider all social duties as equally enforceable. The social consequence of the idea of law is that certain duties can be imposed on the moral agent by force, while the fulfillment of other ones depends on his good will" (Richard 1912a, 92). And Richard concludes: "Comte's attitude and that of those contemporary French thinkers who have accepted his ruinous legacy seems very dangerous. This doctrine does not only contradict itself regarding the nature of an autonomous and specific sociology, but it also could lead to scientific skepticism, and to an alteration, if not an eclipse, of the idea of law" (ibid. 295–296).
6. For Richard, Comte's discourse on women is similar to the ones of Immanuel Kant and Jean-Jacques Rousseau, who think highly of patriarchy: "a wife, if we believe them, can refine the man only if she herself remains humble, subject to him, without legal guaranties, in short, she is eternally subject to the condition which patriarchy has defined for her" (Richard 1909a, 409).
7. Pickering, for example, sees in Richard's article "Sur les lois de la solidarité morale", published in 1905, (Richard 1905, 441–471) the peak of the crisis between Richard and Durkheim, because "for the first time, he [Richard; CP] is openly criticizing him" (Pickering 1979, 168).
8. The Rector of the University of Bordeaux also recognised the important tasks awaiting Richard, "'succeeding to Mr. Durkheim is a very hard task. Monsieur Richard, thanks to his tirelessness, is not exhausted. He is a modest and straight person'" (Fournier 2007: 521).
9. Cf. the letter of Lapie to Bouglé of 30 October 1904, leads the reader to "think that Durkheim would have preferred Lapie, instead of Richard, to teach sociology at Bordeaux" (Pickering 1979, 166) when Lapie writes to Bouglé, "Did I tell you about my visit to Durkheim on Saturday, the 4th of October? He has committed me to teaching sociology, and he declared that 'after what he knows about me, I am quite capable to do it according to the positive method'. Translation: let Richard become professor of philosophy and wait until my chair is vacant in Bordeaux in order the take it" (Mauss et al. 1979, 42).

10. According to Richard, "sociology has taken from theology, correcting it, the idea of human solidarity, and it has used it to shed light on the social facts" (Richard 1892, vii). Richard specified his idea in 1903, saying that "the relations between solidarity and responsibility were the subject of discussions between the supporters of Saint Augustine and those of Pelagus, later between the Arminians and the Gomarists, still later between the Jansenists and the Molinists when they discussed the major problems of the transmission of sin, and of the possibility of salvation by grace. The social sciences have secularized these questions" (Richard 1903a, 131).
11. Richard says, "We know that in the language of jurisprudence, solidarity only refers to some collective responsibility. Montesquieu uses the term in this sense in a passage of l'Esprit des lois" (Richard 1912a, 82).
12. As we shall see later on, Richard has all the more reason to quote Durkheim as the coming of the corporation describes, for Durkheim too, the transition from a society that is organised along the (real or symbolic) relations of consanguinity, towards a society where there is more individualisation, and which is organised along the relations between the actors and their territory (Durkheim 1893a (1922), 161).
13. Richard says: "The picture of the corporate regime is sufficient to show that it bears in itself the cause of its decomposition. Alone, it testifies to the emergence of the enterprise regime" (Richard 1897, 101).
14. Richard details this general rule relating to the evolution from corporation to enterprise and industry by assuming the following three conditions: "1° it was necessary that industrial activity was no longer granted by some authority in the form of monopolies; 2° that the authority would no longer attribute to itself the right to protect consumers from the craftsmen but would allow them to choose their suppliers themselves; 3° that the master craftsmen, becoming individual entrepreneurs, would no longer exert any paternal authority on their workers but became tied to them by reciprocal or bilateral contract" (Richard 1897, 102).
15. Durkheim comments on this lack of adaption as follows: "In principle, so long as artisans and merchants drew their custom more or less exclusively from the town-dwellers or the immediate neighbourhood alone, that is, so long as the market was mainly a local one, the guild, with its municipal organization, sufficed for every need. But it was no longer the case once large-scale industry had sprung up. Not being particularly urban in any way, it could not conform to a system that had not been designed for it. In the first place, its locus was not necessarily the town. It can even be installed far from any existing population settlement, whether rural or urban. It merely seeks the spot where it can be best supplied and from where it can spread out as easily as possible. Next, its field of activity is not confined to any particular region and it draws its customers from anywhere. An institu-

tion so wholly involved in the commune as was the old corporation could not therefore serve to frame and regulate a form of collective activity so utterly alien to communal life" (Durkheim 1893b (2013), 23).

16. As Durkheim puts it: "The ties that arise from living together have not their source so deeply in men's hearts as those arising from blood relationship" (Durkheim 1893b (2013), 146).
17. To Durkheim, this means nationalisation—or even internationalisation—of the corporations which would then be constantly in contact with the state, of which "the state cannot fail to be aware" (Durkheim 1909, 219).
18. Indeed, according to Richard, "Professional organization is necessary to civil society and in fact, has never been outlawed since the end of the Roman Empire" (Richard 1903a, 225).
19. Durkheim writes more extensively on this topic in his *Leçons de sociologie* (cf. Durkheim 1890–1900 (1995), 55–56).
20. Durkheim illustrates this with the example of the unequal distribution of wealth: "the hereditary transmission of wealth suffices to render very unequal the external conditions for the struggle, since it gives to some the benefit of advantages that do not necessarily correspond to their personal value. Even today, among the most cultured peoples, careers exist that are totally closed, or more difficult to enter for those blighted by misfortune" (Durkheim 1893b (2013), 296).
21. This argument can be found almost everywhere in Richard's works, as for example here: "The hierarchy of the classes is only a transient phenomenon of anthropological origin. Very harmful in less complex societies and in little differentiated communities, it loses its importance when the relationships of cooperation become more complex, when the individual's competence has more value, and when exchange between human beings becomes universal" (Richard 1912a, 331). On Durkheim's side, we have almost the same reasoning: "if the institution of class or caste sometimes gives rise to miserable squabbling instead of producing solidarity, it is because the distribution of social functions on which it rests does not correspond, or rather no longer corresponds, to the distribution of natural abilities" (Durkheim 1893b (2013), 294). Therefore, what is needed is "to eliminate external inequalities as much as possible", which would be a "work of justice…still more absolute as the organized type of society develops" (ibid. 297–298).
22. This allows a better understanding of what Richard says against Durkheim when speaking of professional solidarity: "Let us make a distinction, absent in Durkheim's work, between inter-professional and intra-professional solidarity. Only the first one would deserve the name of organic solidarity but only exists to the extent in which the state succeeds in subordinating the corporate interests to the sustainable requirements of national solidar-

ity; the second one is a new form of solidarity by similarity; it is based on the analogy of interests, and on the identity of professional habits. To what extent can this intra-professional solidarity, which is a collective egoism only, be compatible with national solidarity, or, if one prefers, with civic solidarity?" (Richard 1925a, 261).

23. Let us quote Durkheim more extensively: "To co-operate, in fact, is to share with one another a common task. If this task is subdivided into tasks qualitatively similar, although indispensable to one another, there is a simple or first-level division of labour. If they are different in kind, there is composite division of labour, or specialization proper" (Durkheim 1893b (2013), 97).
24. Durkheim repeatedly illustrates this in *The Division of Labour in Society*. See, for instance, "So far as we can judge the state of the law in the very lowest societies, it seems to be wholly repressive" (Durkheim 1893b (2013), 108).
25. Durkheim's assertions in this sense leave no doubt, as for example here: "penal law is not only of essentially religious origin, but continues always to bear a certain stamp of religiosity" (Durkheim 1893b (2013), 77).
26. The penalty, for Durkheim, has nothing to do with vendetta: "Private vengeance is…far from being the prototype of punishment" (Durkheim 1893b (2013), 73).
27. Speaking of the effect of social change on individual consciousness, Richard indicates that social actors and societies have a reciprocal purpose, and he adds: "This reciprocal purpose can be described as voluntary cooperation or organic solidarity" (Richard 1903c, 265). In the note, he comments: "We know that one of these expressions is preferred by Mr Spencer, the other by Mr. Durkheim" (ibid. note 1), before he concludes, expressing his criticism, "but they cannot be correctly explained by the mechanical laws of the division of labour" (ibid. 265). For a similar observation, cf. Richard 1903b, 12–13.
28. This element of will is typical of how Richard understands cooperation. There is, however, another element that can be used to distinguish cooperation from other forms of association, namely the fact that cooperation is linked to contractual exchanges of a material or non-material nature—a point on which Richard and Durkheim agree. "In general, the contract is the symbol of exchange" (Durkheim 1893b (2013), 98). For Richard, "The contract has neither a place in the foundation of the family, nor in that of the nation. Its place refers to production and exchange" (Richard 1892, 133). Therefore, even if cooperation is a phenomenon that is not absent in ancient societies, it is not at the origin of society, a point well underlined by Durkheim and Richard in their critique of Rousseau and his concept of the social contract.

29. Durkheim expresses this most directly in his text *Définition du fait moral*, speaking of the "feeling of obligation, i.e. the existence of duty" (Durkheim 1893c (1975), 282 note 21).
30. The attention that Durkheim pays to the work of his German colleagues has often been underlined in literature in regard to the work of either the German economists (see particularly Jones 1994, 37–57; Nau and Steiner 2002, 1005–1024; Morchõn 2005; Steiner 2011), or the German philosophers and sociologists (for example Marica 1932; Alpert 1939; Lukes 1973; Filloux 1977; Alexander 1982; Gane 1984, 304–330; Watts Miller 1996, 31–42; Feuerhahn 2014, 79–98).
31. Regarding Gumplowicz, Durkheim highlights this dependence by saying that "The moral is coming from law, and it follows all its variations. But in its turn, law gains power only if it is based on moral, or in other words, if it manages to push its roots into the heart of citizens" (Durkheim 1885b, 631).
32. A very good example of Richard's approximations is given on page 299 of his article *Philosophie du droit. La contrainte sociale et la valeur du droit subjectif* (Richard 1909b, 299). Here, we can legitimately think that duty is on the side of morals while law is on the side of obligation. However, at the end of the page, Richard says: "The obligation set by the law is always a coercive one, sanctioned by power, while duty coming from morals does not admit any constraint of this kind" (ibid.).
33. As Richard says, "the fulfilment of the social function, or duty" (Richard 1903a, 117).
34. In morals, this is what Richard was to call the moral law, which is a law of emancipation, "an ideal of autonomy, which we can consider at most as a limit that we shall never reach" (Richard 1903a, 116). It is an ideal or a "hypothesis" which enables us to examine whether morals changes human nature, and if one can observe the effects of such transformation in history (ibid.). Richard observes such effects not only in the history of the European countries, but also in China and India, for example.
35. As Pickering says: "Durkheim keeps silent on that question. Maybe it was Durkheim's will not to talk about that, in order to prevent an open controversy which would have led to dissension, and which would have lowered the spirit of his troops. His prestige in the academic world would have been diminished" (Pickering 1979, 168).

CHAPTER 3

Contact: Gaston Richard and Marcel Mauss on Sacrifice and Magic

Little is known about the relationship between Marcel Mauss and Gaston Richard. All we have are some indirect words by Mauss and Richard that indicate that they did not share any particular affinity towards each other. To Earle Eubank, who travelled to Europe in 1934, and collected about twenty-five interviews of eminent European sociologists, Mauss said: "Gaston Richard is a good man, but honestly, he is of very little importance in sociology. He has not really provided any contribution to this discipline, he is now retired, and I do not even know if he is still alive" (Käsler 1985, 152). Richard sees Mauss as the heir of the latter's uncle, Émile Durkheim, and associates him with Mauss' and Durkheim's joint enterprise, i.e. the sociology of religion, which Richard strongly criticised. For him, "Mess. Durkheim, Mauss, Hertz, Lévy-Bruhl and their disciples [profess; CP] that the essence of religion is not and never has been something else than the collective consciousness of wild hordes" (Richard 1929, 29). This, Richard regarded as an absurdity, which was just as great as the one that led the Durkheimians to seek "the prototype of the ancestors of civilized humanity" among the Maoris or the American Natives (Richard 1897, 177).

Yet Mauss and Richard knew each other well. They worked together in 1896 on the publication of *L'Année sociologique*, a periodical by which Durkheim wanted to extend his scientific programme in sociology. They both had an important position as editors at *L'Année*. Mauss was Durkheim's right hand, recruited the collaborators at *L'Année*, and was,

C. Papilloud, *Sociology through Relation*, Palgrave Studies in Relational Sociology, https://doi.org/10.1007/978-3-319-65073-9_3

with Henri Hubert, responsible for the most important section of the periodical on religious sociology (Mauss 1927 (1969), 178–179; Durkheim 1998, 5; Besnard 2003, 319–329). Richard, as we have seen in our second chapter, knew Durkheim since their early years at *Ecole Normale Supérieure* (Essertier 1930b, 365; Richard 1932, 609). In the first three volumes of *L'Année*, Richard was the single editor of the periodical's fourth section on criminal sociology. Both Richard and Mauss, had been dealing with Durkheim's work. This gives rise to the question whether this professional proximity between them is also reflected in or by their work.

When comparing the writings of both authors, we quickly see that Mauss and Richard converge on what will become their main concern, which is the relational perspective on social phenomena. Their interest in this perspective developed in the context of the investigation of religious phenomena. Nevertheless, it *prima facie* appears that, at both an intellectual and a personal level, Mauss and Richard would have to differ on nearly everything. Mauss followed the intuitions of his uncle and regarded himself and his closest colleagues, such as Henri Hubert and Robert Hertz, as the "disciples of Durkheim" (Mauss 1927 (1969), 178). For his uncle—to whom he referred as his "master" (ibid. 179)—Mauss had deep admiration, which reminds us of the enthusiasm he had felt when he attended Durkheim's lectures as a young man (cf. Durkheim 1998, 5ff.). Literature has since largely contributed to Mauss' image as a scholar who was inextricably linked to Durkheim. The authors writing about the relationship between Mauss and Durkheim very often describe the work of the nephew as the prolongation of the work of the uncle, even up to the point where those who evoke their differences[1] mostly do so in order to highlight their similarities.[2] In contrast, literature paints Richard who, compared to Mauss, was little read after World War II, either as a "second Durkheim" as purported by Pickering's expression (Pickering 1979, 164), or as his direct opponent (Aron 1938, 413) and the head of a counter-programme opposing Durkheimian sociology (compare also Pickering 1975, 347). However, the similarities between both authors remain and exceed the institutional divide between Durkheimians and Anti-Durkheimians, not least because Mauss did not always remain true to the work of his uncle or to his own reputation as Durkheim's follower.

Working on Mauss' religious sociology, Mike Gane wrote an interesting article (Gane 1984, 308–309), calling the image of Mauss as a faithful and loyal nephew into question. For Gane, it is anything but certain that Mauss blindly followed his uncle with the single aim to continue his uncle's work or to support the further growth of the Durkheimian School. Analysing his writings on religion, Gane suggests that Mauss, while declaring himself explicitly to stand in the service of Durkheim, does no less than deliver a critique of Durkheim's sociology of religion. In his argument, Gane refers to a disagreement—actually a minimal one—between Mauss and Durkheim regarding the definition of religion.

For Durkheim, religion and society are inextricably linked, even if their relationship is asymmetric in the sense that society is the lifeblood or—as Durkheim says—"the soul of religion" (Durkheim 1912 (1995), 421). Religion "is a unified system of beliefs and practices relative to sacred things, that is to say, things set apart and forbidden—beliefs and practices which unite into one single moral community called a Church, all those who adhere to them" (ibid. 44). Durkheim says that this intimate link between society and religion was revealed to him in 1895 when he read Robertson Smith (Durkheim 8.11.1907 (1975), 404). Having become deeply aware of such a link, Durkheim provides a variety of explanations of how it should be understood (cf. Durkheim 1890–1900 (1995), 188, 1897, 352). The most radical one appears in the lecture that Durkheim writes on the origins of religious life, where he indicates identity between religion and society:

> As to know why men need gods, and why gods need men, this is easy after what has been said above about the true nature and the objective basis of religion since, as we have seen, the divinity is nothing else than society itself, and it becomes real because it is only one mode of representation of the collective; the soul, in turn, as a religious being, is the social in us. (Durkheim 1907b (1975), 121–122, 1912, 323; cf. also Pickering 1984, 61; Fournier 2007, 261ff.)

With his very first major writings on religious sociology, Mauss already differs from Durkheim in how this link between society and religion is to be understood. For him, religion and society are not as consubstantial as Durkheim claims. This difference is particularly visible when Mauss speaks of sacrifice,[3] a topic that runs like a major theme through his scientific work up to his famous essay "The Gift (1925)". Sacrifice is also the topic on which Richard relied in order to propose an understanding of society as well as of religion, which too is different from Durkheim's understanding of both concepts. Therefore, if there is an intellectual affinity between Mauss and Richard that can be deepened, the notion of sacrifice gives our investigation a starting point. Sacrifice is intimately linked to another subject matter that is of major interest to both Mauss and Richard: penalty, and the broader subject to which it refers, namely that of the origin of criminal law.

Penalty

Penalty is at the converging point of sacrifice and criminal law, whose meaning Mauss attempts to reconstruct. He starts with the discussion of Sebald Rudolf Steinmetz's theses on the relationships between the practices of vengeance and the cult of the dead.

For Steinmetz, societies practising the cult of the dead take revenge for the death of one of their members in order to satisfy the dead, and to prevent them returning as spirits to settle old scores with their former society. Steinmetz explains this practice of vengeance by the cruelty of the actors in those ancient societies whose members, once one of them died, killed all foreign actors they came across in order to appease the deceased, and to protect themselves from his anger. Contrary to what Steinmetz suggests, Mauss thinks, however, that "the relationship between the cult of the dead and bloody vengeance was better established by the practice of the funeral sacrifice" (Mauss 1896 (1974), 678–679). Therefore, bloody vengeance that can be found in ancient societies cannot be understood as a crime whose origin would be found in the psychology of cruel individuals. It is instead part of a set of rites that Mauss calls funeral or mortuary sacrifices. "In these societies, murder is not a crime but it is damage done to a family group, an insult; in these societies, it was not an offense as compared to incest or sacrilege. Murder was recognised by criminal law only very late; it was certainly not there at its origin" (ibid. 679). Bloody vengeance in its most extreme form—murder—was not a public matter, but a private one.

Richard expresses the same idea when he notes that, in the same societies, "there is no intervention of neither power nor reason between vengeance and criminal aggression" (Richard 1892, 14). Vengeance is above all the business of families, the "relatives of the victim are the ones who must punish the perpetrator" (ibid.). Consequently, vengeance does not have a public character. It is not considered a crime in those societies that, to the contrary, uphold it as a generally accepted institution (ibid. 88). Thus, we are confronted with a social group whose punishment by vengeance has nothing to do with criminal law. "Where vengeance exerted by the victim's relatives is the only penalty for the crime, the concept of offense is unclear or even stifled by the associated ideas of punishment and vengeance" (ibid. 123). For Mauss as for Richard, it can be said that if vengeance is not at the origin of criminal law, then the origin and the motivation of criminal law have to be found in the fact that "society removes these private wars" deriving from vengeance (Mauss 1896 (1974), 689). For Richard too, the idea of penalty and its presence in modern criminal law grows out of the same root. "Penalty is aimed at protecting society from private wars brought about by vengeance or other conflicts" (Richard 1892, 145). The idea of penalty assumes a "debt not of the defendant towards society, but of society towards its members" (ibid.). For Mauss, this is the reason why penalty "cannot therefore concern the clan, except in very rare circumstances; in its origin, it concerns the individual" (Mauss 1896 (1974), 693).

One of the emblematic illustrations of this idea of debt that Mauss and Richard found in the history of societies is "composition", i.e. the compensation of the injured party in money or property by way of redemption (ibid. 668–670; Richard 1892, 129). However, this "composition" does not evoke an idea of debt only. It is also linked to a promise, which for Richard "represents the obligation of society to prohibit private vendettas and settlement of conflict by private warring" (ibid. 143). Here, Mauss sees the origin of the systems of sanctions that are the prerequisite for executing public penalties in the first place (Mauss 1896 (1974), 670). Mauss' and Richard's reasoning rests on an identical assumption, namely that law depends on religion.

For Mauss, this is the most important point of his critique of Steinmetz who does not see that public criminal law has religious origins (Mauss 1896 (1974), 678–679). At the same time, this argument allows Mauss to recall his attachment to Durkheim's sociological theory, explicitly mentioned as one of the important sources in his text on Steinmetz (ibid. 679, note 115, 680, note 116).[4] For Richard, there can be no doubt about the intimate relationship between law and religion because the various types of law are all based on religion (Richard 1892, 192–193). Thus, Richard seems to fully agree with Mauss. Nevertheless, he underlines an important point, saying that the development of law becomes in time independent of the development of religion.[5] This gives rise to the question: how to reconcile the intimate relationship between law and religion, and the fact that law and religion are evolving independently of each other in history?

In order to solve this problem, Richard asks what is meant by religion (ibid. 193), which, for him, is neither a religious institution—the Church—nor a religious doctrine but is, instead, a religious practice. Religion is above all "the cult, the rite" (ibid.), and the object of these cults and rites is "the sacrifice given to the divinity" (ibid. 194). This leads to the following question: "Does participation in the sacrifice represent…the condition of law?" (ibid.). There is no obvious answer to this question because there are various forms of sacrifice that have a variety of purposes, as Mauss and Hubert show in their essay *Sacrifice. Its Nature and Functions* (1899). Richard likewise observes: "Sometimes, the purpose of the sacrifice is to obtain forgiveness of sins and the moral force necessary to obey the divine commandments. Sometimes it is to avert natural scourges, above all disease. And sometimes, it is to know the future. But nowhere do we see sacrifices with the express purpose to cause human beings to give each other guarantees" (Richard 1892, 194). Should we then conclude that in spite of the appearances, there is no relationship between sacrifice and law?

For Richard, there is indeed a relationship between sacrifice and law, which we can observe when we look at the role of the intermediary in sacrificial ceremonies. In their *Sacrifice* of 1899, Mauss and Hubert follow the same path. They particularly highlight the importance of the intermediary for the sacrifice, to the point that, for them, "with no intermediary, there is no sacrifice" (Hubert and Mauss 1899 (1964), 100). The intermediary is not exclusively the victim of the sacrificial killing who links the world of human beings to the world of the gods. It is also the priest who is going with the sacrificer (the one who performs the killing) when the latter enters into the sacrifice. The priest "stands on the threshold between the sacred and the profane world" (ibid. 23). He is the "mandatory of the sacrifier", and he is "sealed with a divine seal" (ibid.). Due to his proximity to the gods, the priest is often exempted from the rituals that the sacrificer must perform in order to enter into the sacrifice. At the same time, he is a supervisor, guiding the sacrificer, as well protecting society against any possible harmful consequences of the sacrifice.

In animal sacrifices, for example, the priest consumes the portions of the sacrificed animal to be sure that the animal disappears completely from the temporal world (ibid. 38–39). The priest, is playing the role of an intermediary between the profane and the sacred world acts, according to Richard, as arbitrator. Such arbitration does not itself lead to legal rules but, as Richard says, limits the legal rules through religion and the practice of cults and rituals of which the practices of sacrifice are the most emblematic ones (Richard 1892, 196).[6] Mauss and Hubert give an illustration when they say that the rights of the sacrificer to the portions of the sacrificed victim he is entitled to consume are most often "restricted by the ritual. Very often, he had to consume it within a limited time" because "the effects of his consecration lasted only for a while" (Hubert and Mauss 1899 (1964), 40). In these temporal limits, law has all the external aspects of religion, so that sacrifices can be interpreted as contractual practices. "Fundamentally, there is perhaps no sacrifice that has not some contractual element. The two parties present exchange their services and each gets his due" (ibid. 100).

Indeed, if human beings need gods, gods also need human beings in order to exist. This ambiguity is directly linked "to the presence of the intermediary" (ibid.) without which such an exchange in both directions—from humans to gods and from gods to humans—would not be possible. The role of the intermediary that the priest and, by extension, the sacrificer play is therefore an element that proves the unity of law and religion in ancient societies. Nevertheless, unity does not mean causation. From this viewpoint, it is symptomatic that Mauss often speaks of a *religious* origin of law, and never of an origin of law in religion. This nuance is very important because Mauss refers to *ritual practices* between humans and gods in ancient societies where law and religion are complementary but not sequentially interconnected, as shown by the various forms of sacrifice. Thus, in sacrifices, law and religion coexist. But then, how do they become different from each other?

According to Richard, we can answer this question when considering the utilitarian character of sacrifice (i.e. the way in which sacrifice benefits those who practise it) as well as the anthropomorphic character of the god and its resemblance with human beings. The former element is directly found in Mauss and Hubert who identify it in the typical framework of sacrifices that directly benefit the sacrificer (Hubert and Mauss 1899 (1964), 62). The same is true of agrarian sacrifices where it is not the sacrificer who is at the centre of the sacrifice, but where the sacrifice centres on the objects given to the god(s). For Richard, this utility is most emblematic as regards the character of sacrifices whose goal is always to gain the favour of the gods or to appease their anger, i.e. to make the gods into allies (Richard 1892, 203). These cases are reflected by the fact that the objects of sacrifice are more concrete.

In the agrarian sacrifices of which Mauss and Hubert speak, the wheat used as offering represents the spirit of the wheat only while the wheat sacrifice itself aims to ensure most immediate effectiveness for the sacrificial rite. As Mauss and Hubert say, the spirit of the wheat "leaves the fields only to return to them immediately" (Hubert and Mauss 1899 (1964), 78). The spirit of the wheat in agrarian sacrifices warrants to society that the wheat will continue to grow in the fields and that the fields remain fertile. However, this sacrifice of wheat in agrarian rites has only an effect in relation to the wheat itself and to the fields of wheat it represents. For the sacrificed object to have an effect not only on wheat fields but also on the agricultural environment as a whole, the spirit of the wheat must be given a "personality" (ibid.). It is then necessary to give the wheat another name, either by replacing it with an animal, or even a human being. "In this way, the spirit of the fields' life gradually becomes exterior to the fields and becomes individualized" (ibid. 79). This is the prerequisite for the sacrifice of the divinity itself, the ultimate form of sacrifice for Mauss and Hubert, because in such sacrifice "the god who sacrifices himself, gives himself irrevocably" (ibid. 101). Here, the god gives himself to himself regardless of any returned offerings by human beings. Without wanting to claim that agrarian or divine sacrifices do already contain the essence of the sacrifices practised in contemporary religions—for example the sacrifice of the Paschal lamb in the Christian religion—Mauss and Hubert nevertheless describe the successive transformation of the sacrificed object. This transformation contributes to the emerging distinction between the sacrifice's religious and legal character. This explanation is also endorsed by Richard, who speaks of the humanisation of the sacrificed object in order to describe the same phenomenon.[7] Although they do not use the same vocabulary there is still perceivable accord between these authors when it comes to sacrifice, as seen in the summary below.

First, Mauss and Richard observe a convergence of law and religion in the practices of sacrifice in ancient societies. The religious practice gives law its internal boundaries, blocking in some way its application to any objects outside these boundaries.

Second, they describe an evolution of the practices of sacrifice, which they reconstruct by following the transformations of the means used for performing those sacrifices, i.e. the sacrificed objects. The more they become personalised, humanised, the more the sacrifices refer to religious practices only, and the more these practices differ from legal practices. The same can be observed in relation to penalty. If, in ancient societies, religious and legal penalties are considered to be intrinsically interconnected, the evolution of the practices of sacrifice shows a corresponding evolution in the classification of transgressions and their respective penalties. Where "composition" replaces sacrificial killing, its penalty becomes a payment and ceases to involve vengeance and death.

In modern societies, acts of transgression are no longer considered actions that affect the whole of society because transgressions are judged by the idea of individual responsibility towards society and its rules. Therefore, in contemporary societies, the law now applies where in ancient societies religious practices dominated. "Progress has been uninterrupted and it consisted in moving from religious and instinctive origins to the rational and social ideal towards which our justice tends" (Mauss 1896 (1974), 698). This idea is the same as the one found in Richard's work. It is a fundamental idea, which is required if one wants to understand the key elements in Mauss' and Richard' reflections on sacrifice. Sacrifice does not only allow us to gain a better understanding of the relationships between religious and legal cults and rites. It also enables us to highlight the fundamental elements of a relational approach to religion and law as found in the observation that "social practices [are] not strictly religious" (Hubert and Mauss 1899 (1964), 103).

The most important of these elements is the contact that sacrifices establish between the profane and the sacred in the relationships between human beings and gods, or, speaking of daily practices, between the individuals and society (Mauss 1896 (1974), 685–687; Richard 1899, 484). Contact gives the sacrifice its two dimensions—i.e. an individual and a collective dimension. These dimensions depend directly on the sacrifice's effectiveness not just as a rite but especially as a relation, where elimination of the individual transgression is nothing without "the religious solidarity of the group" (Mauss 1896 (1968), 688), without a society being "profoundly in solidarity with the offender's sins" (Richard 1899, 484). This touches on the meaning of penalty as a debt, as a form of contract between the individuals and society. On a more theoretical level, the penalty represents a specific contact between individuals and society. In ancient societies, the forms of sacrifice are manifestations of that contact (for example, Hubert and Mauss 1899 (1964), 95–99; Richard 1892, 206). In Mauss and in Richard, contact is certainly more fact than concept and we can therefore ask if it can be relevant as a concept. This is what we are trying to do when we take a deeper look at penalty in relation to pain.

Pain

Let us start with Mauss. If the relation between the profane and the sacred world on a religious level, and between offender and society on a legal level must be established again and again and if the sacrifice contributes to highlight regular "communication"[8] between human beings and gods as well as between human beings amongst each other, then these societies and their actors do not start from nothing. Instead, they start from the contact between the profane and the sacred world, from the contact between human beings and gods, and between human being and human being. This contact is already present as a presupposition in the practices of sacrifice in the ancient societies of which Mauss and Hubert speak. Here, there is neither a world of human beings without a world of gods, nor are there individuals without society. This is why such contact is the concrete starting point of a mobilisation of actors and society that could lead to the relation between them.

For Mauss, pain is a key argument in his critique of Steinmetz's interpretation of vengeance as the product of the cruelty inherent in human beings. If cruelty could explain the imposition of penalties and the sacrifices, this would mean that instead of the relation, there would be a state of permanent violence between actors and society (Mauss 1896 (1974), 680). This contradicts the periodicity of the practices of vengeance and sacrifice. They do not constantly occur but instead appear at well-defined times. This leads Mauss to suggest that instead of being cruel, the family group that exerts vengeance is, in fact, merely angry: "Vengeance relates more directly to anger than to cruelty" (ibid.). Anger allows us to understand that, for ancient societies, manslaughter out of vengeance was not regarded as murder. Rather, it expressed the need to eliminate the pain caused by the loss of a group member by killing someone else (ibid. 678–679). The fundamental point Mauss underlines is that of pain as the origin of anger, a pain that is felt by the individual as well as by society. "[A]ll suffer from the pain felt by a single one" (ibid. 685) because all are in contact with each other. Mauss, reviewing Steinmetz, remains however on a general level in his explanation of pain. He provides no detail of how this kind of empathy by the group or by society for the individual actor's suffering actually occurs other than by Durkheim's argument of "family solidarity" (ibid.).[9] The character of such solidarity goes back to the "religious nature of the family" (ibid. 676), which Mauss, in 1896, takes still for granted. "Whatever the differences between the historical and the anthropological schools that put either the totem or the patriarchal family at the origin of the evolution of the family, the religious nature of its origin is taken for granted unanimously" (ibid. 685). Here, we recognise the pivot of Durkheim's thinking, namely the circular relation between religion and society. On this point, however, Mauss differs from his uncle.

He certainly takes the religious nature of the family for granted, but he does not think that it provides a sufficient explanation for vengeance, penalty and pain. He thus explores the religious nature of the family in more depth in the essay that he publishes with Henri Hubert in 1902–1903, *A General Theory of Magic*. To know the meaning of the family's "religious nature" on which Mauss bases his relational perspective on pain, we must follow his reflections on magic and religion. This occupied Mauss the most when he gave his lectures at *Ecole des Hautes Etudes* between 1902 and 1905, when he defined magic as "a religious phenomenon…apart from religion in itself because it is inorganic and not necessarily determined" (Mauss 1902–1905 (1974), 390). This definition expresses the basic idea that, in their *General Theory of Magic*, Mauss and Hubert have set out to defend

Magic and religion differ from each other because they do not describe the same reality. Magic "has a taste for the concrete", religion "tends to be abstract" (Mauss 1902–1903 (2001), 175). Magic is a "living mass, formless and inorganic, and its vital parts have neither a fixed position nor a fixed function" (ibid. 108). Religion is seen as a specialised system where "ritual and its like on the one hand, and myths and dogmas on the other, have real autonomy" (ibid.). Yet, these differences are described on an analytical level. In the daily life of those societies that Mauss and Hubert examine, there never is a radical separation between magic and religion. Mauss and Hubert even believe that both depend on the same "matrix [of] magical facts", namely the *mana* (ibid. 168), a kind of magical power that would be their "common source" (ibid.). The meaning of *mana* is difficult to grasp and Mauss and Hubert do not find any accurate definition. They say that *mana* symbolises the collective forces that force the magicians to play their role (Hubert and Mauss 1904 (1974), 369), or that it is on the same level "as the idea of the sacred" (Mauss 1902–1903 (2001), 146). However, they are not satisfied by these definitions. "We might end here and conclude that magic is a social phenomenon, since we have uncovered the notion of collectivity behind all of its manifestations. However, in its present form, the idea of mana still seems to us to be cut off from social life; there is still something too intellectual about it" (ibid.

150). This is an interesting quote, because it shows that for Mauss, magic, in contrast to religion, is linked to the practical life of human beings.

In this practical life, everything is mixed up. The gestures "by which the needs of the individuals are expressed" remain "poorly coordinated and impotent" (ibid. 175). Magic has the function to give a "shape" to this lack of coordination: "it does this through ritual, it renders them effective" (ibid.). In the framework of magic, this effectiveness is measured by the "physical" effects of rites (Mauss 1947 (2007), 67). Whereas in religion, the rites already have an effect as rites, a "sui generis" effect as Mauss says (ibid.), without always affecting the natural environment or human beings. And here, we are at the heart of the problem posed by Mauss' relational perspective on pain. Indeed, if the pain experienced by the individual might be also felt by his social group because of the social group's religious nature, the word "religious" then refers to more than religion only—it also refers to magic, and especially to the *mana*. Behind this unclear notion of *mana* is society's practical life, which the *mana* symbolises. This practical life, similar to what we have seen in magic, is made of more or less uncoordinated activities, which neither have efficiency nor any power in themselves. They acquire both by the development of rites that give them the power to act on the physical world (in the case of magical rites), the moral world, and the world of gods (in the case of sacrificial rites). Therefore, there is, in the societies that Mauss and Hubert examine, a certain vulnerability of activities which best expresses what contact means. It is the concrete ground of a relation developed by putting humans, things, activities, symbols, and gods together—which is necessary but, however, does not in itself suffice to mobilise actors and society.

In this context, the pain inflicted on an actor takes a meaning that does not make sense only to the actor who is suffering. It also affects the contact between all individuals. It directly threatens the relational orientation that these individuals give to their activities, a relational orientation which may therefore cease to exist. In responding to the pain by vengeance, the actors avert the danger that threatens the contact that individuals and society need in order to sustain themselves. Against Steinmetz, Mauss says that, in ancient societies, bloody vengeance and, in general, sacrifices are not directed at specific actors but at anyone because these practices are less about the punishment or, respectively, the protection of an individual or a clan. They are, in fact, about protecting the contact that is threatened by pain.

Richard too comments on Steinmetz but, in contrast to Mauss, he takes another viewpoint. Questioning Steinmetz's hierarchy of populations ranging from "wild" people, i.e. the cruel and ferocious human beings of ancient societies, to "civilised" ones, namely the peaceful human beings of modern societies, Richard discovers not only Steinmetz's closeness to "social Darwinism" (Richard 1912a, 321). He also discovers Steinmetz's affiliation with the organicist thinkers found among anthropologists and criminal scientists of his time. Organicism was a paradigm that, although dominant in the nineteenth century, Richard wanted to overcome. Indeed, Steinmetz's arguments are not very different from the ones Richard found in the works of Charles Letourneau, Cesare Lombroso or Henry Joly. These authors contrast civilised people and their conscience of law to wild people who fear neither god, nor man, and who have therefore no idea of law. According to these authors, "civilised people" obviously capitalise on their comparative advantage over "wild populations" because "civilised people" carry with them biological predispositions enabling them to recognise others and their rights, causing them to evolve from conflict to pacifying competition. For Steinmetz, it is only the "civilised people" who have developed any sympathy for the victim. "Wild people", in contrast, do not outgrow conflict because they do not have such predispositions and therefore can only feel cruelty in respect to other people. Thus, it is not surprising that they remain "uncivilised" and are incapable of developing their lifestyle in the same way as "civilised people" do.

To consolidate their distinction, organicist theoreticians either claim that these two groups of people have no common ancestors—a hypothesis which paves the way for racial theories. Or they adopt the more nuanced view of Herbert Spencer, who distinguished between military (violent and cannibal) society and industrial society. However, Richard observes, Spencer himself admitted that "The radical distinction of these two social types is purely theoretical. Most of the societies offer a combination of the two structures; sometimes one type predominates, sometimes the other" (Richard 1892, 82). If we were to assume, as the organicists do, that non-industrialised societies remain stuck in their own crimes without being aware of their criminality because no individual pays any attention to any individual other than himself, then we would also have to assume that they have remained purely egoistical. For Richard, this would mean that such purely egoistic societies would have necessarily stopped to develop into another kind of society, e.g. the industrial society. Even Spencer does not support such a hypothesis when he speaks of the transition from military to industrial society. As a matter of fact, these societies of "wild" people have built an organisation where we find production of tools, artistic objects and rituals. The organicists provide no credible explanation for such social organisation. For Richard, this social organisation shows that there has always been an awareness of an offence's criminality everywhere, including in so-called "wild" or "criminal" societies.

Therefore, there is no reason to doubt their awareness of criminality. For Richard, this means that there is no reason to doubt that the idea of law is present in all societies, and we cannot assume that the presence of this idea rests on biological predispositions (ibid. 183). Law is not born in humans who have only been driven by their bodily needs—who, according to Richard, they have actually never been. Rather, humans form their society in resistance against their physical constraints, in general, against the constraints of nature. This resistance is not an opposition or a refusal, but the production of an activity aiming at developing a "social rational relation" (Richard 1915, 212–213). This prospect might never be truly achieved, but it remains the ideal or unsurpassable horizon of life in society for Richard. What guides social life is a relational perspective. In its most elementary expression, it is already present when the individual is in contact with his own impotence to be other than what he is, namely to be something other than a sensitive being, i.e. a being who is at once emotional, rational and physical. Such contact where the actor is feeling rather than understanding his own inability to be someone other than the particular human being he is, is the original experience of pain at the origin of his awareness of criminality (Richard 1892, 75).

This experience is first a physical one (ibid. 222), assuming the individual's experience of his own body and emotions, and through them, of his own limits. This limitation is what Richard calls the "fundamental injustice" (ibid.), which is the root of the feeling of injustice as demonstrated in the relation between offence and law. This fundamental injustice is fed by everything that can hamper contact, such as for example the physical pain resulting from beatings or voluntarily administered deprivations, particularly those related to the satisfaction of basic needs such as food, drink, clothing or protection from environmental events (ibid.). To any actor, pain means "that society does not attain its goals when its members suffer from foreign invasion, famine, epidemic diseases and other scourges. In addition, pain means to him that sacrifices offer a solution, either in the formal sense of the term where sacrifices are acts of propitiation intended to calm the irritated divinity, or in the figurative sense, in fostering a more energetic cooperation of the individuals in social activity" (ibid. 3). Pain is therefore a vector of the mobilisation of social actors in order for society to attain its goals, namely the development of this relational perspective which is present as a possibility in concrete contact, and which, according to Richard, contributes to an ideally rational social bond. As we can see, if Richard's reasoning differs from Mauss' in its form, as the latter writes about religious and Richard rather about legal phenomena, the arguments converge on a relational theory based on contact. But something is still missing.

Indeed, for Richard and Mauss, pain is an essential element of alertness, warning both individuals and society that they are in danger of losing contact. The pain caused to a social actor is not only a danger for this actor alone, but for the entire society. For example, when it takes the form of crime or transgression, it threatens the relationship between the individuals and their society. However, we can imagine situations where pain seems to matter little to the actor who feels it, that the actor does not react to attacks or that groups abandon an injured member. Mauss, for example in his essay on the *Seasonal Variations of the Eskimo*, speaks of such abandonment when they, during hunts, leave wounded, infirm or elderly people behind: "once they are incapable of keeping up with the family in its migration, they are abandoned" (Mauss 1904–1905 (2004), 71). How can we reconcile such behaviour with the idea we have developed so far, namely that, for Mauss and Richard, societies tend to preserve a minimum of existence shared with their actors, i.e. contact and thus usually react to conduct that would threaten them? Looking at Mauss and Richard, we must interpret these acts of abandonment not as an indifference to the other members of the group, but rather as manifestations of an inhibition.

Inhibition

Inhibition is a fundamental act of human behaviour that is at the bottom of the relational character of any social actor. "Not to do something is still an action, an act of inhibition is still an act" says Mauss (1947 (2007), 183), and he adds that inhibition as "resistance to the invading emotion is something fundamental in social and mental life" (Mauss 1934 (1989), 385). Inhibition is an act of control, "self-control", "presence of mind", or "dignity" towards the social world, the physical world, as well as towards the world of gods (ibid.). It is about keeping a distance between oneself and one's surroundings in order to not loose contact. Mauss finds examples of inhibition everywhere in sacrifice, and in different forms. Any sacred thing causes inhibitions (Hubert and Mauss 1905 (1929), 27) since all things sacred have a prohibiting character. Once it becomes detached from the sacred things as such and is generalised in a set of rules, it survives in a way that is both typical and public. Inhibition is "delayed action" (Mauss 1934 (1989), 385) which we can observe when we look at how priests and mages practise sacrifices and rites. They require extensive preparations and precautions if the priest or mage wants to celebrate them safely, and to avoid being devoured by the powers he has summoned. Even if the priest is "naturally nearer to the sacred world" (Hubert and Mauss 1899 (1964), 23) and therefore needs to take fewer precautions than the sacrificer when he enters into the sacrifice, he nevertheless must take "certain extra precautions…He had to wash before entering the sanctuary. Before the ceremony he had to abstain from wine and fermented liquids" (ibid. 24). He must keep apart from his family, and stay awake at night to prevent involuntary impurity (ibid. 23–24). These measures are safeguards for the priest as for the society in which he practises his magical rites, ensuring that he is not going to die during the sacrifice (ibid. 118, note 115).

Once the sacrifice has been made, the priest must perform rituals in order to step out. He stands apart from the group, washes, changes his clothes in order to be able to come back to the group as one of its members. These different forms of precautions are marked by a distance to the others, by renunciation and reserve. They are manifestations of inhibition, which is even more accentuated when it comes to mages.

> Where religious rites are performed openly, in full public view, magical rites are carried out in secret. Even when magic is licit, it is done in secret, as if performing some maleficent deed. And even if the magician has to work in public, he makes an attempt to dissemble: his gestures become furtive and his words indistinct. The medicine man and the bonesetter, working before the assembled gathering of a family, mutter their spells, cover up their actions and hide behind simulated or real ecstasies. Thus, as far as society is concerned, the magician is a being set apart and he prefers even more to retire to the depths of the forest. Among colleagues too, he nearly always tries to keep himself to himself. In this way he is reserving his powers. (Mauss 1902–1903 (2001), 29)

All these practices highlight the "irreligiosity of magical rites" (ibid.), as well as the little homogeneous and harmonious character of magic, which directly links to the practical necessities of daily life. This is why Mauss says that “When somebody has recourse to a medicine man, the owner of a spirit-fetish, a bone-mender or a magician, there is certainly a need, but no moral obligation is involved” (ibid. 29–30). This need comes from daily life and has thus neither a fixed time nor a fixed place where or when the magic has to be performed and is therefore different from religious rites or religious cults, which are governed by strict periodicity.

Becoming a mage, rather than a priest, is also not easy and people are reluctant to enter or to perform in the “profession”. “The majority are wary of employing magic, whether through scruple or lack of self-confidence; there are also those who might refuse to pass on a useful remedy” (ibid. 31). The reasons for these hesitations are related to the fact that the mage is not a member of society like any other, but a member who takes a more distant position from the society he or she is in. This is the reason why mages are often elderly, women, children or social actors on the periphery of the usual daily activities in societies. There are also, and for the same reason, mages among physicians and blacksmiths, whose “complex techniques makes it inevitable that their profession should be considered marvellous and supernatural” (ibid. 36).

The same applies to barbers, shepherds, gravediggers, and executioners because of the occult nature attributed to the surroundings in which they follow their profession—the body for the barber, nature for the shepherd, death for the gravedigger and the executioner. Similarly, people of power or renown can also become mages because they are just as much in a distant position (ibid. 36–37). The same applies to people who are persecuted, such as the Jews or the members of religious sects (ibid. 38). What makes an actor into a mage is the social position he takes or is placed in, meaning that the actor, although living amongst other actors, is at a distance from them, has almost exclusively contact only with those actors in his vicinity and a more or less virtual relation to the rest of society. Mages are therefore isolated people whose degree of isolation depends on whether the mage makes a profession of his magic or exerts it only from time to time alongside his other profession or role in society. We admire mages as much as we fear them. They are surrounded by superstitions such as the belief that the soul of the mage leaves his body and travels the world in different shapes (as a bird, insect, etc.). Mages also take advantage of such superstitions and beliefs in order to maintain the “mystery which surrounds their activities” (ibid. 42). The mage’s social position is reflected by the way in which he acts, in which he practises the magical rites, which consists of initiating contact between all possible things. In magic, everything is in contact:

> Everything which comes into close contact with the person—clothes, footprints, the imprint of the body on grass or in bed, the bed, the chair, everyday objects of use, toys and other things, all are likened to different parts of the body. There is no need for contact to be permanent or frequent, or actually made—as in the case of clothes or objects of everyday use. A road, objects touched by mere accident, bath water, a fruit that has been bitten into, etc.—all can be used magically. Magic performed over the residues of meals—which is practiced throughout the world—follows from the idea that there is a continuity and complete identity between the remains, the food consumed and the one who has eaten—the latter being substantially identical to the food partaken by him. A similar relationship of identity exists between a man and his family. It is through his relatives that he can be harmed most effectively…There is also continuity between a wound and the weapon that caused it: a sympathetic relationship is involved in the curing of the wound through the intermediacy of the weapon. (ibid. 80–81)

This is also the character of the "universal sympathy" that Richard is assigning to magic (Richard 1911b, 125), which he, like Mauss, understands as a way to give a relational direction to things by putting them in contact, to make them exchangeable in order to produce a relation (Mauss 1902–1903 (2001), 78–79; Richard 1925b, 44, 142). Everything that characterises the inhibition in the mage refers to the precautions taken in order to be able to act on the objects with a maximum of efficiency. This "action" being nothing else than to put objects and beings into contact, to ensure that once established, the contacts are preserved, or, on the contrary, can be broken.

From this point of view, magic appears to Mauss and to Richard as "a primitive science" (Mauss 1902–1903 (2001), 79), "at once a science, a poetry, an industrial technique" (Richard 1911b, 124). It exists in a different sphere to the practices of the sacrifice,[10] namely the sphere of everyday life and everyday help and assistance that the members of a society provide to one another. However, the magic world remains a world of "hopes in the form of magical formulas" (Mauss 1902–1903 (2001), 171), which are "still a very simple craft" (ibid. 175). "All efforts are avoided by successfully replacing reality by images. A magician does nothing, or almost nothing, but makes everyone believe that he is doing everything" (ibid.). Such is the effectiveness of magic which "by these methods fully [satisfies; CP] the desires and expectations which have been fostered by entire generations in common" (ibid.). However, how to explain magic's disappearance given that Mauss and Richard see magic as losing its ground when it transforms into science and technology?

If magic loses its mysticism, this is because the images it provides in order to explain the world are no longer satisfactory. They are questioned by the mages themselves. By exerting his power on nature, the mage cannot avoid looking at nature inquisitively and thus starting to specialise and refine his practice:

> Magic…attaches great importance to knowledge—one of its mainsprings… as far as magic is concerned, knowledge is power…magic—which we have shown to be more concerned with the concrete—is concerned with understanding nature. It quickly set up a kind of index of plants, metals, phenomena, beings and life in general, and became an early store of information for the astronomical, physical and natural sciences. It is a fact that certain branches of magic, such as astrology and alchemy, were called applied physics in Greece…Magicians have sometimes even attempted to systematize their knowledge and, by so doing, derive principles. When such theories are elaborated in magician colleges, it is done by rational and individual procedures. (ibid. 176–177)[11]

This last point is very important for Richard too, who understands it as the prerequisite of any pedagogy and any education of the individual. Inhibition such as Mauss found it in magic and among mages is, for Richard, an action too, which presupposes a "consciousness of the obligation" towards society (Richard 1903a, 116). It supposes a voluntary effort that each individual produces, first in relation to his own egoistic tendencies towards self-satisfaction, and then on the representations he has about the world. This effort allows the individual to "aim at this relative autonomy which leads him to judge the social norms and to assimilate them only after he has found a rational reason for them" (Richard 1895a, 129).

Richard however says that such voluntary effort is not the victory of individuality over society or of rationality over social determination. Indeed, if there is an individual commitment, there is no free will that would not be affected by society. This is why Richard calls such a will the "moral will" (Richard 1903a, 11). It syntheses two ideas, i.e. the idea of an individual commitment that cannot be totally predetermined by society, and the idea of the presence of the social rule within the individuals, who are never completely free to do what they want. Richard concludes on the one hand that moral will consists of three interrelated elements:

the individual consciousness of the reason of any action, the consciousness of the goals to attain, and the consciousness of the social rule.[12] On the other hand, will is not the origin of society, and therefore, when Richard says "moral", he does not mean "social". A concrete act of will may not always be involved nor is it always required. People may remain in the state of a "natural will" (ibid. 162), which is analogous—but not identical—to the instincts of animal species. As such, it is a symbol of self-protection or self-preservation, but also a symptom of a "development failure" in individuals and societies.[13] This development failure is a permanent element of the human condition anchored in inhibition, and therefore in a more or less enlightened individual consciousness of the social rule, so that for Richard, "the primitive fact without which human morality would not exist is character, or to say it better, inhibition" (Richard 1895b, 96). Thus, it seems that Mauss and Richard converge on the importance of inhibition but differ on how inhibition is to be understood.

For Mauss as for Richard, inhibition leads to the constraint exerted by social rules that have been more or less internalised by individual actors. Such constraint does not only come from the outside, i.e. from society, but is also coming from the individuals who exert it on society. Yet, Mauss accentuates more than Richard the external character of this constraint, i.e. the inhibition brought about by a constraint exerted from the group on its actors. "All social phenomena are to some degree the work of a collective will" (Mauss 1929 (1974), 470) Mauss says. For him, if the mage gradually becomes a scientist, and if religion is a result of specialisation in magic, this then can only be the result of an endogenous transformation. "We feel justified in saying that medicine, pharmacy, alchemy and astrology all developed within the discipline of magic, around a kernel of discoveries which were purely technical and as basic as possible…techniques are like seeds which bore fruit in the soil of magic. Later, magic was dispossessed. Techniques gradually discarded everything coloured by mysticism" (Mauss 1902–1903 (2001), 176).

For Richard, this transformation is instead coming from inhibition on the level of the individual, because "the sources of the energy of society have to be eventually found in the individuals" (Richard 1911b, 128). The individual is important because the development of societies presupposes that the variations introduced into society by the individuals are taken into account for society to be freed from traditions even if they can never be completely detached from them.

> As soon as science distinguishes itself from magic and begins to change the techniques, a very powerful cause of variation is introduced into the relationships between generations. Confidence in the infallibility of the tradition is weakened, and, therefore, progress ceases to be entirely unconscious and involuntary. The radical elimination of original characters and minds is no longer the supreme rule of social preservation. Public opinion not only accepts the changes imposed by the transformations of technical skills, but it also admits that, to a limit, the variability of skills and characters is legitimate, and that it can be socially useful. (Richard 1905, 464)

Although agreeing with Mauss on the idea that science moves gradually away from magic and becomes, over time, increasingly independent, Richard does not regard the relationship between individual and social rule—a relationship at the heart of inhibition—as a result of some predominant affinity by which the individual and the group would harmoniously make up the two sides of the same coin, i.e. society. On the contrary,

> the substitution of personal moral life for subjection to collective habits marks a rupture with magic…allowing the individual to gain or regain possession of his own thinking as well as of his own will and his own consciousness. Until then, he had accepted magic without difficulty because it was in every mind, actually in every Me who was as much depersonalized as the individual Me. As soon as the individual has taken command of his conscience and thought, he does no longer recognize himself in this fantastic world. (Richard 1926, 505)

For Richard, inhibition reflects the above mismatch between the individual actors and the social rules—a maladjustment that becomes concrete in their contact. Individuals and society are strangers to one another because each side constrains the other. Society exerts pressure on its individuals just as the individuals exert pressure on their society. Both do this by the means of rules.

This is why contact symbolises a double externality in the relationship between individual and society—the individual does not find his meaning in himself or in society just as society takes its meaning neither from the individuals nor from itself. They find their meanings in their contact, which very fact is expressed by the inhibition between an individual and a social rule in its most basic way. This is why inhibition is not the same as indifference and why renouncement, reserve, abandonment, and refusal too are concrete manifestations of contact. They too refer to a position shared by the individual and society, namely the position that each of them tries to impose their respective perspective on the other and aims to have that perspective introduced to all things and practical activities. Even if this insistence on the individual's equal importance seems to characterise Richard's explanation and distinguishes him from Mauss, who favours the power of the social group, we should still not place them in opposition.

Mauss says about magic, for example, that belief in magic and the justification of a permanent magical character that the mage derives from his contact with a spirit do only work because the mage is in a trance—because he is not in his normal state but in a state where "the magician's personality has been profoundly modified" (Mauss 1902–1903 (2001), 51). If we move this conclusion closer to Richard's discourse, it seems clear that, for Mauss too, there is nothing scientific that would come from magic as long as the mage does not work rationally on his practice by looking for the best techniques that suit his magic. If the mage, however, does exactly that, then he is moving away from magic in order to work scientifically, which, in turn, requires an individual effort to focus on the magical art per se.

Yet, if Mauss, in contrast to Richard, does not pay much attention to this aspect of the problem, this is because he remains attached to the problem of survivals, which he had inherited from English anthropology. He is thus looking for the traditional elements of social life in order to know if all or parts of such elements may always be found in present societies.[14] The perspective on survivals assumes that there is a relative continuity of societies despite the changes affecting them. It assumes a permanence of some social patterns, social practices and institutions in time and space. This perspective then does not need any assumption regarding the "will" of social actors in order to describe such survivals. Moreover, it can also strengthen the understanding of contact as a concrete manifestation of a relational orientation given to things and to the activities of daily life, which can survive the ruptures of contacts between social actors—contacts that would then exist even if there were no manifest social relationships. As Mauss says in the context of social groups practicing magical rainmaking rites, "Although they [the social groups; CP] may get divided and contact may cease, a sympathetic connexion continues and produces mental actions and reactions which, despite the separation, are no less intense" (ibid. 165). This connection reinforces the idea according to which nothing can destroy contact. Because, even if it is the most elementary manifestation of a relational perspective in society, it is based on habits and collective representations, on the history of subjects and societies having survived individual secession. Contact has its own resistance that ties generations of individuals together. If this argument of resistance of contact in time and space makes sense for Mauss because, for him, it refers to a permanence of contact that allows for survival of social institutions (habits, collective representations, history of subjects and societies etc.), it is quite surprising to also find it in Richard's discourse.

Resistance

Penalty, pain, and inhibition are three different manifestations of the same resistance in the contact between human beings and their material, spiritual or social surroundings. Even when the contacts are empirically broken, the relational perspective that they represent does not disappear. This is why something religious remains in law, and something magical in science. They can evolve apart from each other in the history of societies. But the relation between them remains, even if constantly reimplemented, if not directly, then indirectly, if not with these actors, then with other ones, if not concretely, then virtually, if not as this configuration, then as another one. If this perspective could disappear from daily life, then this would mean that the individuals as well as the societies could become radically indifferent to not only what unites them, but also—and this is why penalty, pain and inhibition are so important—to what sets them apart. Magic provides Mauss as well as Richard with many examples of such resistance, but both of them look at it from different viewpoints.

For Mauss, resistance refers to collective representations and habits well anchored in the generations of individuals and societies. For Richard, who thinks that inhibition operates against tradition, resistance comes directly from inhibition as a "more or less powerful resistance by the internal to the external", from the actor to himself and to society (Richard 1894b, 1999). Richard understands resistance as "primitive moral predisposition" (Richard 1895b, 97) and as the root of any effort and any human activity (Richard 1903a, 116). We become social actors because we resist our natural inclinations towards quick satisfaction and immediate pleasures. Resistance involves, at the same time, the recognition or the awareness of the social rule in us, and the personal will not to be dominated by this rule. Penalty, pain and inhibition are the three conditions of individual resistance to society "because his own purposes [of the individual; CP] will be the means to achieve the purposes common to all, and because the completion of the social purposes is the means without which the individual's real purposes, I mean his self-preservation and rational development, will not be achieved" (Richard 1903b, 265). This resistance is "spontaneous" or "direct" (ibid. 83) and it is present in contact. In other words, because human beings are beings of contact, their (dis)position within society is, at the same time, one of resistance against society. Now that we have described the difference between Mauss and Richard, let us take a closer look at what it entails.

Mauss' discourse on resistance has the advantage that it puts the concept in relation not only to empirical facts, but also to entire groups or collective social phenomena. For Mauss, resistance is a resistance of habits as, for instance, in bloody vengeance (Mauss 1896 (1974), 669–670), where the groups that practice this kind of vengeance do not want a system that would substitute anything for the act of killing—i.e. compensation in money for the loss of a clan member.

Resistance is also a resistance of societies and civilisations "which explains the limits of civilization in a number of cases, as well as the limits of societies" (Mauss 1929 (1974), 471). Resistance is anchored in "collective habits" which, for Mauss and Fauconnet, are "the proper object of sociology" (Fauconnet and Mauss 1901 (1969), 146–148). Collective habits are "ways to act or think consecrated by tradition and which society imposes on individuals" (ibid. 146). Of some of these habits, we are "aware", of others we are not (ibid.). The individual is not directly the producer of such collective habits "since he receives them from the outside" (ibid. 149). They seep into the individual through education as "models of conduct" (ibid.). This is why Mauss and Fauconnet think that 'the social' *is* the collective of habits, namely "the predetermined ways of thinking and acting…usually transmitted by education" (ibid. 150). These elements are important because they allow us to draw parallels to Richard.

Indeed, for Richard, education has just as much importance as for Mauss because it inculcates individuals with the rules of social life. The family and the school, for example, have a responsibility in the education of children because both parents and teachers have the role of educators. They have to have a certain authority in order to help the child to develop its consciousness and will in a way that makes it autonomous (Richard 1903a, 212). The child must therefore obey its parents and teachers. When Richard speaks of obedience, he does not do so because he would be insensitive to the problem of habits and their transmission. According to him, "obedience would be…the proper effect to expect from habit" (Richard 1911b, 276). But how can habit produce obedience? By warranting recognition of the social rule, by representing it in a collective as well as in an individual form and by warranting such recognition of the rule both by those who apply it and by those to whom it is applied. On this point, Richard shows his difference to Mauss. Because if habits are actually collective habits, then all actors are subject to them. All actors more or less obey them. Everyone including any chief recognises the power of these habits in themselves as well as in others: "The chief commands with much more insurance in that he shows himself all the more subject to the rule that he enforces" (ibid. 279).

If obedience is not the recognition of domination by one individual over others but the recognition of the domination of social rules over everyone, i.e. of rules that the actors have given to themselves and that are transmitted through socialisation and that, for Richard, represent the social order (Richard 1903a, 85), then those rules' collective character symbolises nothing else but the individuals' resistance to society. The relational character of such predetermined social rules comes precisely from the fact that a social rule does not correspond to anyone in particular, but applies to all. The power of habits lies in the fact that they apply to all social actors.

However, the weakness of habits is that they symbolise a way of living that does not really match the concrete daily life of the individual actors to whom they apply. Not to mention the questions, which those habits could stimulate in the actors who are taking them up, this is exactly the reason why it is difficult for any actor to settle in the mould of habits without batting an eye. If, like Mauss, we consider these habits as collective habits directly coming from society through socialisation, then it is impossible to think that they remain sealed off from any changes in the contact of the actors to whom these habits are transmitted. For Richard, resistance is the most direct expression of this gap between the present state and the traditions of a society. This is why resistance is always spontaneous or, to use the concepts discussed so far, this gap is nothing less than the public manifestation of inhibition in contact, contact here being contact between individual actors and collective habits. This is where obedience to social rules reaches its limit, not because the actors would not obey social rules but because obedience does not eliminate all resistance to these rules.

This raises a number of questions on the present viability of the habits inherited from tradition, their practical usefulness for the construction of a sustainable social order, and their effect on the collective, in particular their segregating effect on society, separating those who want to keep the collective habits and impose them on society from those who do not want them, or want to renew them. If such an imposition of collective habits is understood as a theoretical case of domination over the actors by the rules of their society,[15] this understanding would take up only one of all conceivable possibilities. In fact, the idea of such imposition of collective habits is only credible if it can be proven that there is perfect social inheritance in social life. This would mean that the transfer of collective habits between the generations would have to be the normal or usual process—or the natural process, as would Durkheim say. This, in turn, presupposes that the individual actors identify themselves with their social inheritance (Richard 1892, 68). However, such perfect social inheritance is nowhere to be found. We find, to the contrary, that there is a gap between social actors, particularly in the education system.

If the school is the public institution that, perhaps, best reflects the overall problems of the transmission of habits between generations, it is because the school has been established to promote equality and social justice between individual actors. However, the school does lead neither to equality, nor to social justice. What it, instead, leads to is inequality, which—beyond the difference in individual abilities—reflects the varying individual relationships to educational methods, teachers, and/or the contents taught. This is why, for Richard, the education system, which cannot erase such diversity, must evolve from an unnecessary and ineffective use of the school's authority to a more personalised encouragement of all actors in the educational system, enabling all of these actors to acquire the necessary background for growing and developing as individuals in society. The educational system must "find the methods which save, in the true sense of the word, mental effort, i.e. which are not prematurely imposed on the child, which do not push intensity beyond necessity, and from which it can derive the maximum benefit" (Richard 1911b, 21). The teacher must therefore be above all an educator whose main task is "to methodically collaborate with the student in his personal work" (ibid. 246). Even if the student is in contact with the knowledge accumulated by the generations, he is, at the same time, inhibited in the acquisition of this knowledge. He cannot assimilate it without a teacher who is supporting him rather than constraining him through authority. For Richard, the role of the education system is to foster this relational perspective not only for its own sake but also to enable the actors—here the students—to step into the socialisation delivered at school and, at the same time, to take their position in the educational system as well as working towards knowledge. What resistance has already shown is that the actors, nevertheless, already take a position in relation to other individuals, to society and to social values because they are in contact with their surroundings.

If Mauss seems far away from Richard, then this is especially the case in his early writings that were influenced by Durkheim, having sometimes, in fact, been drafted in collaboration with him. As we have seen, Mauss certainly never denies the loyalty to his uncle nor his fidelity to Durkheim's sociological views on society, which have brought important concepts to the social sciences even today, such as the concept of collective representations that, according to Mauss and Fauconnet, describes the "intimate background of social life" (Fauconnet and Mauss 1901 (1969), 160). Nevertheless, in defining, together with Fauconnet, the object of sociology as collective habits, Mauss shows his difference to Durkheim, just as he does when he defines magic as practical context, i.e. as the religious environment in which religion takes its shape from organised cults and rituals, doctrines and corresponding professions.

This difference can be seen even better when we compare Mauss and Fauconnet's article with Mauss' essay on the *Rapports réels et pratiques de la psychologie et de la sociologie* (1924), in which he says: "In society, there is something else than collective representations" (Mauss 1924 (1989), 287). Mauss emphasises that society consists of concrete collective facts, and this not only in collective representations but also in human beings, social groups and practices that are at the core of collective habits (ibid. 291–292). While he acknowledges that collective representations are an important object in sociology, they must not make us forget their empirical roots which contribute to the formation of those abstract skills that Mauss calls "reason, personality, willingness to choose or freedom, practical habit, mental habits and character, variation of these habits" (ibid. 289). We note that for Mauss, it is not only the habits in the formation of collective representations that are important, but also those faculties that Richard regards as essential players when one considers the individual, e.g. reason, personality and will.

Mauss is sensitive to these faculties because they are involved in the social phenomena he examines. They indicate that the imposition of collective habits, and consequently the power of collective representations on individual consciousness, do not necessarily work. In other words, collective representations and collective habits have their limits. These limits are not abstract but lie in the daily lives of the actors and the groups themselves. It is therefore not surprising to see Mauss making the following observation: "it is part of the nature of the collective representations and the collective practices that, as humanity will not form a unique society, the area of their extension is necessarily limited and relatively fixed because neither they, nor their material outputs can travel beyond where we can or want to bring them, beyond where we can or want to borrow them" (Mauss 1929 (1974), 471). This attention to the complexity of the concrete, where the collective representations and the collective habits are limited by actors and groups, finally leads Mauss to relativise his understanding of endogenous social change, which characterises, as seen earlier, the transition from magic to religion. "One of the serious flaws in our studies of collective history, ethnology and other subjects is that they are only devoted to observing coincidences only. It seems that only positive phenomena happen in history. However, one should examine non-borrowing, i.e. the refusal of the loan even if it would be useful. This research is as exciting as that on the loan" (ibid.). Mauss had this intuition from the beginning. Our comparison with Richard on penalty, pain, inhibition and resistance has highlighted the similarity of their observations without concealing the difference in their positions, i.e. that Mauss, even if he relativises his commitment to the major concepts of Durkheim, nevertheless picks them up and uses them continuously.

Contact symbolises best both proximity and distance between the two authors, as seen when looking at their converging views on penalty, pain, inhibition, and resistance between individuals and society. Although Mauss and Richard have similar views, this very similarity reveals what distinguishes them from each other.

Conclusion

So far, contact as the centre of gravity for penalty, pain, inhibition and resistance provides the context of a relational perspective that is still largely virtual. Indeed, such a perspective needs considerably more than simple contact in order to be developed. The examples found in Mauss and Richard about sacrifice, magic, religion, law and education shed light on the social labour that is to be performed in order to go from contact to manifest social relationships. Such social labour involves not only the mobilisation of many actors, but also the production of objects, as well as ritualistic procedures as documented in the magical and sacrificial practices described by Mauss and Richard.

Mauss sees this individual and collective work as the origin of technology, qualifying magic as "the most childish of skills", "the oldest" technology (Mauss 1902–1903 (2001), 175). Magic looks like a set of "old wives' remedies" (ibid. 31) showing not only the complexity of the religious rites but also the complexity of social activities because their relational character takes concrete shape when they are brought in relation to each other. Such social labour is also highlighted by Richard and plays an important role in his understanding of education where the educator's work to develop the intuition of the child as well as manual work are helpful in building more abstract competences (Richard 1911b, 220), and give the child a taste for effort, which contributes to the child's integration in society. At a more general level, this social labour is nothing other than the effort made by all individuals to put objects into a currency that binds and differentiates these individuals, that is shared by them and which separates them, and which also leads them to occupy a social position. Because if the actors of a given society are in contact, they have to carry and to extend the relational perspective to other actors, other objects, and other activities, whether they keep or change their position in society or not. Even the mage at society's periphery has his moment when he is initiated into magic as such initiation assumes a collective support that might be either concrete or virtual. In other words, the activities that the actors develop on a daily basis have not only the advantage of extending the relational perspective through society; they also have the advantage of allowing the actors to deal with social position. This second aspect of the problem, i.e. the relational understanding of social position, is found especially in Mauss, particularly when he speaks of consecration.

Consecration is, in the religious practices and the corresponding rites, a way both to extend the scope of these practices and rites to more actors, and at the same time to differentiate the actors or groups of actors by giving them a specific power—in the case of religious phenomena a magical or sacred power. Consecration has an "expansive force" that varies in intensity, which is not always easy to limit other than by the establishment of appropriate rituals (Hubert and Mauss 1899 (1964), 76). Consecration is not limited to magical or sacrificial practices. It is found in varying degrees in all social practices and Mauss gives several illustrations in *The Gift* (1925). Richard, in contrast, although speaking on a few occasions of the importance of consecration by law, understanding it in the same sense as Mauss, namely in the sense of an expansion of the legal bonds to more actors and in the sense of an individualisation of the actors consecrated by law (Richard 1909a, 160), does not look at social position directly. Or, to be more accurate, he seems to take up the issue in a more general way as he takes as examples those actors that the law in contemporary societies most neglects, namely children, women and offenders. This, however, is another story that goes beyond our comparison of Richard and Mauss, and should be told elsewhere.

If there is an author whose work has been greatly inspired by Mauss', particularly in relation to the ideas of collective habits and consecration, then this author is Pierre Bourdieu who is also well known for his critique of *The Gift*, an essay Mauss published in 1925 in the new series of *L'Année sociologique*. Bourdieu's critique of Mauss' understanding of "the gift" is not the only one. It is part of a broader critical reception often concerned with whether we can look at the gift as a phenomenon whence we can draw general principles that might explain the *modus operandi* not only of ancient, but also of contemporary societies. In his essay, Mauss introduced a general theory of society suggesting that exchanges of gifts are based on a triple obligation, i.e. to give, receive and return presents, three obligations that, for Mauss, make up the dynamics of all social relationships. Claude Lévi-Strauss who, in his critical introduction to *The Gift*, returns to the problem of the three obligations (Lévi-Strauss 1989, IX–LII) argues that if there were something universal in the gift, then this would be reciprocity rather than those obligations. Reciprocity is at the origin of the structures of kinship, a kinship that comes either from limited exchanges or from generalised exchanges between groups of actors (Lévi-Strauss 1967, 100, 159). Marshal Sahlins extends Levi-Strauss' statement when responding to Mauss and his idea of total reciprocity, which he rephrases as generalised, balanced and negative reciprocities likely to summarise the dynamics of all kind of exchange (Sahlins 1972, 192–195). These reciprocities form a continuum—from extreme sociability to extreme unsociability. This is why Sahlins recommends focusing any analysis of contemporary societies on the conditions that lie at the bottom of the question of how reciprocity is to be reproduced, a recommendation widely taken up in the contemporary literature that has been inspired by Mauss' understanding of the gift (e.g. Mooney 1976, 323–347; Price 1978, 339–351; Weiner 1980, 71–86). In their work on the gift, Georges Bataille (1991) and René Girard (1986), developing a surrealistic cultural anthropology, later overcome Mauss' understanding of the triple obligation inherent in the gift just as they overcome Levi-Strauss' reflections on reciprocity. They open a new perspective by placing the gift into a framework made up of the economy of expenditure and of the sacrifice made to the benefit of social groups. These parallel approaches to the gift, as different as they may be, lead nevertheless to the similar question of whether it is right to see the gift as the single foundation of all manifest social relationships.

If the answer turns out to be "yes", we have to say what it is that is fundamental about the gift—the three obligations or reciprocity or both or even something else. If the answer is "no", do we then have to see the gift merely as a public demonstration of generosity and selflessness, enabling the actors to better hide their private schemes and egoistic interests?

Notes

1. Many authors have underlined these differences, as for example König (1972, 239), Gephart (1990, 137 SSQ.), Martelli (1993, 377, 1996, 51–66), Fournier (1994, 334ff.), Strenski (1997, 132ff.), Mürmel (1997, 214, 217), Cefaï and Mahé (1998, 210).
2. This makes us remember the words of Isambert, saying that Durkheim would not have been able to write *The Elementary Forms of Religious Life* without Mauss (cf. Isambert 1976, 39). As for René König, he sees in Mauss a precursor of structuralism, who extends Durkheim's sociology to a paradigm of the symbolic order (König 1972, 633–657).
3. On the difference between Mauss and Durkheim about their understanding of sacrifice, see Isambert (1976, 35–57), Pickering (1979, 163), and more recently Paoletti (2012b, 301).
4. See Fournier, who indicates to what point Durkheim will be both surprised and pleased to see Mauss develop the intuitions that Durkheim also claims for himself (cf. Fournier 2007, 286–287).
5. As Richard observes, "Although Roman law has been contemporary to three different religions—the cult of ancestors, the pantheistic cult of nature and heroes, and Christianity—it has been internally transformed with majestic uniformity. The religious revolutions have neither managed to accelerate its progress, nor to delay it" (Richard 1892, 197).
6. Richard also says that in the framework of the ancient societies, "Religion consists in making a sacrifice to the divinity in order to obtain its favor" (Richard 1892, 198).
7. If, for Richard, religion and law are progressively becoming distinct from one another in the sacrifice, this is because of the successive transformation of the objects of the sacrifice, as they become less and less material (Richard

1892, 203). Nevertheless, there is still a difference between Richard and Mauss. Richard understands this successive transformation as one from the most to the least material, whereby the Christian god represents the highest abstraction of a sacrifice where the god gives irrevocably. However, Mauss and Hubert explicitly warn against such continuity: "It was doubtless convenient to imagine a steady progress from human to animal sacrifice, then from animal sacrifice to figurines representing animals, and then, finally, to the offering of cakes. It is possible that in certain cases, which moreover are little known, the introduction of new rituals brought about these substitutions. But there is no authority for applying these facts in order to make generalizations. The history of certain sacrifices shows rather the reverse process. The animals made from dough that were sacrificed at certain agricultural festivals are images of agrarian evil spirits and not simulacra of animal victims" (Hubert and Mauss 1899 (1964), 109 note 29).

8. The word "communication" describes the way in which the sacrifice puts human beings and gods into contact. It is found throughout the whole of Mauss and Hubert's essay and is seen as "the primitive purpose of the sacrifice" (Hubert and Mauss 1899 (1964), 89). For Mauss and Hubert, communication, however, means that sacrifices do not involve some direct communion between human beings and gods, against the theses of Robertson Smith and James Frazer (Paoletti 2012a, 301).
9. Durkheim was later grateful to Mauss for having mentioned this argument, and after the publication of Mauss' review on Steinmetz, he said to him, "I owe you, in reading you, and in debating with you, that I have been more aware of my own thinking; and this is the greatest favour that you could do me" (Durkheim 1998, 73).
10. For Mauss, there is a clear link between the sacrifices and the contacts that magic establishes, so that, according to Mauss, "we find the same idea in magic which we found in sacrifice" (Mauss 1902–1903 (2001), 77).
11. See also also Richard for a definition of magic as power: "Magic is therefore power in action" (Richard 1925b, 107).
12. Richard also speaks of "deliberate intent" or "conscious personality" when he speaks about the moral will. This is a way of saying that will always assumes the "consciousness", the "intelligence", and the reflexivity that support it—even if this reflexivity of the moral will is never absolute since there is no individual prospect existing without a collective one (for some typical examples, cf. Richard 1903a, 116, 134, 160, 1911b, 165).
13. In his review of Theodor Elsenhans' ethical psychology, Richard already speaks of this natural will where human beings differ from animal species because human beings can experience both the feelings of pleasure and displeasure (Richard 1895b, 85–97). For Richard, the natural will systematically stimulates human beings to seek pleasure in a self-preserving reflex

in order to protect themselves from the adverse consequences of displeasure. By avoiding all experiences of displeasure, any such individuals would prevent their own moral development, giving society free reign to dominate all social actors (Richard 1902b, 1–16).

14. Mauss claims not to love "the word of survivals, relics, for institutions still alive and proliferating" (Mauss 1938 (1989), 336). And indeed, his understanding of survivals has nothing to do with the admiration and the promotion of the past, but rather with its reconstruction, as would a philologist or an archaeologist, i.e. with the reconstruction of the chain of meanings which allows to understand the development of the institutions of society in time and space.
15. This is the possibility that Fauconnet and Mauss take up when they say that social institutions can impose collective habits on the individuals, and that these institutions are both the output and guarantors of such habits (Fauconnet and Mauss 1901 (1969), 150).

CHAPTER 4

Position: Marcel Mauss and Pierre Bourdieu on Gift, Interest, and the Mobilisation of Actors

In Chap. 3, we saw how Marcel Mauss and Gaston Richard provide elements that help us to see contact as the founding principle of a relational perspective in sociology. At the same time, contact is the converging point of personal and social inhibitions, of the double externality of individuals to themselves and to society, and of societies to themselves and to their actors. If contact is so important, it is because it materialises this relational perspective in daily life. Its concreteness refers to the natural situation of actors or groups of actors close to each other who can possibly, but not necessarily, evolve together, if they generalise their perspective to include other actors, objects, and activities.

Anything can be used in support of such a commitment—an invitation as much as a murder, an expression of modesty as much as an expression of the most absolute contempt. Mauss, maybe more than Richard, has given multiple empirical illustrations in his essays on sacrifice and magic. What the religious practices of magic and sacrifice show are not only ways to ward off bad luck, penalty and pain. They express more fundamentally an inhibition (not a cruelty), a distance (not violence), attention paid to acts (not indifference to them). Mauss and Richard perceive inhibition not only as the result of a constraint that society exerts on its actors. Inhibition also refers to the constraint that actors exert on their society, a constraint that unveils the resistance that actors and societies share and exert when they are in contact with one another. Inhibition is the negative moment when the relation becomes manifest as a configuration bringing together

C. Papilloud, *Sociology through Relation*, Palgrave Studies in Relational Sociology, https://doi.org/10.1007/978-3-319-65073-9_4

things, activities, procedures, techniques, symbols, beliefs and the actors that they mobilise. Mauss and Richard therefore have a very realistic understanding of their relational perspective on social phenomena.

Indeed, for Mauss as well as for Richard, this relational perspective refers to different forms of empirical activities, which assume the practical commitment of actors and societies and their effort to extend the contact between them, without which there is nothing beyond this contact but only forms of inhibition. Comparisons of Mauss and Richard have also shown their differences—Mauss anchors in the Durkheimian School, and Richard in dissent to this school. Despite these differences, we have seen that for Mauss as for Richard, contact—where individual commitment and collective habits meet—is the point they both emphasise. We also find this duality in Mauss' *The Gift* (1925), even if in another form, i.e. in the form of the dualities between freedom and obligation, and interest and disinterestedness. For this reason, we use Mauss' *The Gift* as the starting point of the present chapter, which will allow us to explore more deeply the concluding statement of Chap. 3 on the relational perspective on social positions. We conduct this discussion by comparing Mauss to Pierre Bourdieu. We have already provided motivation for this comparison between Bourdieu and Mauss at the end of Chap. 3, to which we would like to refer briefly.

First, we have seen many parallels between Mauss and Richard, as well as comparable attention paid to key elements that lead them to the concept of contact. However, when we look at the rest of their respective discourse, Mauss and Richard have views that do not match. Mauss insists on the survival of socio-cultural phenomena in history, on their transformation and on their meaning for contemporary society. Richard provides a historical sociology that explains how societies survive social, economic and political crises. Far from weakening them, these crises empower societies, and they have enabled us to describe the several stages of evolution from less rational to more rational societies or, following Richard's relational scheme, from a less to a more rational relation. Second, Mauss links his relational perspective on social phenomena to an understanding of the social positions that actors can take in the framework of their daily activities. He explains this at length in his essay *The Gift*, as we shall see. Richard certainly does not ignore such questions, but he does not provide a thorough analysis of them, or only does so in the form of very specific actors briefly mentioned in the conclusion of Chap. 3: namely, the child, the woman and the offender. These actors are important for Richard's historical sociology, because they enable him to support his thesis about the progress of societies, particularly regarding their understanding and use of law. But, otherwise, Richard does not pay specific attention to the problem of social positions in society.

Finally, what motivates our comparison between Mauss and Bourdieu is not only Bourdieu's perspective on Mauss' understanding of the gift, but more generally Bourdieu's use of other concepts of Mauss', e.g. collective habits and consecration,[1] which Mauss takes up from Émile Durkheim, and for which he gives a new interpretation. In this chapter we explore more deeply this comparison between Bourdieu and Mauss in order to understand better how they make the link between contact and the social positions of actors and groups in society. Their discourse on the gift provides the necessary material to do this. But beforehand, we have to say that this chapter does not represent the first attempt to compare Mauss and Bourdieu on the gift. Indeed, it is well known that Mauss' *The Gift* takes an important place in Bourdieu's ethnological studies on the Kabyle society, which provides some of the most important concepts of Bourdieu's theory of practice.[2] There is even a debate about Bourdieu's interpretation of Mauss' gift in his studies on the Kabyle society, which has been particularly supported by Alain Caillé, the leader of the MAUSS group (Anti-utilitarian Movement in the Social Sciences) in France. We briefly discuss this debate in order to introduce the problem which is the focus of this chapter. First, we provide a summary of Bourdieu's position on Mauss' gift. Then, we introduce Caillé's critique to Bourdieu's interpretation of Mauss, before eventually exploring more deeply the comparison between Mauss and Bourdieu regarding an argument at the heart of the controversy between Caillé and Bourdieu: the maximisation of social positions.

Interested Gift

In his ethnological studies on the Kabyle society, Pierre Bourdieu speaks of the gift, particularly of the important role of the *taousa*, a form of gift of goods and money studied before him by René Maunier, a French ethnologist who specialised in the culture of North African societies, and one of Mauss' former students.[3]

In the Kabyle society, the *taousa* most often takes the form of "a challenge which honours the man to whom it is addressed, at the same time putting his point of honour (nif) to the test" (Bourdieu 1977, 12). The *nif*—the honour that the Kabyle people associate with men—has a fundamental importance in the *taousa* because it forces the person who receives it to accept the challenge that the donor is addressing to him in giving the *taousa*. If the donee does not accept this challenge, or if he tries to postpone or to escape from it, his whole family will exert pressure on him to respect the obligation of the *taousa*. The channelling of challenges can ruin an entire family, a phenomenon that Bourdieu highlights when he describes the ceremonial *taousa* (ibid. 18).

Let us take the example of family A inviting family B to dinner. Family A should give family B a present or, more often, it should give money and/or agrarian products like meat, coffee or vegetables. Family B then has to return the present to family A, and has to give more than it received in order to restore its *nif*. If families A and B continue that way, they will soon be ruined because the *taousa* prescribes escalating challenges, which theoretically have no end. However, if the exchange of the *taousa* leads to the ruin of the two families, the *taousa* loses its meaning (ibid.). Thus, to preserve the *taousa* and, more generally, the exchange between families and the families themselves, the two families most often conclude an agreement that limits gift exchanges while preserving the honour of the families (ibid.). The conclusion of such agreements can lead to rituals and ceremonies, but the agreement itself does not become a ritual. According to Bourdieu, an agreement always corresponds to the individual dispositions of the actors, and it allows the preservation of these dispositions. These actors constantly live according to gift exchanges likely to destabilise not only social contexts or groups (i.e. family), but also the social position of individual actors in these groups, and in society. The agreements concluded between families about the *taousa* therefore allow the continuation of exchanges between these families by preserving the individual disposition to exchange gifts, and thus the social positions of these actors in these exchanges.

Bourdieu summarises this linkage between individual dispositions and social positions of the actors in society by using the concept of habitus (ibid. 17–19). In its most basic form, habitus is a principle of action that, in the case of gift exchanges—as in the case of other forms of exchange—protects actors and societies from the consequences of time passing by. The exchanges develop over time and, as can be seen in the case of the *taousa*, time might have destructive consequences on the exchanges and their actors. Bourdieu provides many examples that indicate how not to give a *taousa* immediately, or how to delay the time of accepting or returning it (ibid. 6–7, 180), which helps the actors to preserve their honour, reputation, or even their existence. To remain in an exchange is the most important challenge with respect to the gift, and this requires the development of individual strategies.[4] These strategies are motivated by the habitus, they rest on the individual dispositions of actors, which, for Bourdieu, are identical to the actors' own interests. A gift exchange cannot happen by chance but according to the interests that actors want to promote. This is why Bourdieu says that "the lapse of time separating the gift from the counter-gift is what authorizes the deliberate oversight, the collectively maintained and approved self-deception without which symbolic exchange, a fake circulation of fake coin, could not operate" (ibid. 6). If Bourdieu seems to insist on this fake character of gift exchanges, it is because the gift might cause the impression that it has been given in the most disinterested way. However, the agreements that the Kabyle families conclude between each other to avoid their own ruin prove the contrary.

The actors want to control their exchanges in order to preserve their own interests, their habitus, and their identity and, at the same time, they want to avoid that this logic, which is driven by individual interests, appears in public, so that the gift can be considered as a "real", i.e. disinterested gift. This is why actors deploy strategies that hide the individual interests that rule their own habitus, and the public presentation of these strategies aims to lend credibility to disinterestedness, which should make them appear to everyone else as objectively committed and attached to the gift.

> Strategies aimed at producing 'regular' practices are one category, among others, of officializing strategies, the object of which is to transmute 'egoistic', private, particular interests (notions definable only within the relationship between a social unit and the encompassing social unit at a higher level) into disinterested, collective, publicly avowable, legitimate interests. (ibid. 40)

What is misleading in gift exchanges, and by extension in all social exchanges, is to think that they are made on behalf of the collective, while they must first and foremost serve the interests of the individual actors of these exchanges. Therefore, all the efforts made by the actors involved in the gift are only made in order to substitute such exchanges for what is really at stake for them, namely the preservation of their habitus. Thus, as time passes by, actors take part in these exchanges without questioning the reasons that motivate such exchanges. As Kabyle society shows, the conduct of actors with respect to the gift is socially legitimised, i.e. recognised by all the protagonists of the gift exchange as the only appropriate conduct in these exchanges. In this context, Bourdieu develops his critique of reciprocity, a concept which he links less to Mauss than to Claude Lévi-Strauss, who sees reciprocity as the irreducible and universal fact of any exchange (ibid. 195f.).

Reciprocity in every exchange, and in particular with respect to the gift, is a concept that has the disadvantage of eliminating the practical reality of these exchanges.[5] Indeed, by analysing the gift with a focus on reciprocity, we forget to take into account the effects of the habitus on the gift. This does not mean that there is no reciprocity in gift exchanges, but rather that ethnologists have replaced the reality of the interests of socially situated actors with reciprocity—i.e. of actors who have a well-defined social position in society and, therefore, corresponding specific interests.

> All experience of practice contradicts these paradoxes, and affirms that cycles of reciprocity are not the irresistible gearing of obligatory practices found only in ancient tragedy: a gift may remain unrequited, if it meets with ingratitude; it may be spurned as an insult. Once the possibility is admitted that the 'mechanical law' of the 'cycle of reciprocity' may not apply, the whole logic of practice is transformed. (ibid. 9)

You can make reciprocity a norm or a rule,[6] but you have to admit that like any norm or rule, reciprocity is nothing other than the product of social actors, all ruled by the logic of their habitus. Bourdieu goes even further, saying that the interests of each social actor are actually driven by economic calculations:

> practice never ceases to conform to economic calculation even when it gives every appearance of disinterestedness by departing from the logic of interested calculation (in the narrow sense) and playing for stakes that are nonmaterial and not easily quantified. Thus, the theory of strictly economic practice is simply a particular case of a general theory of the economics of practice. (ibid. 177)

According to Caillé, this means that actors are egoistic, calculating people, competing to keep the monopoly of their social position, and through this, the monopoly of the social position of their group in society. This is no longer a sociological statement, it is an economic one.

Indeed, Caillé says that Bourdieu defends a kind of political economy that has been applied to society and from which he draws his sociology, and this can be most directly seen in the way in which Bourdieu uses the concept of interest, which he reformulates in *libido* (Caillé 2010, 46, 121). Of course, Bourdieu is delivering an "economy of practice" (Bourdieu 1990a, 50)—the terms he uses in order to describe his sociological inquiry. But he also says that he does not use the word "economy" in the sense of economists or capitalist" economy. He gives it a broader meaning, as he also does with the concept of interest (Bourdieu 1977, 175–177). Moreover, Bourdieu, for example in his book *The Weight of the World* (1999),[7] criticises capitalist" economy, particularly by underlining the social damage that leads to social exclusion, for which capitalism is responsible. He also criticises economics as an academic discipline, which tends to make capitalism into a standard that should be used in order to evaluate other forms of economic regimes, leading in practice to the one-sided imposition of a dominant view on various forms of dominated economies.[8]

Nevertheless, according to Caillé, the theory of practice, as Bourdieu understands it, remains fully subject to the economic axiom of the egoistic interest that drives individual actors, which, for Caillé, is an unbearable assumption. We cannot reduce all social practices to presumed egoistic interests of individual actors (Caillé 1994, 58). This first difficulty leads to a second when looking at Bourdieu's theory of the forms of capital. Bourdieu introduces his theory of the four forms of capital—economic, cultural, social and symbolic capital—in order to summarise the resources that each actor needs to construct his/her social career in society. According to Caillé, Bourdieu, in doing so, makes economy into a principle that—as in economic science—would explain what motivates actors to live together, i.e. the accumulation of resources. In this regard, Caillé observes, it is not surprising that economic capital becomes for Bourdieu "the condition, the mean and the goal" of the accumulation and development of other forms of capital (cultural, social, and symbolic capital), as well as of their mutual conversion (ibid. 80). This means that for Bourdieu, "The social bond is understood as a kind of relation derived from the economic exchange" (ibid. 81), which leads Caillé to say that Bourdieu's social theory can be fundamentally understood as "generalised economicism [*économicisme*; CP]" (ibid. 84).

Caillé provides similar observations on habitus (ibid. 138–164). As a structure producing practices by converting individual interests into public strategies, each habitus rests on the legacy of similar practices that reinforce it, or to put it in other words, habitus accumulates only practices that correspond to it.[9] Among these practices, those that are the most practical, i.e. those that are the most connected with the material world and material aspirations, play a preponderant role. They are related to economic capital, which is the most preponderant form of capital in social life, and which is one of the most important resources for converting the elements of one form of capital into the elements of another (ibid. 153). Taken as his habitus, the social actor is only the subjective sum of his materialised interests (ibid. 167). He evolves in a context of pure and perfect competition—or according to the semantic of economic science, within fields that work like perfect monopolies in society. Against this understanding of sociology, Caillé proposes an anti-utilitarian perspective in social sciences, whose first source of inspiration is Mauss' *The Gift*.[10]

When Mauss speaks of three obligations—to give, receive and return presents—he indicates, Caillé says, that these obligations have nothing to do with any form of economic exchange, or with a utilitarian concept of society.[11] The gift as a cycle of giving, receiving and returning presents is the fundamental structure of social relations in society, and it represents the common heritage of all social actors. According to Caillé, this heritage cannot be reduced to individual dispositions of actors motivated by their own egoistic interests, otherwise we would have to assume that concrete social relationships are only the by-products of actors' strategic actions. Bourdieu confuses the type (social action) and the genus (social relation), which leads his sociology to tautology: habitus produces actions at the origin of its structure, in other words, it reproduces itself. If we generalise this view and apply it to society as a whole, this would mean that we live in a society reproducing itself strictly identically from a structural viewpoint, regardless of the changes that could affect it at one level or another.

Despite their differences, Bourdieu and Caillé nevertheless share some common considerations. The first regards the normative character of their theory—the theory of habitus in the case of Bourdieu, and the theory drawn from Mauss' gift in the case of Caillé. When Bourdieu says that actors hide their personal interests and their calculations, this should not be understood as the logical consequence of the reproduction of habitus. It corresponds to a meta-theoretical principle directly related to the way in which Bourdieu understands the existence of social actors. Bourdieu assumes that individual actors exist not only because they are different from each other, but also because they bring this difference to the competitive markets of exchange, in order to be recognised and legitimated by the others. Although they have a habitus, the actors need to see it recognised by others in order to be reassured that they exist in the social world.

The normative character of Caillé's theory consists in the emphasis put on the obligation to give, receive and return presents in the gift, an obligation which applies to all exchanges, and therefore also to economic exchanges. In this sense, Caillé's anti-utilitarianism is no radical anti-utilitarianism—it is, as he says, "negative" utilitarianism[12]—because Caillé does not deny the presence of social relationships in which egoistic interests and calculations could play an important role. "Saying that the whole subject and his practices can not be reduced to a personal interest, to the interest of a family or a class obviously does not mean that interest does not matter" (ibid. 58). The gift assumes interests, and for Caillé too, interests have an important function in regard to concrete social relations, which Caillé describes in the framework of his structural model of the gift (Caillé 2010, 201f.). This model consists of two pairs of opposite concepts from which Caillé derives the gift as an obligation to give, receive and return presents. Without these two pairs of concepts, there is no gift (ibid. 95). The first pair consists of the concepts of obligation and spontaneity, and the second of the concepts of (material and immaterial) interest and pleasure. Each of these concepts represents an ideal that exists only in theory, and that can never be materialised in practice. The gift too evolves at the crossroads of pure obligation and pure spontaneity, as at the crossroads of pure interest and pure pleasure. Caillé links spontaneity to interest by drawing from Mauss, who, according to Caillé, suggests that "Spontaneity is always the mask of personal interest" (ibid. 201), or in other words, that interest determines spontaneity. In addition, spontaneity and obligation are intimately interconnected, otherwise pure obligation without spontaneity would not lead to gift-giving (ibid.). This similarly applies to the interest that determines obligation.

Finally, as pleasure without interest does not lead to the gift, interest determines pleasure too. In other words, if the relationships between these four concepts are necessary in order for the gift to exist, this necessity comes from the concept of interest. Caillé does not reduce it to economic interest only, but he sees it as a broad spectrum extending from economic interest to *aimance* (ibid. 95), i.e. to an interest which is not conditioned by either an economic or an egoistic calculation but is, instead, purely an interest in the gift and for the actors involved. It is particularly when we look at how this relates to obligation that we can better understand the important role of interest for Caillé. Indeed, according to him, this link between interest and obligation describes the context of primary sociality, namely the relations between "close relatives and allies" (Caillé 1982,

65).[13] This primary sociality is set apart from secondary sociality, from the relations of the individual actors to the state and to economic markets, which Caillé describes as "functional relations" (Caillé 1991, 111, 2010, 205). Caillé's concept of interest also plays an important role in understanding how actors move from primary to secondary sociality, from the world of *aimance* to the world where economic interest and egoistic calculations dominate, a world with which everyone nevertheless has to deal, which must be built with others (Caillé 1994, 158–159).

What does this broader understanding of interest add to what Bourdieu says? According to Caillé, this understanding of interest means that gift exchanges cannot be reduced to strategies and calculations, because the gift is always fundamentally "unconditional" (Caillé 2010, 62). We always have to give something, even if this unconditional gift is never a pure gift, even if it still remains in the practical world of actors for whom their exchanges matter, and who, for this reason, might prove occasionally to be formidable egoistic calculators. Therefore, if the gift is always fundamentally unconditional, it is not possible to see it as fundamentally motivated by the actors' egoistic interests to which they would, by hypothesis, subject their exchanges. Exchange in the form of the gift comes first, and then comes interest, which more or less determines the unconditional character of the gift. We can now better appreciate the difference between both authors.

Criticising the utilitarianism of Bourdieu's sociology, Caillé has undoubtedly highlighted one of the most important ambiguities in Bourdieu's works. Certainly, Bourdieu says that his economy of practice is not to be understood in the sense of an economic theory of social action. In his book *The Logic of Practice* (1990), he observes that:

> There is an economy of practices, a reason immanent in practices, whose 'origin' lies neither in the 'decisions' of reason understood as rational calculation nor in the determinations of mechanisms external to and superior to the agents. Being constitutive of the structure of rational practice, that is, the practice most appropriate to achieve the objectives inscribed in the logic of a particular field at the lowest cost, this economy can be defined in relation to all kinds of functions, one of which, among others, is the maximization of monetary profit, the only one recognized by economism. In other words, if one fails to recognize any form of action other than rational action or mechanical reaction, it is impossible to understand the logic of all the actions that are reasonable without being the product of a reasoned design, still less of rational calculation. (Bourdieu 1990a, 50)

Nevertheless, Bourdieu adds that:

> if one fails to see that the economy described by economic theory is a particular case of a whole universe of economies, that is, of fields of struggle differing both in the stakes and scarcities that are generated within them and in the forms of capital deployed in them, it is impossible to account for the specific forms, contents and leverage points thus imposed on the pursuit of maximum specific profits and on the very general optimizing strategies (of which economic strategies in the narrow sense are one form among others). (ibid. 51; also ibid. 122)

This second sentence clearly shows the ambiguity of Bourdieu's sociological discourse.

Indeed, Bourdieu suggests that sociology understood as an economy of practice would be nothing more than a more general form of economic theory, applied not only to actions conceived from the viewpoint of economic rationality, but more generally to all kinds of social actions. Nevertheless, to Bourdieu this ambiguity is a virtuous one. Economic science can contribute to social theory, as well as social theory can contribute to economic science where social practices are not easy to explain—either because they are difficult to quantify, or because they refer to exchanges not explicitly subjected to a logic of rational calculation and choice, as for example the practices of gift exchange (ibid. 123). This is why sociologists must "abandon the economic/non-economic dichotomy" (ibid.) in order to understand how these practices function "as economic practices aimed at maximizing material or symbolic profit" (ibid.). The maximisation of material and symbolic profits and, in general, of any type of profit still falls under Caillé's critique, and nothing seems to separate Bourdieu's social theory more from a theory of the gift, if, in the expression "profit maximization", we focus on profit only.[14] This was Caillé's strategy in his critique of Bourdieu, which has a side effect, as it tends to simplify Bourdieu's sociological discourse too much by veiling Bourdieu's diverting use of economic concepts. We can explore another way, and focus instead on the idea of maximisation, thus taking Bourdieu's broader understanding and use of the economic semantic into account, a perspective that Caillé also takes in his interpretation of Mauss' gift. However, we do not simply discard the concept of interest—we will see it coming back in the following chapters.

Maximisation

Once detached from profit, the idea of maximisation shows that, for Bourdieu, social actors do not act in an exclusively utilitarian way, but in a useful way, i.e. they favour the strategies that are most practical for them, i.e. strategies that correspond to their interests in a broad, non-exclusively utilitarian sense (ibid. 91). We have seen that Caillé argues similarly that actors act in the sense of their interests, these interests being not exclusively egoistic. Mauss does not provide any very different reasoning, as we can see in his work prior to *The Gift*, as for example in his description of sacrifice. A sacrifice is both "a useful act" and "an obligation" (Hubert and Mauss 1899 (1964), 100). The profane has "every interest in drawing closer" to the sacred because "it is there that the very conditions for its existence are to be found" (ibid. 98). Except for the sacrifice to the god—the only case "from which all selfish calculation is absent" (ibid. 101)—sacrifices do not exclude egoistic calculations, because they are about the preservation of oneself and of one's social group, of one's identity and of social norms. This idea returns in Bourdieu's idea of maximisation where actors' strategies contribute above all to the self-affirmation of the habitus, and therefore of an actor's identity, as well as of the group to which he belongs—we must not forget that for Bourdieu, the habitus always refers to the larger structure of a class of actors sharing the same lifestyle. This self-affirmation of the habitus is thus primarily a principle of preservation of personal and social identity.

Bourdieu gives many examples of this, as in the case of marriages and related matrimonial strategies in Kabyle society.

> Faced with the dangers that every marriage presents for the patrimony and therefore the lineage, owing to the fact that the compensation due to the younger brothers could force the break-up of the patrimony...families respond with a range of actions designed to overcome this specific contradiction of the system. Their responses...have their common origin in the habitus. (Bourdieu 1990a, 160)

This strategy, aiming to preserve family heritage and lineage, has side effects. It creates victims among families, as for example daughters or the youngest son. Daughters, from the eldest to the youngest, represent a risk for the Kabyle families because they do not guarantee the families' preservation.

> [I]f she married an eldest son, her 'house' would be in a sense annexed to another, and if she married a younger son, domestic power (at least after her parents died) would pass to a stranger. And if she were a younger daughter, she would have to be married off, and therefore dowered, since, unlike a son, she could neither be sent away nor usefully be kept at home unmarried, because the labour she could provide would not meet the cost of her upkeep. (ibid. 154)

The same applies to the youngest son, who becomes

> the perfect domestic servant, whose private life was invaded and annexed by his employer's family life, who was consciously or unconsciously encouraged to invest much of his time and private emotions in his borrowed family, especially in the children, and who usually had to renounce marriage as the price for the economic and emotional security of sharing in the life of the family. (ibid. 158–159)

These victims play a role analogous to the role of the victims of whom Hubert and Mauss speak with respect to sacrifice, who play the role of intermediaries between the one who offers the sacrifice and the god, and who protect the participants in the sacrifice from the dangers of the sacrifice. As for the Kabyle families that Bourdieu describes, Mauss and Hubert indicate that the one offering the sacrifice "gives up something of himself but he does not give himself. Prudently, he sets himself aside" (Hubert and Mauss 1899 (1964), 100).

This is no different in Mauss' gift, but Mauss expresses this with a formula directly opposed to the one proposed in the analysis of the sacrifice, which can be confusing. Indeed, Mauss says that "by giving one is giving oneself, and if one gives oneself, it is because one 'owes' oneself—one's person and one's goods—to others" (Mauss 1925 (2002), 59). Should we understand that the gift goes against this idea of preservation of oneself and of one's group? This would then mean that the gift does not present any danger, contrary to the sacrifice, where the danger threatening the participants in a sacrifice is omnipresent. Actually, this is not the case.

With a gift, of course, the donor gives something of himself, "some part of his spiritual essence, of his soul" (ibid. 16), which Mauss identifies with the *hau*, the spirit of the donor in the thing that he gives to the donee. However,

> To retain that thing would be dangerous and mortal, not only because it would be against law and morality, but also because that thing coming from the person not only morally, but physically and spiritually, that essence, that food, those goods, whether movable or immovable, those women or those descendants, those rituals or those acts of communion—all exert a magical or religious hold over you. (ibid.)

We have here an explanation of sacred things that Hubert and Mauss have already delivered with regard to sacrifice. Indeed, the possession of a sacred thing is as desired as it is feared, because it is dangerous—and the same applies to contact to the things and beings attached to the sacred thing. This is why these things can only be accessed by practising the rituals which allow their appropriation without putting one's own life at risk. Why do we want to own these dangerous things? The ritual of sacrifice already shows us—these things shall transmit their sacred virtues to the actors, and this is what we also find in the gifts of the *vaygu'a* in the societies of the Trobriand Islands. "[O]ne cannot fail to acknowledge the eminent and sacred nature of the objects. To possess one is 'exhilarating, strengthening, and calming in itself.' Their owners fondle and look at them for hours. Mere contact with them passes on their virtues" (ibid. 31). The property in the gift in the form of the thing possessed is therefore no less ambivalent than the sacrificed things or the sacrificed victims, and if one appropriates them, it is at once to gain power, and to strengthen one's position in exchange with other actors.[15] As in the case of the Kabyle marriages that Bourdieu describes, gifts are not intended to foster the egoism of the actors and their group or to isolate them from other actors and other groups. They must instead enable them to resist the others, to assert themselves against the others. At the same time, this resistance guarantees the sustainability of the actors and their groups, as well as their maintenance in exchange with other actors and other groups. From this viewpoint, the maximisation of which Bourdieu speaks is close to the habitus, whose optimisation and affirmation in social space is expressed by such maximisation. In other words, maximisation refers to the deployment of social activities symbolising the resistance of contact between actors and social groups, as well as their personal resistance to contact to each other. To this first characteristic, which can be drawn from the idea of maximisation, we can add another one: identification.

We observe that maximisation in its relation to habitus goes hand in hand with the resistance inherent in contact as described in the previous chapter. We have said that this resistance generally reflects an inhibition. We have seen that for Mauss, this inhibition typically means a delay of action. This is evident in the development of strategies and social activities including ritual activities before, during and after gift exchanges. They are intended to preserve actors and their group and, at the same time, to contribute to their self-affirmation. These elements are also present in Bourdieu's understanding of maximisation in relation to habitus, where the self-affirmation of actors and groups leads to the affirmation of their social position—the position they take in relation to other actors and other social groups. This leads Bourdieu to say that, in this way, actors and social groups are "naturally distinguished" from each other (Bourdieu 1990a, 108). Therefore, Bourdieu's maximisation is not only a principle of self-affirmation of habitus, but also a principle facilitating identification of social positions resulting from the practical effectiveness of the habitus.[16]

In the exchange of gifts that Mauss describes, gifts are directly linked to the identification of three social positions—the positions of giving, receiving and returning the presents—and these three positions correspond to specific things and actors entering into the gift exchanges with specific rights and duties (Mauss 1925 (2002), 17–18). For example, the Hausa in Libya are expected to give to poor people and to children not only to please the dead, but also to avenge them "for the superabundance of happiness and wealth of certain people who should rid themselves of it" (ibid. 23). These acts of redistribution not only actualise a principle of justice materialised in the form of alms (ibid.), they also allow one to mark and thus make visible distinct social identities characterised by fortune, gender and generation, as distinctive elements to which several objects are attached. The symbolic marriage of *mwali* (bracelets) and *soulava* (clamps) in the *kula* (ceremonial exchange system) on the Trobriand Islands refers to the marriage between women and men (ibid. 33). The things given express the attention paid by the donor to the social rank of the donee. In the *kula*, for example, these exchanges of gifts may take the form of a contest where the protagonists compete, challenge each other, publicly show their wealth to prove their power and increase the number of exchanges by increasing not only the number of things entering into these exchanges, but also the value of these things. In these competitions through gifts, the social hierarchy of the groups unveils as the exchanges go on, and the thing appears as the mediator of this unveiling.

Among the Kwakiutl for example, things belonging to the family home are personalised. They have names associated with "the titles (which vary) given to nobles, both men and women, and their privileges" (ibid. 158, note 224). In Melanesia, gifts exchanged within the brotherhoods of men and of women finance "the ranks and successive 'ascensions' (promotions) in these brotherhoods" (ibid. 45), and to each rank corresponds a particular thing. Among the Kwakiutl, this is for example the "miraculous box" given on the occasion of initiation or marriage, which "transforms the recipient into a 'supernatural' person, into an initiate, a Shaman, a magician, a noble, the one who possesses dances and seats in a brotherhood" (ibid. 157, note 222). These exchanges of presents thus reflect a whole social organisation, and while Mauss constantly evokes the mix that gifts reveal—a mix of social groups, and even of tribes—the analysis he provides about gifts opens up to the distinction of social positions within and through these exchanges. Gifts bring actors with different social positions into relations, and these gifts do not aim to remove these differences. Rather, these gifts are an opportunity for self-affirmation, for actors and social groups to affirm their social position and the multiple daily operations that they develop in order to supply these gifts as complete as they should be. Because there are various gifts exchanges, giving, receiving and returning gifts supposes "going into details and with scruples, so no error is committed in the way one gives and receives. It is all a matter of etiquette; it is not like in the market where, objectively, and for a price, one takes something. Nothing is unimportant" (ibid. 77). This is all the more so if we assume that the acts of giving, receiving and returning do not describe the same social positions, but a hierarchy of social positions in the exchange of gifts. This hierarchy is not explained by the development of the gift over time, i.e. that the gift begins with the act of giving, followed by the act of receiving, and finally ends with the act of returning. The series of positions related to the gift rather expresses the transition from contact between these actors and groups, to a configuration of activities that mobilises them and potentially other actors and groups in society. The time that passes between gifts is materialised by the activities deployed to extend the relational perspective to the collective, as well as by the things mobilised for this purpose. The openings and closures of these gift exchanges describe "cycles" of the relation,[17] i.e. the transition from one configuration to another of the relation. Let us use this perspective to interpret each position of the gift by starting with the act of giving. This will allow us to understand the link between the maximisation of social positions and the identification of actors and groups in Mauss' work on the gift.

According to Mauss, giving something is characterised by the mobilisation of actors, who should be as numerous as possible. This mobilisation of the collective is a typical characteristic of gifts, where "it is not individuals but collectivities that impose obligations of exchange and contract upon each other" (ibid. 6). The North American *potlatch* and its attenuated form, the Melanesian *kula*, provide clear examples of such mobilisation.[18] The *potlatch* is given by a chief, who can be the chief of the family or of the clan. The prerequisite for the chief for giving the *potlatch* is the mobilisation not only of his family but also of the greatest possible number of actors. The Melanesian *kula* provides a good illustration of such mobilisation. The villages and the clans gather around their leader. Together, they prepare maritime expeditions in order to bring a gift to the villages and clans of other islands. These inter-tribal phenomena are sometimes even "international" (ibid. 126 note 18), as in the example of the North American *potlatch*. Other examples are endogenous phenomena, happening inside the village or the clan. In the case of the Tlingit *potlatch*, "clans and phratries, and families allied to one another, confront one another" (ibid. 38); "the personality of the chief" who gives the *potlatch* "does not make itself felt" (ibid.). "The chief is merged with his clan, and the clan with him. Individuals feel themselves acting in only one way" (ibid. 41). In British Columbia, clan members invite family, friends, neighbours to the *potlatch*, and they give to them their wealth, i.e. "'all the profits accumulated over long years of work'" (ibid. 139 note 131; Mauss quotes Franz Boas). This extravagant expenditure for the *potlatch*, which, when taken too far, may even lead to the destruction of the entire wealth accumulated by these societies, is a matter of prestige and affirmation of the nobility of the chiefs and their clan.

> Nowhere is the individual prestige of a chief and that of his clan so closely linked to what is spent and to the meticulous repayment with interest of gifts that have been accepted, so as to transform into persons having an obligation those that have placed you yourself under a similar obligation. Consumption and destruction of goods really go beyond all bounds. In certain kinds of potlatch one must expend all that one has, keeping nothing back…The political status of individuals in the brotherhoods and clans, and ranks of all kinds, are gained in a 'war of property'. (ibid. 47)

This is why the *potlatch* often presupposes various rituals—for example, the donor must climb to the scaffold, he must hoist the greasy pole—

which refers in a metaphorical way to a double movement of the donors who, giving the *potlatch*, affirm their social position as well as their power over the people who receive the *potlatch*. Once the gift is given, the time of receiving takes place.

The position of receiving the gift personalises or individualises the responsibilities within the village or the clan, and it puts into question the social position as donor that the actor—now become donee—had taken. As donee, the actor "is dependent upon the anger of the donor" (ibid. 76), of whom he becomes the "'partner-candidate'" as the Melanesians say (ibid. 31). This status of partner is variable, and this variety is reflected both in the objects given and in the donee's attitude toward these gifts. This is why it is important to woo the partner by giving him multiple gifts in order to find out who he is (ibid. 35). The act of receiving tests the contact, i.e. the actors' capacity to re-produce and generalise the contact towards the collective. Is the partner only partially committed, or is he really going to commit not only to receiving the gift but, especially, to returning it? If the donee refuses the gift—as for example among the Kwakiutl, where "an acknowledged position in the hierarchy, and victories in previous potlatches, allow one to refuse an invitation, or even, when present at a potlatch, to refuse a gift"—he then invariably loses the "'weight'" of his name (ibid. 52). Even if, as among the Kwakiutl, such refusals may occur episodically, concerning only the specific categories of actors whose social status is generally high, there never is an absolute refusal of gifts. Such a refusal would isolate the donee by interrupting the gift exchanges and, with them, "the circle of the law, rewards and foods" (ibid. 73), like avarice in the act of giving. Thus, there is a double challenge for the donee and the donor related to receiving gifts.

For the donee, his position in the exchanges and his ability to remain in the exchanges—to resist the gifts in affirming his identity—are put into question. For the donor, the donee puts his ability to give to the test, and this is why donors deploy strategies in order to have an effect on the donee, so that the latter takes the gift. For example, the donee on the Trobriand Islands is wary of the thing given, this is why he does not want to take it. Thus, the donor throws it at his feet in order to force the donee to take it (ibid. 80). The Kwakiutl nobles of above, who refuse a gift, are forced to return or to give either more presents, or more sumptuous presents to maintain their position in the social hierarchy of their society. The more they try to get out of the uncomfortable position of receiving, the more the entire society mobilises in order to bring them back to their position. They cannot escape, but they must affirm themselves, otherwise they will suffer the punishment of the social group, from humiliation to banishment, up to killing the refractory, even if he is a chief or a notable member (ibid. 8). For both the donee and the donor, receiving gifts is therefore the culminating point of maximisation, of affirmation of their respective position and identity, and at the same time the point where everything can crash, either in favour, or against, the continuation of the exchanges. Beyond their social identity being marked by their position with respect to the gift, which reflects their position in the social hierarchy, it is about the principle of identification itself. Because in refusing the gift, not only does the donee refuse to show who he is. He also denies others the opportunity to show who they are, how they defend their honour, what power they have or what sacrifices they are capable of. The act of returning the gift appeases these tensions.

"The most important feature among these spiritual mechanisms [of the gift; CP] is clearly one that obliges a person to reciprocate the present that has been received" (ibid. 9). Returning gifts is not only the last act of the cycle of the gift over time. It is also the time when recognition occurs—recognition by the donee of the position of the donor, and by the donor of the position of the donee, as well as recognition of this mutual contact, which has not only been established, but has also been extended to the collective, their family, their clan, their village. This encoding of a relational perspective to the collective favours the mobilisation of this collective for further gift exchanges. Nevertheless, what contributes to this encoding is less the collective as such, which is already mobilised by the act of giving, and already present when it comes to consecrating gift exchanges. It is the thing itself, the object that has been given and that should be returned. The object is at the forefront of the operations of returning the gift, because it is evidence that there has been a gift, it represents what Mauss calls the "surety" or "certainty" that there will be a return of gifts (ibid. 45). The thing which is the gift—i.e. the property or value, no matter whether goods, talismans or masks—enables the actors involved to acquire a rank, a social position, and finally to pass from one cycle of the relation to another.

Mauss' argument on this point is well known, and it refers to the *hau*, the spirit of the donor in the thing given that requires its return to the donor, and which discredits the donee if the latter should not return the thing. The *hau* is the "force of things" (ibid. 55), while representing at the same time "a sign and a pledge of wealth, the magical and religious symbol of rank and plenty" (ibid. 56). But the *hau*, independently of the critiques that have been addressed at Mauss' *Gift* and his interpretation of that Maori word, does not explain everything.[19] On the one hand, returning a gift most often means that the donee gives back more than he has received, that he "repay[s] with interest...in order to humiliate the person initially making the gift or exchange, and not only to recompense him for loss caused to him by 'deferred consumption'" (ibid. 96–97). Humiliating the donor also forces him to give again in order to regain superiority—not only to affirm his social position, but also to challenge the other to do the same. Returning the gift means that actors consecrate the cycle of the relation together—they put it to an end that can lead to another cycle, where actors and things will be brought into further cycles of the relation.

On the other hand, returning presents, particularly in its most demonstrative forms, e.g. the destruction of property in the *potlatch*, indicates that behind the thing circulating in the gift, there are institutions such as the cult of the dead and of the spirits that link the gifts to the practices of sacrifice (ibid. 22–23). In the *kula* on the Trobriand Islands, each thing "has its name, a personality, a history, and even a tale attached to it...one cannot fail to acknowledge the eminent and sacred nature of the objects" (ibid. 30–31). It is not possible to use these things independently of the cults and their institutions, the fact of which is expressed by Mauss when he says "To give to the living is to give to the dead" (ibid. 145 note 152). These objects are all—in different degrees—mediations attached to the institutions of these societies. These mediations circulate and determine not only the pace of the gifts, but also the transition from one position in the gift-cycle to another one—from giving to receiving to returning the gift. When the time comes to return the gift, what is at stake is therefore not only compensation for the donor. For the actors, it is also of critical importance to show that they place themselves in control of the institution to which the things refer. This is why there is a point of honour, a challenge, a provocation involved in returning presents. This is a kind of revenge, where, while the power of the donor on the donee is dismissed, it revives competition between both sides and their groups. This, once again, supports the maximisation of actors' social positions—not only for these actors to affirm their identities, but also in order to rank them in society.

Ranking

Ranking comes from maximisation in the sense that identification of actors and social groups leads to the hierarchical classification of these actors and groups in society. According to Bourdieu, identifying and classifying assumes ranking.

> In most ordinary modes of behaviour, we are guided by practical models, that is, principles imposing order on action (***principium important ordinem ad actum***, as the scholastics said), or informational models. These are principles of classification, principles of hierarchization, principles of division which are also principles of vision, in a word, everything which enables each one of us to distinguish between things which other people confuse, to operate, that is, a diacrisis, a judgement which separates. (Bourdieu 1990a, 77–78)

We find the same idea in Durkheim and Mauss' text on primitive forms of classification. "Every classification implies a hierarchical order for which neither the tangible world nor our mind gives us the model" (Durkheim and Mauss 1903b (2009), 5). This hierarchical order extends to religious cults, rites, related institutions, and to the things used in these rites and cults. "Thus, a sorcerer belonging to the Mallera phratry may use in his art only things which similarly belong to Mallera" (ibid. 9). In other words, the social position of groups in society, and of the actors belonging to these groups, is immediately linked to a set of corresponding things, which these actors and groups use.

In Bourdieu's work, there is a similar idea in the sense that different social groups and their actors are connected to sets of material and immaterial things corresponding to them, which Bourdieu summaries by using the concept of capital. This is why Bourdieu says that "the principle of differentiation is different each time, as are the stakes and the nature of the interest, and therefore the economy of practices. It is important to work out the correct hierarchy of the principles of hierarchization, i.e., of the different forms of capital" (Bourdieu 1985a, 737).[20] Identifying these different forms of capital leads to different principles of hierarchy, where different habitus are linked to the forms of capital that correspond to them—a reasoning which Bourdieu formalises in his book *Distinction* (1984), where the habitus is multiplied by the capital (Bourdieu 1984, 101). The self-affirmation of actors and the maximisation of the habitus remain preserved by the use of appropriate mediations, leading to the maintenance of divisions and hierarchies between social positions—and therefore to the consolidation of social positions. For example, use of language is socially defined in the sense that the style of the spoken or written language corresponds to a specific habitus, which contributes to a person's maintenance in the social hierarchy.

> In ordinary speech as in learned discourse, styles are hierarchical and hierarchizing; an 'elevated' language is appropriate for a 'top-level thinker', which is what made the 'unstylized pathos' of Heidegger's 1933 address seem so inappropriate in the eyes of all those who have a sense of philosophical dignity, namely, a sense of their dignity as philosophers: the same people who acclaimed the philosophically stylized pathos of Being and Time as a philosophical event. (Bourdieu 1991a, 152)

In the field of literature, and more generally, in the arts, we can observe two competing principles of ranking, depending on whether the actors in these fields use the elements of economic capital to maximise their habitus, or whether they favour the elements of cultural capital. For Bourdieu, the first principle, based on the use of economic capital, does not genuinely come from these fields while the second one does. This distinction between these two principles shows that these two fields are under the influence of other fields in social space, even if they remain relatively autonomous from one another. Thus,

> the heteronomous principle, favourable to those who dominate the field economically and politically (e.g. 'bourgeois art') and the autonomous principle (e.g. 'art for art's sake'), which those of its advocates who are least endowed with specific capital tend to identify with degree of independence from the economy, seeing temporal failure as a sign of election and success as a sign of compromise. (Bourdieu 1993, 40)

These two principles contribute to "the delimitation of population" (ibid. 180) inside these fields, i.e. to the identification and classification of different groups of writers and artists in the positions that they claim using either economic, or cultural mediations. The arrival of new actors into these fields (for example, in the literary field at the end of the nineteenth century, the naturalists, with their leader Émile Zola or, in painting, the impressionists with Edouard Manet), the increase of readers and producers of art partly caused by the expansion of education, the formation of cultural industries: all these elements contribute to moves across social positions. As with the Kabyle gift, the particular economy which prevails in the peculiar field of literature and in the general artistic field does not follow the logic of economic profit. If such is the case regarding artists who produce works for cultural industries and the general public, this is not the case for artists favouring artistic creation more than the sale of *oeuvres*. The latter do not seem interested in economic benefit, like the

Kabyle families which apparently give without interest in profit whatsoever—a disinterestedness which nevertheless assumes a strategy of affirmation of the family position, so that it is able to exchange gifts again, and see its position socially recognised.[21] The work of such artists:

> finds its principle in the specific logic of symbolic alchemy that maintains that investments will not be recouped unless they are (or seem to be) operating at a loss, in the manner of a gift, which cannot assure itself of the most precious countergift, 'recognition', unless it sees itself as without return; and—as with the gift that it converts into pure generosity by occulting the countergift to come—it is the interposed time interval which forms a screen and which obscures the profit promised to the most disinterested investments. (Bourdieu 1995, 148)

Thus, if each of the two types of artists uses different mediations, they both aim at maximising their social position in order to consolidate it. This consolidation means public recognition for some, which ranks them in the set of classic cultural references. For others, it means recognition by a cultural elite, and a corresponding ranking in the cultural *avant-garde*.

Durkheim and Mauss provide a similar explanation using North American and Australian societies as examples. Clans have totems, and each group within the clan is subjected to a sub-totem linked to the totem of the clan, similar to how type is related to genus. The clan can be split into multiple groups, a "segmentation" taking place "along the lines laid down by the classification" (Durkheim and Mauss 1903b (2009), 19). Consequently, "individuals grouped around one of the things classed in the clan…detach themselves from the rest to form an independent clan, and the subtotem then becomes a totem…the classification is changed in consequence" (ibid. 19–20). Now, each sub-group has its own classification principles and the things that correspond to these principles, the usages of which in daily activities develop a new classification, which should be applied in the new clan. In each instance, its goal is "not to facilitate action, but to advance understanding, to make intelligible the relations which exist between things" and between social actors (ibid. 48).[22] If, at some point, such development occurs relatively autonomously from the former clan, to which the (now new) clan belonged, "with time this sentiment vanishes" (ibid. 20). The groups become completely independent from one another, and the subtotems become their main totems, from which other subtotems follow, corresponding to a hierarchical order of social positions in these groups. However, Durkheim and Mauss conclude in a strange sentence:

> Far from it being the case, as Frazer seems to think, that the social relations of men are based on logical relations between things, in reality it is the former which have provided the prototype for the latter. According to him, men were divided into clans by a pre-existing classification of things; but, quite on the contrary, they classified things because they were divided by clans. (ibid. 48)

This is strange because, despite the similarities between Bourdieu, Durkheim and Mauss, it highlights some important difference between them in their respective understandings of ranking.

Like Mauss in *The Gift*, Bourdieu takes material and immaterial things (mediations of exchange) into account in order to understand the ranking of social positions whose synthesis is the forms of capital. Considering these social positions, Bourdieu deduces the formal relations in respect to these actors, other forms of capital and, consequently, other social positions, assuming that these formal relations are the analytic equivalents of concrete or manifest social relations. In other words, for Bourdieu, social positions are understood as containing and producing corresponding social relations, not the reverse. Or to put it in a more compact way, Bourdieu assumes that the "Knowledge of the position occupied in this space [the social space; CP] contains information as to the agents' intrinsic properties (their condition) and their relational properties (their position)" (Bourdieu 1985a, 725). Therefore, the manifest social relation is nothing other than the habitus in action—or, to put it in the terms described above, it is the linkage between maximisation and ranking. Thus, Bourdieu argues that there is a manifest social relation when a social position can be maximised, when it has been distinguished from other social positions, and consequently ranked in social space. According to Bourdieu, when we have such a link between maximisation and ranking, we can conclude that social positions are antagonistic, which correspondingly means that the relation itself is an antagonistic relation.

For example, we can say something about the relation between the Decadent and the Symbolist poets at the end of the nineteenth century in France (whose most famous figures are Paul Verlaine for the former and Stéphane Mallarmé for the latter) only if we first consider actors who take antagonistic positions towards them. In this example, the poets of the

Parnasse are these actors, working in the same literary genre as the Decadents and the Symbolists, but with other literary techniques. Thus, Verlaine and Mallarmé can be seen as a unit against the Parnassian. But as time passes, the differences between Verlaine and Mallarmé increase. They affirm their position, they maximise it to the point that they eventually become rivals. "At first objectively united by their common opposition to their elders, the Parnassians…the two poets, Mallarme and his Symbolists, Verlaine and his Decadents, gradually grow apart until they confront one another over a series of stylistic and thematic contrasts…which corresponds to social differences" (Bourdieu 1995, 121).

Whether we speak of literature, school selection, *haute couture* or sport, the explanation is based on the same scheme, namely the social position and its determination by the habitus, the expansion of which produces corresponding antagonistic positions, and therefore, antagonistic relations. The logic of position and relation go hand in hand because the relation reflects the habitus and its corresponding social position, of which it is the product, and the relation consolidates the habitus and its social position to the benefit of its maximisation and its ranking. Bourdieu gives an emblematic example when he speaks of the point and sense of honour in Kabyle societies. His starting point is the "mutual recognition of equality in honour" on behalf of Kabyle actors and groups (Bourdieu 1977, 11). This recognition of honour "presupposes an opponent capable of preparing a riposte to a movement that has barely begun and who can thus be tricked into faulty anticipation" (ibid.). This is why Kabyles always choose their opponents, so that they are up to the attack because otherwise, anyone "who challenges a man incapable of taking up the challenge, that is, incapable of pursuing the exchange, dishonours himself" (ibid.). The exchange is therefore always an antagonistic manifest social relation between opponents who are chosen because they know that they have the same power. They know it because they are of homologous rank, i.e of homologous social positions. "[O]nly a challenge (or offence) coming from an equal in honour deserves to be taken up" (ibid. 12). This affirmation of one's social position is so important that the Kabyles consider it an affront to exchange with actors and groups of lower social positions (ibid.). Mauss also speaks of honour in *The Gift*, most explicitly in the examples of the *potlatch*, the exchange of agonistic gifts. Honour refers to the authority of actors (Mauss 1925 (2002), 48) and, in the societies Mauss examines, it "is as delicate as that in our own societies" (ibid.). Thus, there is an affinity between Mauss and Bourdieu. Honour transforms "into persons having an obligation those that have placed you yourself under a similar obligation. Everything is based upon the principles of antagonism and rivalry" (ibid. 47).

Nevertheless, these struggles of honour do not only happen between actors of the same rank, because honour does not only refer to an idea of authority, but also to an idea of betting. It is the corollary to the ideas of credit and wealth (ibid. 141 note 140), of which the best examples are given when Mauss speaks of honour in Australian societies (ibid. 48–49). This double reference of honour to rank and bet has the effect that in the *potlatch*, for example, we do not want to prove that we are equal to the partner whom we want to challenge. We want to prove that we are not unequal to him—a nuance that changes everything. Indeed, we bet to prove that we are not unequal, or conversely, we are giving credit to the partner that he is not unequal to us, even if this is not true. Honour therefore assumes that gift exchanges occur between unequal actors, with the exception of gifts between actors of the same rank in the *potlatch*, or other extreme forms of gift exchanges between clan leaders, or notables. Like Bourdieu, Mauss says that the partners choose themselves in the gift exchange, but they rarely, if ever, select partners to whom they are socially equal. It is therefore not the logic of social position that prevails—a view that we also find in Durkheim and Mauss' conclusion in their text on the primitive forms of classification. First of all, there is a relation, and then, on the basis of this relation, there are social positions, which are supported in their development by relations to things—in Bourdieu's terminology, to forms of capital.[23]

If we return to Mauss' *The Gift*, we certainly observe that gifts enable the identification of ranks (ibid. 7–8), but this does not happen automatically. In the gift, there is a reversal between the logic of the relation and the logic of social positions. Indeed, the more the relation as configuration extends to the collective, the more difficult it is to maintain a position in the cycle of the gift. Conversely, the more we want to preserve a social position, the less the cycle of the relation develops, and the more the actors are in danger of being socially excluded, even the chiefs and notables. The ability to move from one position to another in the cycle of the gift thus ensures a flexibility of the social hierarchy (ibid. 123 note 79), which is necessary for the whole clan to maintain itself and perpetuate (ibid. 8). Even on the occasion of strongly antagonistic exchanges, like the *potlatch*, this is not only pertinent to the chief, but through him "indeed the whole clan that contracts on behalf of all, for all that it possesses and for all that it does" (ibid. 8). The antagonism surrounding the gift as well as, for instance, invitations, celebrations, dances and courtesies, mobilises and allies. Again, there is no direct link between mobilization and alliance. These are two separate phases in gift exchanges, which, even if they overlap in practice (as Mauss reminds us, "everything is mixed up together" (ibid. 6)), can be analytically distinguished. Giving represents above all a time to mobilise the clan and the group. Receiving the gift represents above all a deployment of activities regarding the objects in preparation for returning the gift. Finally, returning the gift is above all the time to consecrate the alliance between the parties in exchange.

At the same time, this transition through the three positions of the gift describes the complementarity between maximisation and ranking, wherein the maximisation of social positions (mostly during giving and receiving) leads to the ranking of social positions at the moment of returning the gift. In his *Gift*, Mauss not only revives but also arrives at the conclusions that he and Durkheim had developed in their text on the primitive forms of classification. Now, he extends them and gives them new meaning. In the cycle of the gift, maximising a social position means establishing the relational perspective in the collective (to give), working at and with appropriate mediations (to receive) in order to consecrate alliances, and to perform hierarchical classifications—i.e. rankings—of social positions (to return the gift). This cycle determines both the change of social positions and the affirmation of social positions either in favour of or to the detriment of the corresponding actors and groups. It affects both future gift exchanges and the way in which these exchanges produce social positions and assign actors to these positions.

Finally, we can describe this cycle of the relation that the gift illustrates by using the reversed complementarity between relation and social position with respect to the gift. When the gift extends the relation to the collective, all social positions in the clan are put into question because in the societies that Mauss examines, the gift mobilises the whole clan. The social hierarchy of the group is put to the test—either directly as a hierarchy, or indirectly through the representatives of this hierarchy (the chiefs, the notables, the priests). To put all chances at their side and to pass this test, actors give the most things possible and the most valuable ones at the risk of losing everything. In the position of receiving, the one who receives must affirm himself in order for all the actors connected to the gift to maintain themselves in the face of this overflow of gifts, which leads them to the cycle of the relation.

The activity surrounding the things received, surrounding the mediations of the exchange under control of those group institutions that these things symbolise, is the typical expression of this self-affirmation. Things are neither randomly picked up nor given as such, as raw things. The givers work on them, they polish them, they decorate and sculpt them, and if needed, they manufacture other things which will be added to the things to be given. Through these activities surrounding the things, actors affirm their social position either towards their own hierarchy, or towards the hierarchy of another social group. Finally, returning the gift is the time to consecrate the social position, affirmed by each actor and each group in the gift exchange. At the same time, the end of the cycle of the relation, which has enabled the gift exchange, is consecrated, and the next starting point for future exchanges, for a future configuration of the relation is established.

Mauss' explanation here is not far from the one he presented with Hubert in their essay on the sacrifice—communication with ancestors or gods through sacrifices has led to the consecration of social positions in society. Actors can therefore be freed from this communication, and they can come back to their daily occupations. Or to put it in other words, once the social positions have been ranked, once this new hierarchy has been consecrated, contact between the actors remains in order to build other cycles of the relation from this new starting point. This conclusion recalls Bourdieu's argument on society considered as a space of possibilities in the probabilistic sense of the word. Because, whenever an opposition between social positions can be observed, when these positions have been maximised and ranked in social space, a new space of possible positions and rankings appears. Nevertheless, for Bourdieu, these possibilities remain bound to the habitus and social positions of actors, whose affirmation determines the only possible relation that Bourdieu's sociology can take into account: the antagonistic relation structuring social space. "Social identity carries a determinate right to the possible" (Bourdieu 1995, 260).

While exploring the logic of social positions in a similar way, Bourdieu and Mauss differ as to how to link social positions to the relation. We have seen above that, for Bourdieu, the social position of actors is given in their habitus and determines their concrete social relations, so that any concrete social relation strengthens the corresponding social position and the habitus. The relation to which Bourdieu refers, and which structures the social space, is an antagonistic one because it is the by-product of antagonist social positions, i.e. of maximised and thus opposed habitus on the different levels of the social hierarchy. In contrast, Mauss says that the relational perspective existing concretely in contact extends to the collective. It mobilises the whole social hierarchy, including leaders—from chiefs and notables to families, neighbours, and so on to the other actors in this hierarchy. This hierarchy is put into question in the gift exchange. It is put to the test to renew itself, which means a renewal of the social positions that actors claim by self-affirmation in the gift exchanges in order to take these new positions, and to be consecrated in them. This consecration closes the cycle of the relation, and it represents the starting point of new exchanges.

This difference between Bourdieu and Mauss also shows the way in which the authors view the partners of exchanges and the meaning of these exchanges in terms of the social hierarchy. For Bourdieu, actors in the exchanges are looking for equal partners because it would be disgraceful to deal with higher or lower ones. Only equal partners can become rivals, this rivalry being the root of the self-affirmation of habitus. The other actors are immediately excluded, or they exclude themselves consciously or unconsciously from these exchanges—they take part in other exchanges that suit them, i.e. that correspond to their interests, social position, or habitus.

For Mauss, the gift indicates that contact takes place between unequal actors who have to prove that they are not unequal. These actors are looking for the best possible partners of exchange whom they will be able to challenge in order to prove their honour or their generosity—this could be either an actor at the top of the social hierarchy (for example, a Brahman famous for his insensitivity to gifts), or an actor at the bottom of the social hierarchy (e.g. a beneficiary of alms). This difference highlights a more important contrast between Bourdieu and Mauss when it comes to their concept of the relation. This, according to Bourdieu, is a power relationship between antagonistic social positions, while for Mauss, this kind of relation, as observed in the *potlatch*, for instance, is only one kind of social relation among others to which neither the gift nor any other kind of exchange can be reduced. The gap between the two authors increases when we pay more attention to the topic that underlies their reasoning about ranking—hierarchy.

Hierarchy

According to Bourdieu, ranking enables us to understand that social hierarchies—whether we talk about the hierarchy of a particular field, or the hierarchy of society, thus the hierarchy between the fields in society

(Bourdieu 1985a, 723)[24]—form a unity, which consists of relatively homogeneous divisions. These divisions are relatively homogeneous because they are rooted in the social positions and in the habitus of the actors, so that the principles of classification and division that give shape to social hierarchies are the same as the ones that shape these social positions and these habitus. In industrialised societies, as in the Kabyle society, hierarchy refers to the legitimation of unity by division (Bourdieu 1977, 165), and to relation by social positions. For example, in acts of speech, language becomes an instrument "enabling speakers to situate others in the hierarchies of age, wealth, power, or culture, guides them unwittingly towards the type of exchange best suited in form and content to the objective situation between the interacting individuals" (ibid. 26).[25] This is similar for other forms of expression, whether they are related to a symbolic or to a material mediation of exchange. Hierarchies are more or less rigid, and therefore, they more or less enable revolutions of the hierarchical order that prevails in a field. A strongly conservative hierarchy, such as that found in the field of education (Bourdieu 2008, 38), will not be as easy to reverse as a more flexible hierarchy, such as, for example, in the artistic field. In order for such a revolution to take place, it is not enough to change the field from the inside, for example by introducing new principles of hierarchy, new mediations of exchange, and new actors. There must still be a correspondence between the changes inside a given field and the changes outside this field. This correspondence can be brought about by societal revolutions themselves (economic, political, social or spiritual crises, for example), or by the actors, e.g. when they introduce new codes of classification or new products in the field, they address new consumers willing to accept these codes and products. Let us take the example of the field of literature. Bourdieu says:

> The new heretical entrants who refuse to enter into the cycle of simple reproduction, based on the mutual recognition of the 'old' and the 'new', and break with the current norms of production in defiance of the expectations of the field can usually only succeed in imposing recognition of their products by virtue of external changes. The most decisive of these changes are the political ruptures, such as revolutionary crises, which change the power relations at the heart of the field (thus, the 1848 revolution reinforces the dominated pole, determining a provisional shift of writers towards 'social art'), or the appearance of new categories of consumers who, having an affinity with the new producers, guarantee the success of their products. (Bourdieu 1995, 253)

These two conditions are almost identical in the sense that they both refer to a demographic condition, i.e. the number of people involved in the fields. A defined number of actors is an indispensable condition for the transformation of the rules that govern a social field, i.e. for the production of new positions in the field and for the movement of actors between the available positions in a field. Where this condition is not given, it can be created to ensure the conservation of a field and of its boundaries. Bourdieu's entire sociology of the school system describes this. It illustrates perfectly the idea according to which divisions legitimise the unity of the school hierarchy, and therefore, of the societal hierarchy. At the beginning, there is almost an inverse relation between social demography and the education system. Examining social demography, we see a low number of representatives of the privileged classes in society in comparison to a large number of representatives of less privileged classes. The ideal and ideological goal of the school is to make the members of these classes equal, i.e. to give as much chance of success as possible to the members of the non-privileged classes in comparison to the members of the privileged classes. "Such an attitude is part of the logic of a system which is based on the postulate of the formal equality of all pupils, as a precondition of its operation" (Bourdieu and Passeron 1979, 67). Because there are more members of the less privileged social classes in society, we should therefore expect to find more of them in each school form in the school system, regardless of the prestige of the school form.

Yet, this expectation is proven wrong once we take into account the mediations between the social classes and the school system. These are, for example, the type of school, the subjects taught at schools, the teaching staff (supervising students), and the geographical area where the school is situated. We must also take into account that these schools, subjects, teachers, and geographical areas have a different prestige that makes it even more difficult to attain equality at school. These material and immaterial mediations operate as filters, contributing to selection of entry into the school system, and to the attribution of a position. Bourdieu notes that, when we take the effect of this filtering into account, we observe that each representative of a social class takes up the position at school which corresponds to the position of their social class in society (cf. Bourdieu 1981a, 3–70). Therefore, although the privileged social classes are a minority in terms of the number of their members in society, they are widely represented in the schools that cultivate the same values as their social class, i.e. prestigious schools leading to prestigious socio-professional careers. For these actors, such schools present a familiar context where it is normal to expect that these actors will correspond to it (Bourdieu 1984, 122f.). Conversely, the members of the prestigious social classes are in terms of their numbers less represented in less prestigious schools or school forms than the members of the less privileged social classes. At school, they find the analogously less privileged position that their social class has in society. In the example of universities, Bourdieu even says that "the potency of the social factors of inequality is such that even if the equalization of economic resources could be achieved, the university system would not cease to consecrate inequalities by transforming social privilege into individual gifts or merits" (Bourdieu and Passeron 1979, 27).

Whether we speak of art, literature or the school system, of revolutions within a field or between fields (caused by the revolutions within the field of power), or of the maintenance of these fields, Bourdieu's reasoning always operates on the same argumentative base. Divisions guarantee and legitimise the unity and the homogeneity of the hierarchy. Mauss' starting point is almost the opposite—the unity acquired thanks to an extension of the relational perspective to the collective should legitimise the divisions that structure the hierarchies in order for the latter to be maintained.

Mauss already introduces this idea in the article he wrote with Durkheim on the primitive forms of classification, where they say that "the scheme of classification is not the spontaneous product of abstract understanding, but results from a process into which all sorts of foreign elements enter" (Durkheim and Mauss 1903b (2009), 5). At the origin, there are few distinctions, even if there is a division between clans or phratries, whose role is to promote "the transformation of the most heterogeneous things one into another, and consequently the more or less complete absence of definite concepts" (ibid. 3). Mauss also underlines this state of a relative absence of distinction in *The Gift*, which indicates the strong collective character of these exchanges in the societies Mauss examines. "In these societies neither the clan nor the family is able to isolate itself or dissociate its actions. Nor are individuals themselves, however influential and aware, capable of understanding that they need to oppose one another and learn how to dissociate their actions from one another. The chief is merged with his clan, and the clan with him" (Mauss 1925 (2002), 41). Therefore, "the juridical and economic concepts possess less clarity and less conscious precision" (ibid. 45). Gift exchanges, without eliminating this relative absence of distinctions, nevertheless allow recognition of the boundaries between groups of actors and between objects, "In practice, the principles are positive and sufficiently clear-cut" (ibid.). These boundaries and divisions not only have to be understood as the result of the ranking of social positions in these exchanges. They also symbolise how the principles that structure the hierarchy of the groups who are exchanging the gifts are put to the test in these exchanges, at the level of their legitimacy—not in regard to the social positions of these groups, but to their relationship. The honour of the chiefs and notables, as well as the attributes of this honour expressed in the things exchanged (which refer to the attributes of the institutions of the whole clan), are only proven if they resist *in* the exchange of gifts—one should not be "'flattened'" by the partner of exchange (ibid. 52)—and *to* this exchange (one should enter this exchange by giving or receiving, and above all, one has to get out of it by returning presents).

When we say "honour has to be proven", this means, for both Mauss and Bourdieu, the recognition of power. With the *potlatch* of the Kwakiutl, for example, "One 'recognizes' the chief or his son and becomes 'grateful' to him" (ibid. 52). This recognition is not based on any ignorance of the rules that constitute this power—rules that the owners of power would try to dissimulate. On the contrary, in gift exchanges, "society, or men, become sentimentally aware of themselves and of their situation in relation to others" (ibid. 102). In other words, this awareness of oneself and of others, of one's position and that of others in the social hierarchy, is not based on the difference of social positions. It is based on the corresponding recognition that this power "works" in practice because it helps to extend the relation to the collective, thus contributing to the maximisation of social positions and because it enables the actor to get out of the relation in order to put these social positions at stake in further exchanges.

Therefore, power, which, according to Bourdieu, is a by-product of the societal hierarchical structure and, at the same time, is what is needed to dominate in society, takes on a different meaning for Mauss. Power is undoubtedly the imposition of something on someone, and in this regard, Mauss is close to Bourdieu. To give, receive, and return presents means to impose something on the other as an affirmation of oneself. But for Mauss, power should "work" in practice in getting other actors to participate in the gift exchanges, and so it will be legitimated. This is a property that gifts and sacrifices share. They are efficient if they contribute to extending the relational perspective to other actors, their activities and things, and they must enable actors to get out of this relational perspective, because otherwise the hierarchy as a whole is in question and with it its most emblematic representatives—chiefs, representatives of the institutions of the social group, and the objects attached to it (cf. for example Mauss 1925 (2002), 92–93).

The conservation of social hierarchies is therefore not based on ignorance or dissimulation of what legitimises this hierarchy, an ignorance that would be maintained by the dominants and recognised by the entire society. Mauss sees this as practical evidence, which does not need to be as spectacular as in the *potlatch*. The principles that govern the hierarchical order in society can only exist because they support the practical organisation of daily life at all levels of this hierarchy. Thus, we observe an important difference between Bourdieu and Mauss in their explanation of such conservation—and therefore the legitimacy—of social hierarchies. For Bourdieu, hierarchies are maintained because they entail the preservation of the principles of division that compose them, and that are imposed on society. The dominant classes in society, i.e. the groups of actors at the top of these hierarchies, define and impose these principles, so that they can be found in all mediations on and with which actors exert their practical activities.

> Through the mediation of the means of appropriation available to them, exclusively or principally cultural on the one hand, mainly economic on the other, and the different forms of relation to works of art which result from them, the different fractions of the dominant class are oriented towards cultural practices so different in their style and object and sometimes so antagonistic…that it is easy to forget that they are variants of the same fundamental relationship to necessity and to those who remain subject to it, and that each pursues the exclusive appropriation of legitimate cultural goods and the associated symbolic profits. (Bourdieu 1984, 176)

In Mauss, social hierarchies are maintained because the principles of division make sense for the collective, and they make sense because they are efficient in actors' daily lives. These principles are not maintained by coercion or force, but because they are useful. This practical utility consists more fundamentally in giving access to the configurations of the relation, which contribute to building these hierarchies, institutions and actors that these configurations bind together.

This difference between Bourdieu and Mauss also refers to the way they see the link between the demographic condition and the mediations of exchanges—or in other words, between the mobilisation of the collective, and the activities surrounding material and immaterial objects in exchanges. For Bourdieu, these two conditions are opposed, whereas for Mauss, they complete each other. As we have seen, the number of actors is important for Bourdieu, and relevant to their mobilisation. But this mobilisation faces challenges from practical life—the relations to things and to institutions connected to these things. Let us again take the example of the school system. The expansion of education in industrialised societies after the World War II, massively supported by public investments, has contributed to a strong mobilisation of these societies on the principle of schooling, related to the associated promises (employment, growth, well-being). Two popular promises were certainly the democratisation of the school system, and the corresponding meritocratic ideal that everyone would have access to social privileges thanks to education, as Bourdieu describes in his two books on inheritance and reproduction in education. However, what is actually happening in practice? The school system selects and reproduces social inequalities from the first day at school, from the first contact with teachers, the first relation to the mediations of school culture (books, pedagogical methods, infrastructure). The power of the school system and its authority are rooted in the values, the requirements and the lifestyle of the dominant classes who impose them unilaterally on the school system to ensure that school and social hierarchy are reproduced in the sense of their class interests. In other words, mobilisation is countered by mediations of school practice, thus preventing a relation to the school that would collectively make sense. The activities developed by the school system on and with the help of these mediations lead to a gradual demobilisation of the actors to the benefit of the heirs of the dominant classes. This demobilisation is maintained by the institutions, which—as do the school in the field of education and artistic critique, publishers and art directors in the field of art—control that the mediations are operating in support of this demobilisation. Action taken by teaching staff, for example, is one of the ways for the school to check the good use of the school mediations and is therefore nothing more than "symbolic violence insofar as it is the imposition of a cultural arbitrary by an arbitrary power" (Bourdieu and Passeron 1990, 5).

Such an understanding of institutions as enforcers for the dominant classes in social hierarchies would, according to Mauss' *The Gift*, not be possible because such institutions—and the actors that they serve—would immediately lose their collective support, their "authority on the consciences" (Fauconnet and Mauss 1901 (1969), 160).[26] They would attract the hostile reaction of society, or even—symbolically—of the mediations of exchange. In Hindu law, for example, the miser who wants to use the institution of hospitality to his sole benefit—who does not give food to a guest, but keeps it only for himself, or charges a fee for it—is symbolically killed by his own food when he eats it (Mauss 1925 (2002), 73). Correspondingly, he loses every concrete collective support in society. The sorcerer or the priest whose powers "become too important and too terrible, and make him dangerous" attracts the anger of the other actors in society, "who abandon or kill him, because they fear to be destroyed, themselves and all their property" (Mauss 1896 (1974), 671).

There is no reason to think, according to Mauss, that our contemporary societies function in a way that, in the context of the gift, is radically different from the way of these societies.

> Institutions of this type have really provided the transition towards our own forms of law and economy. They can serve to explain historically our own societies. The morality and the practice of exchanges employed in societies immediately preceding our own still retain more-or-less important traces of all the principles we have just analysed. We believe, in fact, that we are in a position to show that our own systems of law and economies have emerged from institutions similar to those we describe. (Mauss 1925 (2002), 60–61)

If this is the case, this is not because our societies show a kind of structural similarity to those analysed by Mauss. It is rather because, for both these ancient societies and our own, the fundamental issue is the relation. In sociology, the relation is clearly a challenge because, without developing an analysis of society through relation, it is impossible to understand both the affirmation of habitus and social positions in society, as well as the conservation and the renewal of social hierarchies in any way other than in a way excluding the relational perspective itself. Even the arguments of ignorance and dissimulation that Bourdieu uses to explain social recognition of the domination by dominant classes and of their affiliated social institutions, reveal their limitations when taken from the viewpoint of a sociology through relation. Because, if the dominant classes want to dissimulate the reasons for inequalities between social positions, this requires nevertheless the development of strategies, i.e. of activities on and with the help of mediations of exchange to produce the desired effect on the dominated. The effect is that the dominated believe in the authority of the dominating, and in order to sustain such a belief, the dominating have to extend ignorance to the entire society. Therefore, they have to mobilise far beyond the dominating and the institutions that serve them. Thus, it is an either-or situation.

Either ignorance will be unveiled as a strategy against society and, once unmasked, will be put into question just as will be those actors who had an interest in supporting it. Or it continues, which means that the actors and the mediations at the origin of this ignorance can be shielded from all other social actors and, therefore, from society. The first case applies if we assume, like Mauss, that the relational perspective still represents a challenge of priorities in our society today. The second case applies if we think, like Bourdieu, that this perspective either is not a challenge of priorities in our society today or is at least subject to social positions in society. However, in the latter case, the whole question of power and domination loses its sociological strength, because—to reformulate a sentence from *The Gift* (Mauss 1925 (2002), 73)—if the domination of the dominating already wins the first round, it is then useless. Why would actors participate in social struggles that, according to Bourdieu, are their daily reality if everything is already decided? Bourdieu answers: "in order to transmit the inherited powers and privileges, maintained or enhanced, to the next generation" (Bourdieu 1990a, 161)—which proves again that even when Bourdieu speaks of relation, he means social position.

Conclusion

The critique that Caillé addresses to Bourdieu has the advantage of highlighting the way in which Bourdieu uses the vocabulary of economic science in his sociology, and it enables us to ask what, in Bourdieu's sociology, cannot be reduced to an economy-oriented explanation of society. The concept of interest offers an example of Bourdieu's distinction between "interest" understood in the economic sense of rational individuals acting by calculations of costs/benefits, and "interest" in the sense of individuals concerned about their personal situation, deploying strategies that more often go against any form of economic rationality, and sometimes even against the personal interest of the actors themselves. There are other examples of such distorted economic vocabulary, as when Bourdieu speaks of the maximisation of profit where maximisation cannot be reduced solely to the idea of profit. We have shown this in comparing Bourdieu and Mauss' understanding of maximisation in their discourse about gift exchanges. This has led us to observe many parallels between Bourdieu and Mauss, not only in relation to the gift but also in relation to the fundamental elements of their relational perspectives on social positions. Both authors see a complementarity between the maximisation and the ranking of social positions. Both emphasise the importance of a demographic condition on the one hand—the mobilisation of actors—and a condition referring to the practical activities of actors on and with the mediations of their exchanges on the other hand.

Nevertheless, Bourdieu and Mauss take different views on the relation between these two conditions because they do not understand the relational character of social positions in the same way. Bourdieu sees these two conditions as being in conflict with each other, in the sense that if the activities on the mediations of exchange support the maximisation-ranking of social positions, they prevent the extension of any relational perspective to the collective by discouraging the mobilisation of actors. Mauss, on the other hand, sees the activities on the mediations of exchange as allowing a continuous extension of this relational perspective, with these activities taking over the mobilisation of actors. Mauss' *The Gift* illustrates this with examples of the transition of actors from the position of donors to the position of donees, i.e. from gift givers, to gift receivers and returners. The process of maximising-ranking of social positions is then completed, consecrating both the classification of positions within social hierarchies and the end of the cycle of the relation of which the returning of gifts is the closing mechanism. The latter simultaneously makes the beginning of new exchanges possible, i.e. of a new configuration of the relation.

If the positions of both authors are put at opposite ends, this is because, on the one hand, for Bourdieu, social hierarchy and the operations preexisting before the establishment of this hierarchy are not put into question, which enables the dominant classes to perpetuate their privileges. Mauss, on the other hand, sees the conservation of social hierarchy and the dominant positions of the chiefs or notables in society maintained only if they are collectively put to the test. Whereas for Bourdieu, the dominating can count on these intermediary actors, which are the institutions that control that the activities on the mediations of exchange reproduce their interests and positions—for Mauss, these institutions operate in order to maintain a relational perspective in society, thus contributing to the renewal of the social hierarchy. The affinity that we underlined between Bourdieu and Mauss does certainly not disappear completely behind the differences in their relational understanding of social positions. Indeed, whether we speak of the gift in ancient societies, or of our contemporary societies, with both Bourdieu and Mauss we are talking about hierarchies that want to preserve themselves in one way or another. Nevertheless, in the framework of Bourdieu's sociology, hierarchies are preserved thanks to the domination by the dominant classes in society, holding the others in ignorance of their domination, exerting to their own benefit. In Mauss' *The Gift*, hierarchies are preserved by the alliances that assume a destabilisation of this hierarchy either through its actors or other hierarchies. To give a brief additional example of this contrast between Bourdieu and Mauss, let us turn to the Kabyle marriage described by Bourdieu.

The maxim guiding the matrimonial alliances that Bourdieu describes in Kabyle societies says "'The inside is better than the outside'" (Bourdieu 1977, 58), meaning that there are two types of possible marriages. There are marriages between families who share the same culture—the same position in the social hierarchy, typically the family of parallel cousins—and marriages with other families not sharing this same culture, and hence the same social position. Bourdieu comments on these two types of marriage by saying that they:

> represent the points of maximum intensity of the two values which all marriages seek to maximise: on the one hand the integration of the minimal unit and its security, on the other hand alliance and prestige, that is, opening up to the outside world, towards strangers. The choice between fission and fusion, inside and outside, security and adventure, is posed anew with each marriage. If it ensures the maximum of integration for the minimal group, parallel-cousin marriages duplicate the relationship of filiation with a relationship of alliance, squandering by this redundancy the opportunity of creating new alliances which marriage represents. Distant marriage, on the other hand, secures prestigious alliances at the cost of lineage integration and the bond between brothers. (ibid. 57)

In other words, the Kabyle marriages are contracted in order to maximise the ratio of risk and prestige, whereby the reduction of risk certainly decreases the prestige of the group but guarantees, at the same time, its social position and the reproduction of this position. A more important risk can increase the prestige of the group, but it may weaken its social position and the reproduction of that position.

Mauss, in contrast, speaks of actors and groups constantly going outside of their social position in order to prove their value.

> Over a considerable period of time and in a considerable number of societies, men approached one another in a curious frame of mind, one of fear and exag-

> gerated hostility, and of generosity that was likewise exaggerated, but such traits only appear insane to our eyes. In all the societies that have immediately preceded our own, and still exist around us, and even in numerous customs extant in our popular morality, there is no middle way: one trusts completely, or one mistrusts completely; one lays down one's arms and gives up magic, or one gives everything, from fleeting acts of hospitality to one's daughter and one's goods. It is in such a state of mind that men have abandoned their reserve and have been able to commit themselves to giving and giving in return. This was because they had no choice. Two groups of men who meet can only either draw apart, and, if they show mistrust towards one another or issue a challenge, fight—or they can negotiate. Until legal systems and economies evolved not far removed from our own, it is always with strangers that one 'deals', even if allied to them. (Mauss 1925 (1989), 104–105)

Therefore, if we take Bourdieu's ratio and apply it to Mauss' gift, we see that, as Bourdieu says, the risk increases in proportion to prestige. Yet, if we want to reduce the risk, we also reduce exchange with others. What represented a regular case in Bourdieu's statement about Kabyle marriages is, if we believe Mauss' *The Gift*, a marginal case, because what matters first in gift exchanges are the activities and exchanges with others actors, villages and countries.

In other words, what matters for an actor is to put to the test not only his social position, but also the social hierarchy within which he finds himself. Mauss' argument of alliance is also at the origin of a relational understanding of power, which affects social positions. A societal hierarchy takes the risk of dissolving itself when it is seeking to prove its power over another hierarchy. If it does, then it is in order to extend the relational perspective to the whole hierarchy, i.e. to each group and each actor within it. This is all the more so because this relational perspective rests in the collective, not only in terms of population, but also in terms of activities on the different mediations that occur in the exchanges. In this chapter, we have focused on the mobilisation of actors as a requirement for extending the relational perspective to the collective. We have more or less left the second dimension out of the analysis, i.e. the activity on the mediations of exchange. In the next chapter, we will look at this second dimension.

Notes

1. These two concepts are not the only ones to which Bourdieu pays attention, but they play a fundamental role in understanding how social norms are embedded not only in the minds of actors, but also in their bodies (for

example Crick 1982, 299; Lock 1993, 137; Adkins 2003, 14; Dianteill 2003, 529–549), and, therefore, in their emotions (Karsenti 2011, 77).

2. Coliot-Thélène, for example, goes even as far as to say that Bourdieu's criticism of Mauss' gift represents for Bourdieu "a fundamental turning point in the development of his theoretical position" (Coliot-Thélène 2005, 118).
3. Mahé (1996, 237–264) has clearly highlighted the links between Maunier's work on the *taousa* in Kabyle, and the conceptions of the gift in Maunier, Mauss, Claude Lévi-Strauss and Bourdieu.
4. As Swartz says, "Bourdieu adopts the language of 'strategy' to distance himself from strict structuralist forms of determination by stressing the importance of agency within a structuralist framework" (Swartz 1997, 98). The concept of strategy is a way for Bourdieu to insist on the creativity of the actors, and in this regard, it represents "the general disposition to maximize opportunity and profit…, which might mean the direct manipulation and even avoidance of established ways of doing things" (Grenfell and Hardy 2007, 24).
5. Dumont says that for Bourdieu "the truth that structural objectivism excludes—the 'full truth'—is the temporal 'structure' of gift exchange" (Dumont 1999, 22).
6. Alvin Gouldner has made reciprocity famous as a general moral norm of human exchanges (Gouldner 1960, 161–178).
7. Lane has also stressed this: "Here, then, Bourdieu was attempting to give practical form to the theoretical role he had elaborated for intellectuals as early as 'Questions de politique' in 1977. The intellectual was to adopt a Socratic role, helping dominated groups to articulate a 'heterodox' discourse, which expressed the truth of a marginalized experience that the 'orthodox' discourse of the dominant class tried to silence and naturalize" (Lane 2006, 150).
8. This can be seen in Bourdieu's posthumous book, *The Social Structures of the Economy* (2005), in which he formulates a critique of the economy through an analysis of the French real estate market.
9. Laine underlines this point when he comments on Caillé's critique of Bourdieu, "As Alain Caillé has pointed out, there was an anthropological assumption underpinning Bourdieu's field theory, the assumption that all agents were driven by the need to accumulate or preserve the different forms of capital on offer in the various fields" (Lane 2006, 148).
10. According to Caillé, there is in Mauss "a powerful social theory which gives the guidelines not only for the construction of a sociological paradigm, but for the construction of the solely thinkable and bearable sociological paradigm" (Caillé 1996, 190).

11. Mauss clearly says that his study on the gift in ancient societies is "incompatible with the development of the market, commerce, and production, and, all in all…anti-economic" (Mauss 1925 (2002), 69). Nevertheless, he also says that "the market is a human phenomenon that, in our view, is not foreign to any known society" (ibid. 5). Thus, Mauss remains ambivalent towards the relationship between gifts and economic exchanges, which do not represent two well-defined or well-separated domains of activity. Yet, when Caillé says that Mauss takes the gift out of the economy, he is actually saying that Mauss does not see the gift as an ancient form of modern capitalist economy. However, Caillé does not go as far as Hénaff, for example, who presents a different idea suggesting that the gift and economic exchanges are two forms of exchange that are fundamentally different (Hénaff 2010).
12. When he speaks of negative anti-utilitarianism, Caillé means the most radical discourses against economic semantics (Caillé 1996, 192–193). According to these discourses, there is an asymmetry between gift and economy that must disappear—this will allow for radical critique of modern capitalism and, as a consequence, its removal in order to build a society on the basis of an anti-economic model.
13. Caillé uses the expression "primary sociality" to describe the "forms of sociability" between close relatives and allies (Caillé 1982, 65), which is the domain of "private life" and "inter-personal recognition" (Caillé 2010, 205).
14. Honneth, for example, restricts interpretation of the term "maximising" to the single idea of profit, and he consequently criticises the utilitarian nature of Bourdieu's theory in terms close to those used by Caillé (Honneth 1986, 55–66).
15. Speaking of the ambivalence of the things involved in the sacrifices, which ambivalence Mauss also finds in the gift, being, as it is, at the same time a poison and a present; Mauss refers to Robertson Smith even if he rejects his theory of religion (Isambert 1976, 41). The ambivalence of objects in sacrifices as well as in gift exchanges makes Mauss pay attention to the variety of sacrifices and gifts, their multiplicity and differences, as well as to the corresponding quantity of exchanges coming from them, which are necessary for the extension of the relational perspective contained in the contact. If we imagine that ambivalence is like fog, i.e. makes the things that come into exchanges indistinct from one another, this is, in fact quite the opposite for Mauss. For him, ambivalence is like a spectrum of colours, enabling us to consider the variety of objects and the corresponding exchanges that societies develop in order to deploy cycles of the relation.
16. Bourdieu says that "The schemes of the habitus" are "the primary forms of classification" (Bourdieu 1984, 466). "The habitus is at once a system of

models for the production of practices and a system of models for the perception and appreciation of practices. And in both cases, its operations express the social position in which it was constructed. As a result, the habitus produces practices and representations which are available for classification, which are objectively differentiated; but they are immediately perceived as such only in the case of agents who possess the code, the classificatory models necessary to understand their social meaning" (Bourdieu 1990a, 130).

17. Mauss prefers to speak of the cycle of services and counter-services surrounding the gift, rather than of a "circle", which evokes the *kula* on the Tribriand Islands described by Bronislaw Malinowski (Mauss 1925 (2002), 27).
18. Mauss understands the *kula* as "none other than the system of gifts exchanged", from which the *potlatch* only "differs...in the violence, exaggeration, and antagonisms that it arouses, and by a certain lack of juridical concepts, and a simpler and cruder structure" (Mauss 1925 (2002), 45).
19. These criticisms are well known today. Let us recall them briefly. Mauss refers to Eldson Best to interpret the Maori term *hau* on the basis of the collection of the Dominion museum and of the articles that Best wrote for the *Journal of the Polynesian Society* (Mauss 1925 (2002), 115 note 30). The *hau* is the object of a great variety of possible interpretations (Best 1900, 190). It generally means a vital essence, or a principle of life (ibid. 189). It is also close to the notions of personality or resemblance ("ahua"; cf. ibid. 186, 189), wind, blows, respiration (ibid. 190), and in this sense, to the term "mana" (ibid.). It also means "king" or "supreme leader" (ibid. 190), and it is located in animate and inanimate objects (ibid. 191). In the tradition of Max Müller (ibid. 190), Best structures the concept to enable European scientists to understand its meaning. Mauss summaries Best's numerous meanings of the *hau*, and he says that the *hau* seems to evoke the personality of the donor in the Maori gifts. This interpretation was the subject of several critiques. Raymond Firth said that Mauss had forced the translation of the *hau*, thus distorting the meaning of the Maori gifts. "In his Essai sur le don he had taken a Maori text as the pivot of his argument about reciprocity in the gift. But I felt he did not really understand the Maori, and in fact he glossed one word of the text quite wrongly. The Maori elder spoke of a gift having an immaterial essence which demanded a proper return. Mauss misread this as implying that part of the personality of the giver was involved. But while this distorted the Maori view, Mauss's concept proved extremely stimulating" (Firth in James and Allen 1998, 23). Lévi-Strauss insists less on this translation issue, and instead underlines that Mauss simply invented this meaning of the *hau*. "In the Essai sur le don, Mauss strives to reconstruct a whole out of parts; and

as that is manifestly not possible, he has to add to the mixture an additional quantity which gives him the illusion of squaring his account. This quantity is hau" (Lévi-Strauss 1987, 47; cf. also the critique of Claude Lefort in Lefort 1951, 1402; also Annette Weiner in Weiner 1985, 211–215). Starting in the 1970s, some authors relativised these critiques and rehabilitated Mauss' contribution (for example Sahlins 1972, 155–170; Leach 1983, 536; Karsenti 1997, 381 note 1).

20. As Wacquant recalls (Wacquant 1989, 26–63), ranking presupposes different principles of ranking according to the field or the sub-field in question. This means that the principles according to which social positions are ranked are specific ones. They concern one specific field and its sub-fields, and do not extend to other fields and sub-fields.
21. Regarding this statement about the affirmation of the personal and social identity of disinterested artists, Sapiro points out the use of the concept of charism in Bourdieu, referring to Max Weber's theory of people mobilising actors in order to support a cause that they want to bring to the attention of the public at their own risk (Sapiro 2003, 638–639). This can be seen as a good example—because it exaggerates a general trend—of the link existing between the maximisation of a social position and the mobilisation of the collective.
22. In the original article "De quelques formes de classification. Contribution à l'étude des représentations collectives", Durkheim and Mauss not only speak of "the relations which exist between things", but more generally of "relations qui existent entre les êtres" (Durkheim and Mauss 1903a (1974), 82), meaning things, spirits, and human beings at the same time.
23. From this viewpoint, we understand Rawls' observation on the recurring misinterpretations of Durkheim and Mauss' writings on the primitive forms of classification. For Rawls, it is wrong to see Durkheim and Mauss as two positivists who assume that the forms of classification are part of the collective representations in society, which actors would only use in their daily life. "An empirically valid category of classification only develops, according to Durkheim, when practices that enact moral relationships produce feelings of moral force" (Rawls 1996, 454). In other words, it is only when actors' practical activities lead to manifest relations that they see their forms of classification as empirically valid. In our last chapter, we return to this type of legitimisation *a posteriori—a posteriori* because, as we shall see, legitimisation presupposes the establishment of a relational perspective in society in order to mean something to the collective.
24. Bourdieu understands the fields and sub-fields that form a social space as being subjected to the field of power, one definition of which is "the space of relations of force between agents or between institutions having in common the possession of the capital necessary to occupy the dominant posi-

tions in different fields (notably economic or cultural)" (Bourdieu 1995, 215). The struggles within the field of power, i.e. between dominant actors in the other fields of society, determine the hierarchical order of the fields in society in determining the value of the different kinds of capital present in these fields.

25. On the relationship between language and habitus in Bourdieu, see for example Kögler (2011, 271–300).
26. One remembers Paul Veyne's book, which takes up the same idea as applied to Greek mythology, according to which Greek myths generated reactions in Greek society, which range from belief to fiercest scepticism (Veyne 1983).

CHAPTER 5

Mediations: Pierre Bourdieu and Bruno Latour on Objects, Institution and Legitimisation

In Chap. 4, we saw similarities between Bourdieu and Mauss, as well as crucial differences that we can more generally understand as the asymmetric way of the former and the symmetric way of the latter to support their kind of relational sociology. Indeed, Bourdieu understands social life as a relational asymmetry. Relation is seen as a concrete social relation whose unique type is the relation of power produced by polarised habitus and corresponding social positions.

Mauss, in contrast, offers in his *essay The Gift* a relational perspective based on symmetries of giving, receiving and returning material and immaterial presents whereby donors and donees have to prove that they are not unequal to each other.

By exploring more deeply the comparison between Bourdieu and Mauss, we can highlight the analytic moment where this difference between their relational perspective shows up in the most typical way, namely in the coordination between the two conditions leading to maximisation and ranking of social positions. One of these two conditions is the mobilisation of actors, the other is the actors' activity on and with the mediation of exchange. Bourdieu's understanding of the asymmetry of social life and the corresponding reduction of the relation to a concrete relation of power between antagonistic social positions means that the activities involved in the mediation of exchange lead to the demobilisation of social actors to the benefit of the dominant classes. This happens because such mediation is related to institutions that control the use of mediation

C. Papilloud, *Sociology through Relation*, Palgrave Studies in Relational Sociology, https://doi.org/10.1007/978-3-319-65073-9_5

to ensure that the interests and social positions of the dominant classes are reproduced.[1] From this viewpoint, an institution such as the family acts similarly to other institutions such as the school system, for example. In both cases, the mediation of exchange is used to classify the actors, and contributes to ranking them within the social hierarchy, always to the benefit of the hierarchy's reproduction.

However, there is a difference between these two institutions—family and school—as there is between all the other institutions in society and, therefore, between the mediations of exchange, and it is expressed in a compact form in Bourdieu's theory of capital. Indeed, these institutions are governed by interests. These interests are specific because they depend on the field to which they belong. They are also reflected in the special position that the dominant classes—and the dominant members of these classes—have in each of these fields.

In Mauss' *The Gift* too, we can observe a relative demobilisation of the actors in the cycles of the gift because gift exchanges are risky. They threaten the individual actors as well as society. However, the relation to the mediation of exchange enables actors and society to protect themselves against the gift's dangerous effects and against the demobilisation that it may entail because mediations extend the contact between the actors and society. The activities involved in the mediation of exchange allow both maximisation and the ranking of social positions in hierarchies to continue. They contribute to closing the cycles of the relation, and open the way to other possible configuration of the relation, as well as other possible cycles. This is why, in Chap. 4, we said that Bourdieu's relational sociology does not pay much attention to the relation itself. It is rather a sociology of social positions that have been polarised by concrete relations of power. Mauss' symmetric understanding of gift exchanges is open to social diversity, which, when the collective is going to demobilise, is sustained by the things and the actors' activities with these things. Mediations contribute to the extension of the relational perspective towards the collective. What Bourdieu regards as a general fact, i.e. the polarisation of social positions, the corresponding preservation of the social hierarchy and the individual and collective identities upheld by concrete relations of power, is, in the approach taken by Mauss in his *Gift*, only of peripheral importance. Power relationships rule neither the actors' individual life, nor society, not even if there is power in all kind of alliances. Indeed, although alliances are neither immune from power, nor from domination or violence, they cannot be reduced to them. However, in our comparison between Bourdieu and Mauss in terms of the mediation of exchange, we gained little more than some few general observations because it became more and more difficult to sustain such a comparison. Mauss certainly talks extensively about the mediation of exchange. He constantly underlines the importance of things, speeches, gods, which take part in the exchanges between actors. However, he does not provide a theory that would be comparable to Bourdieu's theory of capitals. Mauss does not provide any synthetic view on the mediation of exchange other than saying that the actors have always to deal with total social facts. We can see this with more clarity when we look at Mauss' discourse on technique, a topic connected to the question of the mediation of exchange.

According to Mauss, technique in ancient societies is the magical rite free from mystical or religious characteristics (Mauss 1902–1903 (2001), 176). This rather general statement will be expressed in more specific terms in Mauss' article on the techniques of the body. In this context, technique appears as "an action which is effective and traditional" (Mauss 1973, 75; also Mauss 1947, 24).[2] The effectiveness Mauss speaks of means the production of an "effect" that is not only an effect *sui generis* as in religion, but is also a "physical effect" (Mauss 1947, 24–25). Technique allows one to feel the things and to physically act on them (Mauss 1927 (1969), 197). It is at the bottom of "practical reason" (ibid.) and it transforms the things—an argument which, even if Mauss does not use the word "technique", already appears in his *essay The Gift* when Mauss says that "the res need not have been the crude, merely tangible thing, the simple, passive object of transaction that it has become" (Mauss 1925 (2002), 64). The same applies, for instance, to what the Romans called *stips* or to what is known as *festuca notata* as used by the Germanic tribes, that is, the deposit (ibid. 62), the things used as security or *mancipi* "always stamped by a seal, as a mark of family property" (ibid. 64), or to the loans codified in the Roman law which always presuppose an "ingot of copper" (ibid. 170 note 10). The things exchanged never remain identical to themselves. They are increased (in quantity or in quality), they are given together with other things, or they are destroyed. The thing is constantly modified, and these modifications confer power to the thing, giving it a practical effectiveness brought about by technical operations performed on the object that is given, received or returned, so that it "binds the honour, authority, and mana of the one who hands it over" (ibid. 80). The work on things is a prerequisite to the gift of things in the exchange between actors who transform them either when they receive the thing, or later when they return it. We can see here perhaps more distinctively how, according to Mauss, the activities on things extend the mobilisation of actors. Because the actors—regardless of whether their mobilisation weakens or takes time—make things circulate in order to mobilise the collective and form alliances. It is therefore not surprising that Mauss puts technique more and more to the foreground of his view on social morphology.

This cannot be seen straight away. In the article on sociology that Mauss wrote together with Fauconnet, for example, social morphology is only defined as a special part of sociology devoted to the number of individuals that make up a group, and to their distribution in space (Fauconnet and Mauss 1901 (1969), 176). Nevertheless, in later works, Mauss sees social morphology as the most important part of sociology (Mauss 1927 (1969), 180), and in the *Manual of ethnography* (1947) technique becomes one of two central categories (the other being population) (Mauss 1947, 14–15, 25).

However, Mauss does not explore technique as a subject matter related to the mediation of exchange in all depth. Although technique is indirectly present in the phenomenon of the gift, and although Mauss recognises its tremendous role in society, he says that he has never had the time or the necessary energy to explore it in a satisfactory way (Mauss 1927 (1969), 194).

Another sociologist, although he does not refer to Mauss, offers a similar reflection—with the difference that he goes considerably deeper than Mauss and incorporates it in his relational sociology. This sociologist is Bruno Latour.

In the present chapter, we want to take a closer look at the mediation of exchange by comparing Bourdieu's and Latour's views on the things that are involved in such exchanges in the context of daily social activities.[3] We will summarise Bourdieu's views on the relationships between the mediation of exchange and the institutions on which they depend in order to put it into contrast to the stance taken by Latour on the same topic. This will lead us to observe that, unsurprisingly, Bourdieu and Latour have different ideas about the mediation of exchanges as well as about its relation to institutions. What is surprising, however, is that they still arrive at a similar conclusion, i.e. that there is a correspondence between the actors, the mediations on which they exert their activities, and the institutions that control these activities on these mediations. What, in relation to such correspondence, both authors emphasise is the legitimacy of both the actors and the institutions and the claim that this legitimacy stems from the reciprocity of the actors' and the institutions' interests. Let us begin our comparison by looking at Bourdieu and Latour's understanding of the actors' work on the material or immaterial mediation of exchange.

Work on Things

'Work' or 'labour' are words Bourdieu uses in order to summarise actors' activities. They tend to be little noticed because of Bourdieu's insistence on his main concepts—habitus, capital, and field—but are not less present in the major parts of his sociology as he does not only describe the relation of power in society, "but also the social labour that it requires of those who perform it and above all the labour that is needed to produce and reproduce both its agents…and its very logic" (Bourdieu 2001, 44). Like Mauss, Bourdieu also thinks that the objects on which the actors exert their activity do not remain passive objects. Taking the relation that the Kabyle peasant has to his land as an example, Bourdieu says: "The land is never treated as a raw material to be exploited, but always as the object of respect mixed with fear" (Bourdieu 1977, 175). Therefore, not anyone can work the land but only those actors who are reputed to pay it sufficient respect—typically the fathers of Kabyle families, not their sons. This respect returns to what is valued in the labour of Kabyle peasants, which "is activity for its own sake, regardless of its strictly economic function" (ibid. 175).

This said, Bourdieu argues that activity has always two complementary aspects, namely a technical and a symbolic aspect. Depending on the social proximity of the actors, these two aspects of labour are not always combined in the same way. The symbolic value of labour has more importance in the eyes of the actors as they are familiar with the activity to be performed, or as they are familiar with the actors to whom the product of the activity has to be given. This symbolic value decreases when labour is done in the name of principles that are unfamiliar to the actors who perform that labour, or when their labour leads to exchanges with strangers (ibid. 172, 175). The Kabyle people try to avoid exchanges of the latter kind because they would reduce their labour to technical aspects only and would deprive them of the honours usually related to their labour and the related activities on things (ibid. 176). If the Kabyle people want to preserve the meaning of their labour, this is because, for them, the symbolic value of their labour is more important than its economic value. Indeed, producing this symbolic value means for the actor that, in his work on things, he is able to transform the technical character of his activity into art, which is recognised as such if it is unique, singular, and as personalised as possible.

According to Bourdieu, labour on things therefore leads to a maximisation of any actor's habitus and social position, even more so as that the practical operations which labour presupposes are sublimated by the production of the labour's symbolic value. The actors are then able to put an end to "the primal undifferentiatedness", to their social anonymity that is part of "the play of individual and collective misrecognition" (ibid. 176) or, to put it in a synthetic way: the personification of labour presupposes a substitution where class habitus replaces the relation, thus becoming the new reference framework that determines the understanding of the mediations (the elements that constitute capital) and therefore of the exchanges in which these mediations circulate. Thus, the production of the symbolic value that represents the labour on the mediation of exchange becomes the symbol of the actors' productive value that influences the social position held by the actor individually (as habitus) and collectively (as habitus of a class of actors). The individual and collective ignorance of the interplay of exchange is, so to speak, the natural outcome of the production of symbolic values based on the recognition of social positions. This does not mean that labour on the mediation of exchange makes social actors blind to these exchanges. Labour rather stimulates the denial of the relational orientation that the actors give to their activities. This leads to an increase in the standardisation and naturalisation of the distinctions between actors and social groups, i.e. it increases the antagonistic polarisation of their social position. Such denial is inherent in the actors' labour, and is the case for both the dominant and the dominated social classes in society, and thus sets the ground for the idea that Bourdieu uses in his interpretation of the Kabyle peasants' practical activities, namely the idea of familiarity or unfamiliarity with the principles attached to, or with the actors benefiting from, such labour.

In his sociology of the school, for example, Bourdieu criticises the ideology of the gift, saying that the school, through its teachers, attributes qualifications to students by distinguishing gifted from less gifted students. This distinction is not based on the relation that the student has to school, school contents, school disciplines, or teachers. It is based on the correspondence between their habitus and the school's or the school system's values and standards, which are the values and standards set by the dominant classes. In school, the ideology of the gift is the "negation of the social conditions of the production of cultivated dispositions" (Bourdieu and Passeron 1990, 52). In other words, this ideology denies the relational orientation towards school culture even before a child enters school—it starts in the family and then continues throughout school—and is a denial whose degree is strongly connected to the social classes. This ideology of the gift goes hand in hand with the pretence of a meritocratic ideology and an ideology of democratisation of schools and social trajectories. These ideologies make believe that the school has the social and political mission to recognise students' equality in their relation to school culture. In practice, however, through the teachers, the school evaluates the students' production of symbolic values and sanctions the correspondence between these symbolic values and the values the school expects, which is "nothing other than the relation to culture to which each is socially assigned by birth" (Bourdieu and Passeron 1979, 24). When, as in the Kabyle society, the father has authority over the land because he is recognised as having made an art of his labour, in school, the students who give primacy to the "manner and style", to "naturalness and lightness" (ibid. 130) have, for similar reasons, authority in the eyes of the teachers. They are recognised as having made an art of their knowledge. They are directly opposed to those students whose labour speaks of effort (ibid. 130), of "laborious pedantry suspected of making up for a lack of talent" (Bourdieu and Passeron 1979, 24). Selection in school denies any relational perspective other than the one of familiarity/unfamiliarity between social positions.

For the students of the dominant classes, denying their labour on the mediation of school culture is a matter of course because they have been socialised accordingly in their younger age and such mediation is part of their habitus and social position. Therefore, in school, they only need to recall their familiarity with this culture by expressing their relative detachment from school requirements in order to be recognised by the teachers and the school system as inheritors of the school values, i.e. the values supported by the school system. The students of the dominated classes however rather attempt to hide the effort and the labour they must make in order to climb to the height of a culture that is not theirs. Such a strategy is all the more difficult to develop in that these students are unfamiliar with the principles of school culture. Therefore, willing to prove their good command of school subjects, they inevitably make mistakes that reveal them to be pale imitators of the real inheritors. This is something that the school system punishes.[4]

Latour, in his sociology of science, also pays attention to the symbolic values of labour where we can observe parallels to Bourdieu. In Bourdieu, the difference between the technical and the symbolic values of the activity can be understood as a difference between skill and authority. In society, it is not enough to have skills in order to be recognised. It is also necessary that these skills create authority. Latour sees this mechanism at work also in science when, for example, a scientist is writing a scientific article. If the body of the scientific article must demonstrate its author's scientific competence, the footnote "quite to the contrary, is intended to convince the reader: I could not believe in the existence of the TRF substance—now, I cannot not believe in it; I could believe that Shibuzawa had isolated it—now, I can no longer believe it....If someone can accumulate enough authority in an article in order to definitively convince the readers that he has demonstrated the existence of the TRF substance, then he dominates the others in this new field" (Latour and Fabbri 1977, 91).[5] If authority is so important and prevails over skills, then this is because it gives credit: "The right to say something...produces a power to convince which, because it leads to recognition, creates a new right...to say something" (ibid.). In Bourdieu, this scientific credit is awarded by two different institutions, namely by the institution where the scientist is employed (the social or symbolic side of credit) and by the peers who review the scientific article in order to check the validity and reliability of the published results (the professional or technical side of credit) (Bourdieu 1991b, 7). Like Latour, Bourdieu sees that these two origins of scientific credit have progressively grown in strength.

> Strictly scientific authority tends to convert itself, over time, into a social authority capable of opposing the assertion of a new scientific authority. Further, social authority within the scientific field tends to become legitimized by presenting itself as pure technical reason, and also the recognized signs of statutory authority modify the social perception of strictly technical ability. (ibid.)

This reinforcement triggers a strategy by scientists to extend their credibility in order to get a dominant position in the scientific field (Bourdieu 1976, 93). This, Latour and Woolgar call "extending the credibility cycle" (Latour and Woolgar 1986, 207) and it is the reason why "scientists invest their credibility where it is likely to be most rewarding" (ibid. 206), or, in Bourdieu's terms, "The tendency of scientists to focus on issues considered to be the most important (because some authors with a high degree of legitimacy have, for example, identified them as such) is explained by the fact that a contribution to or discovery in relation to these issues brings a more important symbolic profit" (Bourdieu 1976, 90).[6]

According to Latour and Bourdieu, there is a strong affinity between symbolic value and credibility because both concepts refer to the reliability not only of an actor, but also of his labour, and of the mediations on which this activity is performed. Speaking of a fictional scientist called Dietrich, Latour and Woolgar say that he "has produced credible data using two sorts of methods, and now works in a new and important area at an institution with an enormous accumulation of resources. In terms of his pursuit of reward, his career makes little sense; as an investor of credibility it has been very successful" (Latour and Woolgar 1986, 198). The credit and credibility of which Latour and Woolgar speak mean a recognition that comes from the group of scientists to which Dietrich belongs. It is a recognition of the reliability of Dietrich's labour. This recognition comes also from the scientific institution where Dietrich works, and which grants him social credibility as a scientist. Dietrich benefits from such recognition. It gives him an authority, i.e. it allows him to mobilise other scientists and other infrastructures that he needs to continue his research activity. As Bourdieu says:

> credit, it is the power granted to those who have obtained sufficient recognition to be in a position to impose recognition: in this way, the power of constitution, a power of making a new group, by mobilization, or of making it exist by procuration, by speaking on its behalf, as an authorized spokesperson, can be obtained only at the end of a long process of institutionalization, at the end of which a representative is chosen, who receives from the group the power to form the group. (Bourdieu 1990b, 137)

Taken in this broad sense, credit is the best illustration of Bourdieu's idea, according to which capital goes to capital (Bourdieu 1977, 181, 1990a, 120), or, in the terms of Latour, according to which conversion between different forms of credibility is now possible, namely "conversion between money, data, prestige, credentials, problem areas, argument, papers, and so on" (Latour and Woolgar 1986, 200). Credibility makes conversions between capitals possible—conversions that determine the efficiency of capitals according to Bourdieu (1990a, 128). This is why the actors are above all looking for symbolic capital in order to gain other capitals. This "requires constant labour in the form of the care and attention devoted to making and maintaining relations" (ibid.), which means in the case of Latour's scientists, "Scientists are thus interested in one another not because they are forced by a special system of norms to acknowledge others' achievements, but because each needs the other in order to increase his own production of credible information" (Latour and Woolgar 1986, 202–203).

Bourdieu's and Latour's explanations are similar not only regarding the cohabitation of the technical and the symbolic values in the labour on mediations. They also take the same direction. Both authors explain that symbolic value/capital is important because it brings credibility, i.e. it brings authority to skills. Without authority, skills will not be recognised (for example by peers) and socially legitimised, not only by academic institutions as in the example of the scientists, but also by others (political or economic institutions, the media) and the state—but to this we shall return later. Let us for now keep in mind that the acquisition of symbolic value/capital and corresponding authority presupposes labour on mediation, and that both contribute to the maximisation of the actors' social positions.

So far, we have seen that, in Bourdieu, the acquisition of symbolic value/capital can only be performed against work on mediation, i.e. by a denial of the effort that such acquisition requires, leading to a naturalisation of the actors' skills and their social position. Latour, on the contrary, thinks that acquisition of symbolic value/capital does not deny the efforts made in the work on mediations but rather extends it, which contributes to associate the actors with one another, thus renewing the cycle of their credibility. If the acquisition of symbolic value/capital does not go against labour on the mediation of exchange, this is because, according to Latour, the actor does not primarily look for a social position. He does not do so because "A position does not exist 'out there', simply waiting for someone to fill it...Indeed, the nature of positions to be seized is constantly the focus of negotiation in the field. The feeling that a constraint on taking a position is dependent on the field is also the upshot of constant negotiation" (Latour and Woolgar 1986, 213–214). Why are these positions constantly subject to negotiations? Because, so Latour suggests, there is not necessarily any correspondence between the positions expected by scientists at a given time, and the positions that scientific institutions can provide. In other words, a scientist may not necessarily anticipate the position that he will have at the end of his socio-professional career. Otherwise, we would have to say with Bourdieu that the position that this scientist takes at the end of his career is—structurally speaking—the same as the position he has at present. This would mean that the actors' expectations conform to the institutional expectations which themselves conform to the expectations of the dominant classes to whose benefit these institutions act. In Bourdieu, this series of correspondence always follows the idea according to which capital goes to capital, an idea which the institution must uphold and protect, and which Bourdieu introduces here from an institutional viewpoint when he says:

> The law of exchanges between agents and institutions may be described like this: the institution gives everything including, first, the power over the institution, to those who have given everything to the institution because they were nothing outside of the institution and without the institution, and because they cannot deny the institution without denying themselves purely and simply, depriving themselves of what they are through and for the institution to whom they owe everything. In short, the institution vests in those who have vested in the institution. (Bourdieu 1981b, 19)

When we speak of schools, universities or research laboratories, as well as of literary journals, bookshops, artistic criticisms, political institutions, or of the family, the same control mechanism is at work whereby institutions determine that capital is going to capital. On this point, Latour differs from Bourdieu.

Institutions

When Bourdieu says that institutions determine that capital is going to capital effectively, this means that the institutions ensure the transmission of traditions, values and norms by which the institution—of whatever type—ensures its own durability, i.e. the sustainability of its principles of vision and division of the social world (e.g. Bourdieu and Passeron 1990, 152). Here, we have to distinguish two aspects of Bourdieu's reasoning on institution. On the one hand, the institution guarantees the existence of a relational perspective in the collective by putting past actors and past states of a social field in contact with current actors and states. It therefore contributes to supporting this relational perspective over time, to giving it some duration. On the other hand, the institution fosters recognition of this relational perspective by the collective through "rites of institution" (cf. for example Bourdieu 1982, 58–63), which consecrate the labour performed by the actors on the mediations of exchange. Thus, the institution assists in the partial release of the collective from its work on its mobilisation. Moreover, according to Bourdieu, an institution never exists independently of the dominant classes.

Indeed, the dominant classes have an interest in delegating to the institutions the authority to reproduce these classes. This puts these dominant classes above any suspicion of meddling since they do not themselves seem to favour their actors to the detriment of other classes, but instead, have this performed by institutions that have their own rules. Correspondingly, it is important to the institutions to publicly show their independence of the dominant classes in order to gain legitimacy in the eyes of all social actors. This is another example of Bourdieu's dialectics of ignorance and recognition in the relationships between institutions, dominant classes and society—a dialectics that is at the heart of the institutional activities. To be credible as institutions and, at the same time, to be recognised as agents providing public legitimacy, the institutions must preserve public ignorance of their affiliation to the interests of the dominant classes, which have delegated to them the task of reproducing their dominant power. The institutions reproduce this dominant power by reducing the "uncertain relation between capacity and status" (ibid. 165), which requires control operations (e.g. evaluations of students at school, accreditation of public institutions by dedicated agencies, quality audits, etc.). The collective must believe that skills reflect social status. Bourdieu calls this a "production of belief" (Bourdieu 1980a, 1–93) that involves the deployment of activities intended to stabilise the attribution of qualities to the actors—qualities materialised by titles, uniforms, and symbols of distinction.[7] In this sense, the institution institutes the actors, and Bourdieu describes this act as an "act of social magic" (Bourdieu 1982, 59). It is about the survival of the institution as autonomous institution, the legitimacy of its control, and the success of the substitution produced by the institution, a substitution where authority takes priority over technical skills.

However, this kind of reasoning is not as clear cut as it looks because Bourdieu, at the same time, says also that this substitution works best where skills are less independent from social authority, i.e. where it is more likely that the actors combine them, namely in less autonomous fields of society as those are the ones that are more sensitive to external requests from politics, the economy, or the media. This is illustrated by the example of science where:

> the contamination of the properly scientific authority by the statutory authority based on the institution is all the stronger as the autonomy of the scientific field is reduced. Similarly, as autonomy lessens, there is increased ability of the holders of a strictly temporal power over institutions (and in particular over mechanisms of institutional reproduction) to exercise a nominally scientific authority (at least in its effects). (Bourdieu 1991b, 7–8)

Nothing is more logical than this reasoning since it recalls Bourdieu's general idea of familiarity/unfamiliarity that should explain the actors' alliances based on their practical activities.

Indeed, the substitution of technical skills with authority is likely to work in the most optimal way in fields where it is not too difficult to bind them together because, for the actors, authority and skills resemble each other in such fields. This is what happens in science because scientific skills are socially valued and in demand by other fields in society. Therefore, the prestige of science does not strictly apply to scientific skills. It allows a build-up of capital that virtually gives the scientists an authority beyond the scientific field, for example in the fields of politics, the economy, or in the media. However, if such a heteronomous field as science almost automatically produces the substitution of skills by authority, then the institutions of the scientific field which have the responsibility of performing—and not only of consecrating—this substitution would only exist in order to intensify the dynamics in the field, i.e. in order to ensure that the field produces its effects where these institutions are located. The logic of the institutions therefore presupposes the logic of the field, or, in other words, the institutions are necessary intermediaries that preserve the dynamics of a field in that part of the social space that is covered by the field.

We have assumed that this reasoning applies only to heteronomous fields, i.e. to fields influenced by other fields. This is however not the case. Let us take an example from one of France's most emblematic writers from the late nineteenth and early twentieth century, Émile Zola. With the help of his specific cultural capital of writer and intellectual, Zola "will be able to break with the political indifference of [his; CP] predecessors in order to intervene…in the political field itself, but with weapons that are not those of politics" (Bourdieu 1995, 131; see also Bourdieu 1988). How is Zola able to take a position in the political field? Bourdieu says that "it is the autonomy of the intellectual field that makes possible the inaugural act of a writer who, in the name of norms belonging to the literary field, intervenes in the political field, thus constituting himself as an intellectual" (Bourdieu 1995, 129). Zola's position in the political field does therefore not depend on institutional support by the literary field, which has been "little institutionalized" (Bourdieu 1991c, 18). On the contrary, Zola fought against these institutions by taking a position against the literary taste of his time. Zola brought the vulgar and misery into literature, "carrying to term the evolution of the literary field towards autonomy", and extending "into politics the very values of independence being asserted in the literary field" (Bourdieu 1995, 129). This strategy worked because Zola contributed to the autonomy of the literary field against the political field. This hostility, combined with the professionalisation of the political field, contributed to the "break with the political indifference" (ibid. 131), which characterised French writers before Zola and, with them, the French intellectual elites.

In all of this, we do not see an effect by any specific institution. We see the effect of the literary field itself, namely the effect of the literary field's "rules" on Zola's intellectual production, driving him to take a position in the political field. This "effect of field"[8] reminds us, at the same time, of Bourdieu's conviction that the autonomy of the literary field is an illusion sustained by those actors who champion these "rules" of the literary field, which Zola, pushing his autonomy to its extreme, exposes as being exactly such an illusion. There is therefore no genuine difference between heteronomous and autonomous fields. There is only a difference of degree. This explains why all fields are subject to the same general rule that is imposed on the institutions. This is what Bourdieu's definition of institution already suggested when he said: "The reason and the raison d'être of an institution (or of an administrative measure) and of its social effects is not in the 'willingness' of an individual or a group, but lies in the field of antagonistic forces" (Bourdieu 1980b, 6; cf. also Bourdieu 1991c, 18, note 35). Therefore, saying that institutions only appear as a sounding board for the field means that the dialectics of ignorance/recognition explaining how institutions substitute skills with authority actually works as a variant of the dialectics of familiarity/unfamiliarity. Or, in other words, saying that the institutions have to make capital go to capital means that they have to control that similar capitals remain together because the aggregation of similar capitals structures the global dynamics of the fields. This principle explains the struggles between socially positioned habitus following Bourdieu's antagonistic relational perspective. At this point, the difference to Latour appears more distinctly because in Latour, even if institutions also assemble, they assemble the most heterogeneous actors and things, forming a heterogeneity represented by the institution as a particular assembly of heterogeneous actors and things.

Latour's starting point in his understanding of institutions is analogous to Bourdieu's when the latter says that institutions provide everything to the actors. Indeed, according to Latour, "the institutions provide all necessary mediations to an actor in order to ensure the sustainable and valid existence of a substance" (Latour 2001, 328). Nevertheless, Latour considers that sociology fails to satisfactorily understand what an institution *is*. Indeed, sociologists do not pay attention to the conditions that favour the emergence of institutions, in particular because sociologists assume that institutions represent human beings only (Latour 1994a, 49, 2011, 2). However, an institution is "a corporate body including passengers, engineers, controllers, and many nonhumans, all safely 'black boxed'" (Latour 1994a, 49). An institution is an assembly of heterogeneous actors and things, an association between humans and non-humans, which is sustainable only if it is actively developed. This activity on this heterogeneous association is shown, for example, by the difference between the two French automatic public transportation services ARAMIS, in the Ile de France, and VAL, in the French city of Lille (Latour 1996). While ARAMIS fails to generate such continuity of association between humans and non-humans, and eventually becomes a mere museum, VAL manages to generate such associations constantly. VAL does it so well that it not only exists as a proper service in Lille but has also become an institution. The continuation of associations did not lead to a decrease of heterogeneity of the associated humans and non-humans; quite the opposite is the case.

The map of tornadoes that the *Smithsonian Institution* wanted to develop at the end of the nineteenth century illustrates this point (Latour 1988a, 21). The *Smithsonian Institution* recruited 600 correspondents across the entire North American territory. They did meteorological surveys and also had to send stuffed animals to the *Smithsonian Institution* in order to better understand, describe and locate tornadoes. The *Institution* recruited additional staff members, who were responsible for the proper conduct of the surveys carried out by the correspondents. They visited the correspondents in order to check that they performed their work with discipline and did their surveys at the same hours and at the same locations every day. "The practical question of obtaining at the same time fixed dedicated weathermen and mobile dedicated naturalists is enormous, and is as much part of the building of an institution" (ibid.).

Latour suggested that in order to build such an institution as the tornadoes' map, one does not only need money, infrastructure and time. Such tasks also require the mobility of the humans and non-humans involved, their loyalty to the *Smithsonian Institution*, and associations between these humans and non-humans. To these heterogeneities of space and associations we have to add the heterogeneity of time, which is important for Latour because it sustains the duration of an institution. This last heterogeneity is only possible under the condition of alliances. "No development of instruments, no conquest of autonomy for [scientific; CP] disciplines, no foundation of new institution is possible without involving the third loop that I have called the loop of the alliances" (Latour 2001, 107).

Building alliances means working at the mobilisation of other humans and non-humans. At the same time, it means completing a cycle of associations and starting a new cycle to repeat this labour and to establish associations anew, in a different space-time, with different humans and non-humans likely to support the labour on the mediations of exchange. On the example of science and scientific institutions to which Latour devoted the major part of his writings, we see that "large groups…have to be mobilized in order to extend the ramifications of scientific labour, in order for the explorations to proliferate, to go always further, for the institutions to grow, for the professions to develop, to lead to academic chairs and other counselling or expert positions" (ibid.).

These alliances, consisting of multiple associations, also change in the way in which we are going to associate over time, which therefore more or less strongly interrupts the activities on at least certain mediations of exchange. The reason for such interruptions is always the same, namely the heterogeneity of humans and non-humans coming into or going out of the different cycles of association, thus renewing or breaking-off alliances and associations. This provides us with a clearer picture of the difference to Bourdieu's views on institutions. Certainly, there is, in Bourdieu as in Latour, an attention paid to the duration of institutions, to the different contacts that institutions initiate and control, and to the means that they mobilise in order to achieve their goal—the reproduction of the domineering actors' order. Nevertheless, Bourdieu believes that institutions operate in support of the homogeneity of social fields in time while the structure of these fields remains fundamentally the same. Even if different actors may occupy the same social position over time, the position is always occupied by actors with the same class habitus.

For Latour, the institution is a place of controversy and negotiations, of changes and novelties,[9] where the game is not over before it has been played, where social positions are determined along the activity on the mediations of exchange and along alliances. The institution operates only in support of heterogeneity because, without heterogeneity, and therefore without alliances with heterogeneous humans and non-humans, the institution would stop operating. It would fail to reproduce itself as an association of heterogeneous elements, of humans and non-humans.

Latour's emphasis on heterogeneity must also be distinguished from Bourdieu's concept of heteronomy as he uses it in his theory of social fields. We see this difference best when we observe the closing mechanisms that institutions apply in order to preserve their legitimacy. In Bourdieu, the general principle that immunises institutions against controversies and negotiations—coming either from the domineering or from the dominated actors—is the substitution of symbolic value for technical skills, which substitution the institutions perform alone, i.e. without any dependency on third parties. We have given various examples of such substitutions, such as the fathers' agricultural art in the Kabyle family, the formal and less formal techniques of evaluation at schools (students' marks etc.), Zola's aesthetics of social misery and his strife for writers' independence in France.

In Latour, institutions legitimise the associations between humans and non-humans in dependency upon a third party. This third party can be the public or the observers of an institution, "the journalists, the critics, or average man or woman on the street" (ibid. 109). Latour understands this third party as "public representation" (ibid.), which, for example, in the case of science becomes "the representation of science in society" (ibid. 110). For an institution, it is important to groom and to convince the public of the institution's value and merits. On the one hand, this is an indispensable step—Latour says "the most important one" (ibid. 109)—if an institution is to stabilise its existence. On the other hand, this step ensures the institution's extension over space and time—which will give it power. Here, we see that Latour proposes a very different argument that rests on relational logic and not on any logic of social positions as Bourdieu's. Nevertheless, Latour comes to the same conclusion as Bourdieu but makes it more radical. Indeed, if the heterogeneity of institutions is the *sine qua non* of their existence, this existence is only stabilised when the institution has power. Furthermore, when Latour says that the institution obtains its power depending on its representation in society, he is close to Bourdieu who says that the institution is all the more able to operate its closure, i.e. to stabilise its authority and the independence of its operations, as it takes care of its image in society. Or, in other words, it stimulates the collective belief and the public trust in its power all the more as it takes care of its image, so that the public cannot know all associations that have led to its existence. Thus, the institution makes the public take part indirectly in the construction of its own authority. Therefore, institutional authority is the more stable and legitimate as the institution is able to convince, and to attract the support of, more humans and non-humans.

Symmetry leads to asymmetry, which leads to new symmetries, and so on.[10] Each time, asymmetry is consecrated by an operation that, for the institution, consists in closing the cycles of associations that led to these cycles in the first place. In this regard, Latour speaks of closing "black boxes", an operation which only the institution can perform. "Only corporate bodies have the capacity to absorb the proliferation of mediators, to adjust their expression, to redistribute professions, to force the boxes to become black and to close them" (ibid. 203). Yet, even according to Latour, debates between institutions and the public can never be hermetically closed because institutions need debates if they want to reproduce the asymmetry between themselves and the public. This is why any closure is only temporary. It represents a short, compared to the long time, of debates, but is only more or less perceived as a closure in society. However, closing the debates as much as possible has an important function for institutions in Latour's view. Indeed, it means that the accumulated institutional power is put off the debates, which fosters the stability of institutions as well as of the associations they represent (Latour 2004, 3). Finally, what remains is to protect the benefits such closure brings and to ensure that black boxes cannot be easily reopened. In doing so, institutions contribute to the customary recognition of their power, of the power of the associations they contain, and of the humans and non-humans brought together by these associations. Black boxes stabilise institutional power and generate social inequalities.

From Social Inequality…

Black boxes are markers to distinguish individual cycles of associations. They mark the differences between past and more recent associations of humans and non-humans, whereby the difference to past associations depends on the heterogeneity that an institution is able to mobilise. Thus, black boxes lead to a social space and time that are structured by social positions—to a kind of field in Bourdieu's terminology, but a field that is transformed by the accumulation of other black boxes and other asymmetries that the institutions produce. While these black boxes accumulate associations and while institutions gain correspondingly in legitimacy, it becomes very difficult to reopen these black boxes and to put the power of institutions into question (Latour and Woolgar 1986; Latour 1987, 80ff.). Whoever wants to reopen a black box is confronted with numerous associations that have to be dissociated.[11] This is not impossible, as Latour says:

> It is always possible to discuss an article, an instrument, a figure; it is always possible for a reader-in-the-flesh to move off the path expected of the reader-in-the-text. In practice, however, limits are reached. The author obtains this result by stacking so many tiers of black boxes that at one point the reader, obstinate enough to dissent, will be confronted with facts so old and so unanimously accepted that in order to go on doubting he or she will be left alone. (Latour 1987, 59)

Indeed, institutions build their power from the associations they contain, which refer to humans and non-humans and to their concrete history. These humans and non-humans should again be dissociated if one wants to understand the black box they are in. This presupposes an investment of time and labour, even of infrastructure, in any kind of actors that have to be mobilised in order to perform this work on black boxes. This alone discourages many adventurers who can never be sure of their ability to dismantle such black boxes successfully. Black boxes are so powerful that even if we can open them, they remain opaque or black. This argument of discouragement, as is produced by the black boxes' social complexity, is also at the bottom of the dominants' power Bourdieu is speaking of when he says that:

> The paradox of the imposition of legitimacy is that it makes it impossible ever to determine whether the dominant feature appears as distinguished or noble because it is dominant—i.e., because it has the privilege of defining, by its very existence, what is noble or distinguished as being exactly what itself is, a privilege which is expressed precisely in its self-assurance—whether it is only because it is dominant that it appears as endowed with these qualities and uniquely entitled to define them...The properties attached to the

> dominant—Paris or Oxford 'accents', bourgeois 'distinction' etc.—have the power to discourage the intention of discerning what they are 'in reality', in and for themselves, and the distinctive value they derive from unconscious reference to their class distribution. (Bourdieu 1984, 92)

However, Bourdieu's argument rests on the idea that power is most of all the power to define the rules of social life, which make up the dominants and their domination in all social fields (for example Bourdieu 1990b, 142–143). Latour criticises this idea of power in very direct terms when he says "Like the 'dormitive virtue of opium' ridiculed by Molière, 'power' not only puts analysts to sleep, which does not matter so much, it also tries to anesthetize the actors as well—and that is a political crime" (Latour 2005, 85). For Latour, such a homogeneous and unilateral concept of power as Bourdieu's does not take the actors' activities into account. Moreover, it takes neither non-humans and their corresponding activities nor their role in supporting the diversity of associations with humans into account, i.e. it disregards a diversity that refers to the intrinsic multiplicity of the non-humans themselves. Power, such as Latour understands it, is nothing but this diversity, a diversity of associations that would not be possible without the diversity of non-humans. As Latour says, "It is the thing itself that has been allowed to be deployed as multiple and thus allowed to be grasped through different viewpoints, before being possibly unified in some later stage depending on the abilities of the collective to unify them" (ibid. 116).

Still, let us consider that "multiplicity is a property of things, not of humans interpreting things" (ibid. 116 note 165). Here, we then have a reference to the asymmetry that, according to Bourdieu, characterises any power relation. Latour's understanding here is however very different. Indeed, if, for Bourdieu, this asymmetry is at the bottom of the legitimisation of power, for Latour it makes the multiplication of associations between humans and non-humans by the multiplication of non-humans possible and, therefore, makes possible the multiplication of activities with and on these non-humans. This is why Latour says, challenging Bourdieu:

> Critical theory is unable to explain why artifacts enter the stream of our relations, why we so constantly recruit and socialize nonhumans. It is not to mirror, inscribe, or hide social relations, but to remake them through fresh and unexpected sources of power. Society is not stable enough to inscribe itself in anything. On the contrary, most of the features of what we mean by

> social order—scale, asymmetry, durability, power, hierarchy, the distribution of roles—are impossible even to define without recruiting socialized non-humans. (Latour 1994a, 53)

Nevertheless, there is a significant similarity between Bourdieu and Latour, which does not return to their notion of power but to the opacity of power. An institution has more power the more associations it generates, the more non-humans it multiplies and the more black boxes it accumulates, which makes it progressively opaque to the public. Even if it seems to be open to the public, the institution is in truth closed because it goes on with its routine activity of associations without making the public know how this is done. Certainly, all humans and non-humans can participate in this work, they can browse the black boxes of institutions in every possible direction, and they can explore their content. However, they never get a chance to really see the associations in the black boxes because they do not take part in the social labour invested in building them, and according to Latour, this is an "essential property" of black boxes (Latour 1993a, 216). It is therefore inevitable that institutions contribute to social inequalities as those institutions grow and as they become more powerful. As Latour puts it when talking of the example of scientists:

> How can inequality be introduced into a set of equally probable statements in such a way that a statement is taken to be more probable than all the alternatives? The technique most frequently used by our scientists was that of increasing the cost for others to raise equally probable alternatives...when Burgus used mass spectrometry to make a point, he made it difficult to raise alternative possibilities because to do so would be to contest the whole of physics...The mass spectrometer is the reified part of a whole field of physics; it is an actual piece of furniture which incorporates the majority of an earlier body of scientific activity. The cost of disputing the generated results of this inscription device has been enormous. (Latour and Woolgar 1986, 241–242)

Producing social inequalities is nothing other than operating a "black-box" (ibid. 242), which requires strong credibility. In Latour's example, credibility is provided by the "mass spectrometer", namely a "black box" (ibid. 150, note 12) standing for the credibility that physics has in science, which would be another black box much richer in associations and much more opaque.

But what are the consequences of social inequalities for institutions? For Bourdieu, social inequalities reinforce the power of institutions and their identity. They create homogeneity, group spirit, and solidarity between the members of institutions, so that in order to preserve their power and identity, institutions favour the actors who fit them better and who are more likely to defend the institutional interests. Bourdieu demonstrates this through the example of the rivalries between the members of two major Parisian schools—*ENA* and *Polytechnique*—how the members of the latter mobilise actors in order to avoid administrative positions in France to fall into the hands of *ENA* members. As he says, "the defense of the corps is not abandoned to the whims of individual initiatives; rather, it mobilizes a large fraction of the corps under the leadership of members specifically chosen for the task and equipped with specific tools of action" (Bourdieu 1998, 204). In Latour's previous example about the mass spectrometer, we have also seen that in order to earn power and to produce inequality, the scientific laboratories do not mobilise just any non-human. They mobilise non-humans that are more powerful than the non-humans of other laboratories—in the context of Latour's example, a mass spectrometer proven to be more powerful than a chromatograph. Nevertheless, even if the process is irreversible once the black box has been set, the intrinsic asymmetry does not last forever. "It's precisely because it's so difficult to maintain asymmetries, to durably entrench power relations, to enforce inequalities, that so much work is being constantly devoted in shifting the weak and fast-decaying ties to other types of links" (Latour 2005, 66). In other words, acquired power is difficult to preserve because it is based on associations that presuppose a continuous mobilisation of actors and constant work with and on the mediations of exchange in order for power to affect the collective. Therefore, in order to avoid disruptions, once it has started to accumulate power, any institution develops other associations and is looking for other alliances.

But how to look for other associations without sacrificing pre-existing associations? Indeed, as Latour says: "Without the presence of the past, the presence of the far away, the presence of nonhuman characters, we would be limited, precisely, to interactions, to what we can manage to do, right now, with our own social skills" (Latour 1994b, 792). Let us reformulate this question in the terms of a sociology through relation: If the development of a relational perspective in society presupposes the mobilisation of the collective and not just the interactions or the manifest concrete social relations of daily life, how can such a perspective survive the unceasing quest for associations? Is there not a kind of exhaustion as time passes by? "Politics provides the answer: by delegating powers to others. But delegation to other men would be as unreliable and shaky as the human bonds themselves. Why not delegate some powers to a few non-human actors that would thus be in charge of their fellow non-human actors?" (Latour 1988b, 21).

Latour suggests that non-humans are not only the receivers of the power that institutions delegate to them. They are also likely to be more reliable than humans when it is about continuing the work of association that institutions delegate to them by giving them their power because their existence depends only on their associations to humans. In other words, non-humans are likely to meet the challenge posed by the delegation of power better than humans, and therefore are better in ensuring that institutions can look for other associations without losing anything of their power. Here, Latour does not seem far away from Bourdieu who thinks, when it comes to power, that the unilateral and channelling delegation of power from dominants to institutions, and from these institutions to their different services, ensures that the power of both dominant classes and their affiliated institutions is strengthened and reproduced.

However, there is a significant difference between Bourdieu and Latour, appearing not necessarily where we believed it to be—namely in the delegation of power to non-humans. In Bourdieu, power rests on the sublimation of skills by the quest for authority, for symbolic value/capital, whereas in Latour, authority is nothing without skills, and these skills are not a human monopoly, but a labour of all possible human and non-human actors in order to develop associations between them. This difference leads Latour to reformulate, on the one hand, the very prospect that Bourdieu wanted to achieve in his sociology, i.e. the explanation of social inequalities, and, on the other, to move this problem from the centre to the periphery of sociological investigation. According to Latour, we cannot understand the origin of social inequality if we do not take the associations between humans and non-humans into account. These associations contain the conditions that determine the way in which the actors are able to more or less invest in the mediations of exchange according to whether or not they have access to mediations facilitating their investment. "By putting aside the practical means, that is the mediators, through which inertia, durability, asymmetry, extension, domination is produced and by conflating all those different means with the powerless power of social inertia, sociologists, when they are not careful in their use of social explanations, are the ones who hide the real causes of social inequalities" (Latour 2005, 85).

At the same time, if we understand social inequalities like Latour, then it becomes clear that the problem of social inequality itself, in particular the way Bourdieu sees it when he speaks of dominant and dominated classes, is no longer the ultimate purpose of sociological investigation. It only is a point of transition towards a theory of associations where the variability of these associations depends on the variability of the mediations of exchange.

> Even if the ethnologist occasionally risks being accused of heartlessness, of 'underestimating the weight of inequalities,' or even of 'ignoring power relations,' the only way to help overturn inequalities, in her view, is to refuse to yield to any illusion about their relative size. And thus never to slip surreptitiously toward the 'bad' transcendence, the one with two levels. The scales are already uneven enough not to be charged in advance with a whole weight of injustices. Here is her mantra: when domination is at issue, whatever you do, don't add to it. (Latour 2013, 420)[12]

We are no longer talking of social inequality as a corollary of the discourse on institutions but speak instead of the inequality of mediations of exchange as that which stimulates the heterogeneity of associations and, therefore, the relations between actors and institutions. Or, in other words, inequality is no longer directly linked to social injustice, but to social pluralism. Nevertheless, the difference between Bourdieu and Latour is less important than it seems as Bourdieu has clearly paid attention to the inequality of the mediations of exchange, and to such inequality's contribution to social inequality.

To the Inequality of the Mediations of Exchange

The mediations of exchange circulate in society, and this circulation is not only an act of transmission, i.e. of passing mediations from actors or groups of actors to other actors or groups. It also presupposes a transformation whereby the mediation undergoes changes in its circulation, which affect its meaning and nature, and the actors' relation to that mediation. Bourdieu says, for example, that "the material circulation and the circulation of production are inseparable cycles of consecration which, in an additive way, produce legitimacy and, at the same time, sacred objects and converted consumers willing to perceive them as sacred and to pay the necessary material or symbolic price to appropriate them" (Bourdieu and Delsaut 1975, 28). For Bourdieu, there would be no "sacred objects" and "converted consumers" if there were no conversion of capitals. The actors must necessarily perform this conversion in order to maximise their social position within a field (see, for instance, Bourdieu 2001, 48). The conversion of capitals is organised and sanctioned by institutions, which check that this conversion produces the practices that fit the field in which these institutions are located. Bourdieu labels them "'regular practices'" (Bourdieu 1977, 40)—and they are nothing but the practices that support the interests and the power of the dominant classes in any given field (Bourdieu and Boltanski 1976, 60). This is why any operation of conversion can be described as an operation of adaption where the actors must "transmute 'egoistic', private, particular interests…into disinterested, collective, publicly available, legitimate interests" (Bourdieu 1977, 40).

Even if all actors have the same four types of capital available (economic, cultural, social, and symbolic capital), not all of them have each capital in the same volume, thus cannot combine their capitals in an identical way. This is what inequality of the mediations of exchange means for Bourdieu. Considering that the actors are also subject to institutional control serving the dominant classes—which is the control of the combinations of capitals—then we understand that these actors do not combine their capitals as they like but according to the rules of the field. What we see here is a double inequality that affects the actors. It is made up of an inequality in volume and of an inequality in the structure of the capitals as it results from the converting operations that the actors perform between their capitals. This double inequality produces a third one, which directly concerns the actors' labour on the mediations of exchange once they have converted their capital. Indeed, the conversion of capitals is not free of cost since it creates a new situation, i.e. a situation with which the actors are not familiar but in which they have to operate, and to which they must adapt. Correspondingly, the actors encounter difficulties in maximising their social position, thus their labour on the mediations of exchange becomes more complicated. Bourdieu describes this situation as acculturation, saying that "a technique can be learned and understood perfectly and then forgotten because the conditions of practising this technique have not been provided, and because it is not integrated into the total system of attitudes and customs which alone can give it a foundation and a meaning" (Bourdieu et al. 1997, 104).

Acculturation leads to permanent re-socialisation. As a result, we would expect the actors to regularly come back to what we have described as contact where, despite the accumulation of labour on mediations, the regular renewal of these mediations along the actors' social trajectory does not make accumulation and conversion of capitals any easier but makes them more difficult instead. However, Bourdieu does not come to this conclusion. Indeed, if we take his viewpoint on social positions, then we see that the actors are not equal when having to deal with this triple inequality. The actors of the dominant classes, having more capitals and being more familiar with power, also have more chances of success in combining their capitals to create a combination that meets institutional expectations and, in general, fits the dynamics of the fields in which they take positions. They can afford or amortise the costs of the conversion of capitals better, and they can do it longer. Therefore, it is more likely that they can take power positions in the fields, rather than those actors who have less capital and therefore fewer possibilities of converting it.

Nevertheless, we can see that this explanation leads to a perverse effect that we can see clearer when we take a relational viewpoint. This perverse effect can first be described on the level of the capitals themselves. They are, in fact, not equal or, in other words, each type of capital requires an unequal time for its acquisition and has its own volatility. Moreover, if we take the determinism affecting the acquisition of capitals into account (for example inheritance, demography, geography), then we understand that the conversion of capitals works well if the actors have a comfortable volume of all the types of capital. Therefore, the conversion of capitals is more likely to produce its expected effect (the maximisation of social position) for the dominants, i.e. those who have the least need to convert their capitals. Indeed, for them it would be enough to use more of the one or, depending on the field, any other capital for adapting to the structure of the field. In all other cases, i.e. in the cases of dominated actors, the conversion of capitals is far less likely to contribute to the maximisation of their position simply because they lack capital and because it takes time and energy to acquire it.

The same perverse effect also appears in relation to the fields themselves. As the existence of fields rests on the struggle between dominant and dominated classes, this struggle presupposes the inequality of capitals both in volume and structure. However, as power and domination only exist if, in these struggles, the dominants and their interests always keep the upper hand, then we can say that, once power and domination exist, they automatically neutralise any benefit of the conversion of capitals that would favour the dominated classes. Such benefit obviously exists, but if we take Bourdieu's explanations of power and domination in the context of his theory of fields seriously, such benefit would have no effect on the structure of social positions, which would remain unchanged. Here, we find a variant of our previous observation on the inequality of capitals. Those dominated could theoretically fight against the dominants, but, in practice, they do not really have the means to do so. As for the dominants, they would have no practical reason to fight against the dominated classes because they would already have all the social resources they need. Therefore, it would be the struggle itself which, for Bourdieu, happens to be the major principle of the dynamics of fields, that would lose its reason for being and, alongside it, the very relation between the antagonistic social positions on which it rests, which Bourdieu regards as a relation of power. If we are left with no practical reason to fight, the same must be true for the mobilisation of actors to take up any fight, and for the labour on the mediations of exchange that could strengthen such mobilisation or compensate for possible demobilisation.

For Bourdieu, the dynamics of the field are always winning and the institutions are always getting the upper hand. However, if our observations above have been correct, it rather seems that the very foundations on which he has made his case dissolve as their ground of existence has vanished into thin air. Latour's concept of association seems to avoid the impasse to which Bourdieu's sociology leads because associations result in alliances that do not only bind humans to one another, but also humans to non-humans.

In his analysis of scientific laboratories, Latour spends time describing their equipment. He speaks of their necessary diversity because "some items of equipment are more crucial to the research process than others" (Latour and Woolgar 1986, 65). Regardless of the problem of having different machines to perform scientific tasks, scientists need to achieve "a particular configuration of machines specifically tailored for a particular task" (ibid.). In order to do this, a scientist must be able to rely on the skills of his scientific staff, and in particular, on his staff's ingenuity if there are no machines or techniques yet but they have to be invented if one wants to conduct the experiment in question (cf. ibid. 68–69). In all these cases, what is at work is a real mobilisation of various mediations that are both human (skills, inventiveness, mobilisation of theories, knowledge of related scientific fields) and non-human (acquisition and configuration of hardware). In scientific practice, these mediations have to be associated in order to obtain a scientific result that is interesting enough to be published and discussed by colleagues. However, as in Bourdieu, Latour indicates that these associations presuppose that scientists are able to convert their capital of credibility.

> Our scientists only rarely assessed the success of their operations in terms of formal credit...The success of each investment was evaluated in terms of the extent to which it facilitated the rapid conversion of credibility and the scientist's progression through the cycle. For example, a successful investment might mean that people phone him, his abstracts are accepted, others show interest in his work, he is believed more easily and listened to with greater attention, he is offered better positions, his assays work well, data flow more reliably and form a more credible picture. The objective of market activity is to extend and speed up the credibility cycle as a whole. (Latour and Woolgar 1986, 207)

Latour gives a particularly complete example of what the conversion of the capital of credibility means when he speaks of the professional trajectory of the endocrinologist Pierre Kernowicz (Latour 1993a, 107–129).

As a good "capitalist of evidence" (ibid. 123), Kernowicz has to work at the maximisation of his socio-professional position in order to take a dominant position in the field of research on contraceptive pills.

> What is this work? It is necessary to ensure that the different conversions from one form of credit to another are performed on the market at the highest possible rate. This requires considerable work: it is necessary to ensure that grant applications focus on the most interesting topics, that the important files arrive in the best hands, it is likewise necessary to negotiate the largest amount of money possible for each of these grants, to watch that this money is invested into the best instruments, and that the best technicians and the best young doctoral students are recruited. All these people have to be put at work and have to be forced to continuously convert their data into arguments, and their arguments into articles...And all of this is only one part of the lab director's job. There are many other tasks located upstream of every authority capable of performing a conversion of credit. (ibid. 122–123)

The point on which Latour wants to insist is a double one. On the one hand, there is a dimension of symbolic power involved in the development of these activities because the goal of scientists like Kernowicz is to assert their authority in a particular area of science. But on the other hand, this symbolic power is acquired at the price of an individualisation of the scientific practice reflected in the singularity or the inequality of the mediations mobilised. "The idea to start not with hormones but with contaminants of impure preparations is, in terms of habit, unusual and is, therefore, an important information, at least for the small world in which Pierre evolves" (ibid. 117). By acting not like the others, i.e. by choosing a mediation on which nobody works, Kernowicz manages to make his work stand out, mobilises other actors and maximises his social positions. But it is a dangerous game that may turn bad at any time, could undermine Kernowicz's efforts, and isolate him permanently from his competitors. Because if the inequality of the mediations promotes the originality of Kernowicz's work, it is still necessary that the general principles of the scientific institution are observed, most of all the principle of scientific legitimacy. It is important to be able to construct asymmetries, but it is also important to be able to restore symmetries for preserving credibility. In order to do this, correspondence must be established between the "stratification among scientists' productivity", the "stratification in the means for making science" (Latour 1987, 166), and the stratification of research institutions at which these scientists work with and on these mediations. "Without this requirement of institution, the discussion would never come to an end, and one would never succeed in knowing in what common, self-evident, certain world collective life ought to take place" (Latour 2004, 111).

Without institutions in favour of or opposed to Kernowicz and without competitors who work at these institutions and who are likely to discuss his work, Kernowicz's activities on his contaminants would not enable him to mobilise other actors and to maximise his socio-professional position. If, for Bourdieu, the conversion of capitals and the corresponding maximisation of social positions in society are always subject to the dynamics of a field and especially of its institutions, for Latour, the mobilisation of various mediations by scientists in the quest for the recognition of their originality is also subject to institutions. These institutions eventually decide their own control procedures—in Latour, for example, on the publication and discussion of scientific results by a community of peers—if the heterogeneity that an actor brings corresponds to the heterogeneity that these institutions want to value in order to stimulate associations and alliances. Therefore, Bourdieu and Latour answer the question of how the actors' labour on and with mediations of exchange supports the mobilisation of other actors or prevents their demobilisation in a similar way. It depends on the correspondences between institutions, actors, mediations, as well as on the institutional consecration of these correspondences, and last but not least, on a political entity, i.e. the state (Latour 2004, 204; Bourdieu et al. 1994, 12).[13] Nevertheless, Bourdieu and Latour have a different, even opposite understanding of the state.

In Bourdieu, the state is acting "in the manner of a bank of symbolic capital...[and it, CP] guarantees all acts of authority" (Bourdieu et al. 1994, 12), therefore, the acts of the institutions are delivering symbolic marks of distinction. By concentrating not only physical power, but especially symbolic power, the state "impose[s] and inculcate[s] in a universal manner, within a given territorial expanse, a nomos...a shared principle of vision and division, identical or similar cognitive and evaluative structures...the state is therefore the foundation of a...tacit, pre-reflexive agreement over the meaning of the world which itself lies at the basis of the experience of the world as 'commonsense world'" (ibid. 13). The state guarantees that the character of power relations between social positions and therefore the order of these social positions legitimised as social order cannot be questioned. If, for Latour, the state must ensure the preservation of a certain order, it primarily must ensure "the continuity of public life" (Latour 2004, 205), i.e. the transition from black-boxed asymmetries to symmetries, the re-mobilisation of the collective and the redeployment of associations. As Latour puts it, "Good government is not a government that offers politics the senseless privilege of defining the common world in the place of all those whom politics assembles, but the power to follow up...to choose the trackless path that goes from a less articulated collective to the better-articulated next state" (ibid. 206).

However, how can the state guarantee the continuity of the collective? By freedom from politics, and therefore by being limited "strictly to the art of governing", which means "preventing all the powers, all the partial competencies, from interrupting the exploration of the learning curve, or from dictating its results in advance" (ibid. 206). State power thus becomes the simple ability "to stir up the collective as a whole and get it moving" (ibid. 203), which is nothing but the ability to associate past and future associations and, at the same time, to exclude dissension by making black boxes more difficult to open and more opaque.

Unfortunately, Latour does not explore the concept of the state in more depth. Instead, he generalises the principle of action that he sees in the state, namely the association of associations. Therefore, the question of how asymmetries can be resolved and lead to symmetries is dropped in favour of the idea of a permanent transition between asymmetries and symmetries, which these associations of associations represent. Latour identifies these associations of associations as the "social", which he defines as "a very peculiar movement of re-association and reassembling" (Latour 2005, 7). In defining the concept of society in the same way (ibid. 62, 66; Callon and Latour 1981, 277–303), Latour manages to generalise his concept of association to the point that dissociations are no longer disruptions of associations. They are merely other ways of associating and make up the "re" of the concept of "reassembly", i.e. they make up another mode of existence of associations, another "agency" (Latour 2005). Other than qualifying as conversion of the capital of credibility, the association–dissociation pair describes the maximisation and transportation of credibility from one state of associations to another. This fine point is of some consequence for a question that directly concerns the state, the institutions and the actors' credibility, which is the question of legitimacy.

Legitimacy, a word "rarely correct in sociology", is, for Latour, only "another, simpler form of association" (Latour 1993b, 135). This, however, is not void of difficulty. State and institutional legitimacy rest in their respective mode of operation, which rests on associations. However, according to Latour, it is all actors who associate, regardless of whether they are individual actors, or human or non-human mediations, or collective/corporate actors. This means, however, that, against his very idea that the state legitimises all associations by bringing them together to close the cycles of credibility, Latour has in fact no grounds to say that the state would be more legitimate than the institutions, or institutions more legitimate than humans and non-humans. And indeed, Latour himself provides examples where recognition of legitimacy and the corresponding transition from past to new associations is brought about by individual actors only, i.e. by their interpersonal relationships. In the example analysed by Latour and Woolgar, the scientists' credibility can, of course, come from the renowned institution where these scientists work. However, this is no sufficient criteria for the scientists' legitimacy.

> For a working scientist, the most vital question is not 'Did I repay my debt in the form of recognition because of the good paper he wrote?' but 'Is he reliable enough to be believed? Can I trust him/his claim? Is he going to provide me with hard facts?' Scientists are thus interested in one another not because they are forced by a special system of norms to acknowledge others' achievements, but because each needs the other in order to increase

> his own production of credible information. (Latour and Woolgar 1986, 202–203)

If the "most vital question" is the interpersonal recognition of scientific credibility, what about the credibility that is awarded by the institutions or the state? Who is closing the cycle of associations in the end? Do we have to think that the institutions and the state only ratify the cycles of credibility to be closed among scientists? If so, then how do we explain both the competitiveness between scientists who want to work at the most prestigious laboratories, or in countries that invest the most in scientific research? And how do we explain the competitiveness between these scientific institutions or countries? How do we explain Pierre Kernowicz's multiple moves, his desire to capitalise his credibility by travelling from France to the west coast of the USA, where, according to him, the scientific environment is more liberal and competitive?

We could think that on this point, Bourdieu's theory provides the better explanation of the relationship between the unequal prestige of institutions and the unequal legitimacy of the actors dealing with these institutions. However, as we have seen, Bourdieu thinks that legitimacy is based on the recognition/ignorance of the imposition of a social order consecrated by law and guaranteed by the state (Bourdieu 1986, 3–19; Bourdieu et al. 1994, 1–18). Since this social order is imposed on the actors in a pre-reflective phase, i.e. at an early stage of the actors' socialisation, the game is over before the die is cast. Legitimacy thus escapes all questions. We are therefore at a dead-end.

We either must admit with Bourdieu that legitimacy is imposed by the state and the institutions on the individual actors, who recognise this legitimacy because they are unaware of the conditions of its production. Or we must admit with Latour that the question of legitimacy is ambivalent and has no clear answer because legitimacy can come from interpersonal associations, or from institutions and states. This dilemma, however, may be dissolved as we will attempt to do in the next chapter.

Conclusion

There is a substantive difference between Bourdieu and Latour regarding the analysis of society, which comes down to the position/association antinomy. Bourdieu's sociology of social positions highlights the structure of social inequalities, which are inequalities between the positions of social actors whose majority is dominated by a minority of dominants. This unequal social structure is reflected in the labour of actors on the mediations of exchange, and the inequality is reinforced by the different institutions in the social fields and by the state, which, in the final analysis, guarantees the legitimacy of these institutions.

Latour promotes an "associology" where "The story is not that of men called 'the People', and women being replaced by machines. The story is of a complete and continuous redistribution of roles and functions, some of them being held in place by human ties, others by non-human ones" (Latour 1988b, 38). The attention paid to non-humans moves the sociological perspective from human actors to the mediations of exchange, and to the inequalities between these mediations and the ways they are used. This has consequences for the assemblages of humans and non-humans, and humans and other humans. This labour on assemblages and agencies is necessary both in the field of science and technology—Latour's preferred field of investigation—and in society as a whole if past or existing associations are to lead to new associations. Yet, this important difference between Bourdieu and Latour cannot wipe out the many similarities between them when it comes to the labour on and with the mediations of exchange, and the consequences of such a labour. Working on and with the mediations of exchange means for the actors to convert capitals in order to maximise their own social position, to rank this position within a field of activity in order to be credible and legitimate. This process is controlled by institutions to which the mediations are related. These institutions have, in Bourdieu as in Latour, an important role in the distribution of recognition to social actors. This distribution is unequal and operates along these actors' ranking in the social hierarchies. At the end of this distribution of recognition, there is the state whose role is to ensure the legitimacy of institutional operations. As we have seen, Bourdieu and Latour do not agree on what legitimisation here means. For Bourdieu, legitimisation strengthens the position of the dominant classes to the detriment of the dominated classes. For Latour, it strengthens the credibility of the actors in space and time, i.e. it contributes to extending the associations to more human or non-human actors. Nevertheless, both cases are equally ambiguous.

For Bourdieu, institutions in each field of activity institute and legitimise the dominant classes and their actors without taking the influence of the dominated classes on this process into account. However, such reasoning weakens Bourdieu's understanding of relations as power relations. Indeed, if the distribution of legitimacy presupposes the pre-reflective imposition of the existing social order, then the distribution of legitimacy cannot depend on the outcome of social struggle. Such a struggle—i.e. the asymmetric relations between social positions—loses its reason for being.

Latour oscillates, in contrast, between two explanations of distribution of legitimacy in society, one focusing on the institutions and the relations between actors and institutions, the other on the interpersonal relationships between actors. The ambiguity as shown by both authors can be explained by their ambiguous use of the same argument. This, we call the argument of the reciprocity of interests. We have seen that, in Bourdieu, the legitimate actors are those who have an interest in legitimacy, namely the actors who invest the most in one another's legitimacy, who are the actors of the dominant classes and institutional actors who represent them in the various fields of activity. In Latour, the reciprocity of interests follows a similar pattern, where the legitimate scientists are those who need other legitimate scientists, as well as the non-humans associated with them, in order to increase their legitimacy. As in Bourdieu, it is a question of homologous social positions, of elective affinities, and of familiarity. The history of the scientist Joao Dellacruz that Latour and Woolgar tell in *Laboratory Life* illustrates the importance of these affinities between associated actors by looking at them from a reversed position. Indeed, "if the others are not there, or are too far apart, the few scientists and engineers become still fewer, less powerful, less interesting, and less important" (Latour and Woolgar 1986, 173–174) and, therefore, less legitimate. Isolated in Brazil at an institution that does not offer the mediations needed by Joao to continue his work on the MOS electronic chips he develops, and dropped by his professor, Joao finally decides to do something other than scientific research to which he is progressively becoming indifferent. This means that his colleagues neglect his work even more. No one associates with Joao at his institution. There is no longer any interest in any reciprocal relation with Joao.

Looking at this example, reciprocity of interests may mean more than meets the eye as, in their work, both Latour and Bourdieu put the same emphasis on interest, rather than on reciprocity, giving the expression "reciprocity of interests" a peculiar meaning that makes the use of the expression ambiguous. But why do they emphasise "interests" rather than "reciprocity"?

Reciprocity has an important disadvantage that Bourdieu well underlines. Reciprocity tends to define in advance a determined state of all social relationships that, in practice, are not always reciprocal relationships.

> 'Cycles of reciprocity', mechanical interlockings...exist only for the absolute gaze of the omniscient, omnipresent spectator, who, thanks to his knowledge of the social mechanics, is able to be present at the different stages of the 'cycle'. In reality, the gift may remain unreciprocated, when one obliges an ungrateful person; it may be rejected as an insult, inasmuch as it asserts or demands the possibility of reciprocity, and therefore of recognition. (Bourdieu 1990a, 98)

Therefore, "The simple possibility that things might proceed otherwise than as laid down by the 'mechanical laws' of the 'cycle of reciprocity' is sufficient to change the whole experience of practice and, by the same token, its logic" (ibid. 99). Such rejection of reciprocity can be understood as an attempt to deliver a sociological theory that does not use any *a priori* understanding of what a relation is. This criticism of reciprocity—in the quoted context, reciprocity such as Claude Levi-Strauss understands it—goes in fact much deeper since it eliminates any relational perspective from sociology, which is, in fact, an untenable position. Because in order to be able to analyse the way in which actors and social groups determine each other, the sociologist and, *a fortiori* Bourdieu, has to think relationally to understand how attraction and repulsion between actors and groups are structured. This is essentially what Bourdieu does when dropping reciprocity in favour of the power relation because power relations make it possible to minimise the bidirectional meaning of reciprocity in order to insist on the unidirectional characteristic of power—from dominants to the dominated.

In Latour, there is no comparable rejection of reciprocity, and this fits his sociology of associations best. He nevertheless puts the bidirectional dynamics that reciprocity suggests into perspective when he says:

> If the only acceptable exchange is a simple one-to-one bartering, the account of the origin of society will be different from that which admits many degrees of reciprocity. For example, contrast Mauss' potlach (1967) with Hobbes' war of all against all and it becomes obvious that it is not the morality of men that is different, but rather the time delay and degree of reciprocity that each author finds acceptable. For Mauss, reciprocity is transitive and the time delay is as long as a year, while Hobbes' actors need only

repay those from whom they have received and must do so instantaneously. (Latour and Strum 1986, 174)

The degrees of reciprocity, the transitivity of reciprocity, and the time that passes in exchanges are three arguments that put the idea that concrete social relations are always and everywhere reciprocal relations into perspective. In practice, we however rarely, if ever, see a complete sequence of reciprocity. We are confronted with associations that are not (only) going from A to B, or return from B to A (only). Latour does not reject reciprocity but does not look at it either, merely picking out some ideas, the most emblematic one certainly being the idea of attachment because Latour's focus on attachment enables him to emphasise his differences not only to Bourdieu's sociology but, more generally, to the French sociological tradition, and particularly to its founding father, Émile Durkheim.

Having seen that Latour's associology is on many points not so different from Bourdieu's sociology, we still have to find out how it differs from Durkheim's sociology. This will be investigated in the next chapter.

Notes

1. As Faveraux points out, Bourdieu sees "the institution…as what, first, serves reproduction only, and second, as what establishes [some actors or groups; CP], rather than what has been established [by them; CP]" (Favereau 2001, 301). This single observation actually reminds us of many French contributions to sociology that attempt to extend Bourdieu's critique of institutions. They try to analyse how this encoding of habitus works in relation to institutions (for example, Lahire 1998), and how it sustains the criticism that individual actors address to institutional frames in society (Boltanski and Thévenot 1987)—in other words the resistance of individuals to their society, as discussed in the first two chapters (cf. also Lamont 2010, 136; Guggenheim and Potthast 2012, 157–178). Such perspectives suggest that more attention has to be paid to the question of institutional control, as has already been pointed out by former relational sociologists such as Harrison White (cf. Chap. 1). In Chap. 6 this question of institutional control will be given special attention.
2. Vogt has already proposed also reading Mauss' discourse on the techniques of the body for a more general view on technique (Vogt 1976, 33–44).
3. For a short introduction to a comparison between Bourdieu and Latour in the perspective of relational sociology, see Schinkel (2007, 707–729).

4. We recognise here the influence of Erwing Goffman on Bourdieu, to which Bourdieu pays tribute elsewhere (Bourdieu 1983, 112–113).
5. As Breslau says, "Uniting the two meanings of the word 'representation', the concept shows that representing a social group and representing an object of science are identical in network terms" (Breslau 2000, 305). Breslau suggests that authority on the mediations of exchange gives authority over the group—in the context of the quote from Latour, a group of scientists.
6. Knorr Cetina underlines this by saying that there is therefore no longer any need to postulate that scientists and all other actors would hide their strategies in order to get their symbolic profits. On the contrary, scientists immediately show their interest in credibility, and they act correspondingly in their daily scientific practice (Knorr 1979, 373 note 36).
7. To say it in Schubert's words, the production of belief in Bourdieu is "the work of socialization necessary to produce agents endowed with the schemes of perception and appreciation that will permit them to perceive and obey the injunctions inscribed in a situation or discourse" (Schubert 2008, 196–197 note 10).
8. For Bourdieu, the effect of a field is the deterministic effect by this field on any kind of production within that field—which is another way to stress the unilateral power of the field over the institutions within or, therefore, to stress the subjection of institutional logic by the logic of fields (cf. for example Bourdieu 1975, 139, 1985b, 73, 1991c, 3–46).
9. Gooday emphasises that, for Latour, institutions—and in particular scientific institutions—have the specific function of transforming the world (Gooday 2008, 794 note 30), which is a direct consequence of their constitution as heterogeneous assemblages of heterogeneous humans and non-humans. This attention paid to heterogeneity and renewal distinguishes Latour's understanding of institutions from that of Bourdieu, who considers that institutions contribute to the reproduction of the structures of fields.
10. Riis sees in Latour's reasoning on black boxes the origin of a "'political ontology'", which we observe all the more when we link black boxes to institutional authority (Riis 2008, 288).
11. This also means that building black boxes is for every institution a way to simplify the complexity that those institutions face when they develop. Thus, black boxes have a critical function for institutions because they provide means to simplify their reproduction (cf. also Schmitt 2009, 216). Nevertheless, what is true for institutions is not true for the public—black boxes represent the complexity of an institution to the public, and thus protect the institutions against possible criticism coming from the public.

12. From this viewpoint, we cannot say with Law that the prospect of *ANT* (Actor-Network-theory) such as Latour conceives it, leads to a study of social inequalities (Law 1992, 379–393). By the way, the relativisation and the shift of this question away from the centre to the periphery of sociological inquiry is not only specific to *ANT* but it is a common feature shared by those sociologies.
13. This is also why we cannot put Latour and Bourdieu into radically opposite positions because the former only speaks of associations while the latter speaks of fields. These two concepts certainly enable us to underline important differences between both authors as we have seen. However, there are noticeable similarities in their views on state, institutions, individual actors, mediations of exchange, and labour with and on these mediations (cf. on this point, on the example of the scientific field, Kale-Lostuvali 2016, 273–296).

CHAPTER 6

Reciprocity: Bruno Latour and Émile Durkheim on Reciprocity and Control

Bourdieu's work contains a concept that Latour particularly likes—the concept of habitus. As Latour says, "Bourdieu's notion of habitus, once it is freed from its social theory, remains such an excellent concept" (Latour 2005, 209 note 280). The reason for Latour's enthusiasm is that, in his view, habitus translates most concisely his own sociological perspective. Indeed, habitus as

> Cognitive abilities do not reside in 'you' but are distributed throughout the formatted setting, which is not only made of localizers but also of many competence-building propositions, of many small intellectual technologies. Although they come from the outside, they are not descended from some mysterious context: each of them has a history that can be traced empirically with more or less difficulty. (ibid. 211)

Therefore, it is not the dialectic character of habitus that Latour appreciates in Bourdieu's concept—habitus as the interface between the private and the public, the outside and the inside, the social structure and the mental structure. Instead, it is the idea that human and non-human actors stem from groups of other humans and non-humans, of which they represent one particular association developing other associations.

From this viewpoint, the concept of habitus suggests that every actor must be considered as a collective actor. This changes the way in which we distinguish between individual and collective actors:

C. Papilloud, *Sociology through Relation*, Palgrave Studies in Relational Sociology, https://doi.org/10.1007/978-3-319-65073-9_6

> As if the personality becomes moral by becoming collective, or collective by becoming artificial, or plural by doubling the Saxon word body with a Latin synonym, corpus. A body corporate is what the pipette and I...have become. We are an object-institution...the point I am making is symmetrical: What is true of the 'object'—the pipette does not exist by itself—is still truer of the 'subject'. There is no sense in which humans may be said to exist as humans without entering into commerce with what authorizes and enables them to exist. (Latour 1994a, 45)

This reasoning motivates Latour to say that sociologists must understand society as a "'flat society'" (Latour 2002, 117–132), meaning they must reconsider the distinction between the two levels of micro- and macro-sociology.

> It's not that there are a macro-sociology and a micro-sociology, but that there are two different ways of envisaging the macro-micro relationship: the first one builds a series of Russian Matryoshka dolls—the small is being enclosed, the big is enclosing; and the second deploys connections—the small is being unconnected, the big one is to be attached. (Latour 2005, 180)[1]

These two metaphors refer to two perspectives on the relations between the micro and the macro, and to two views on associations, which do not correspond. Indeed, the Matryoshka doll metaphor assumes that all individual and collective actors fit into one another, while the network metaphor suggests that individual actors are not interconnected, unlike collective actors. However, if we take the concept of association in the sense of Latour into account, we cannot strictly speak of disconnection at the micro-sociological level. Indeed, Latour's association presupposes that every individual and collective actor, all humans and non-humans, can only exist on the basis of their interconnection. Therefore, Latour's example is somewhat misleading. Because if we take the idea of a possible disconnection at the micro-sociological level seriously, then there is no reason to assume that such disconnections do not occur at the macro-sociological level as well. This is not only what the Matryoshka doll metaphor presupposes. This is also due to the fact that—as we saw in Chap. 5—connections and disconnections are two modes of associations.

Latour attempts to remove this difficulty by postulating that associations have a syntagmatic structure (e.g. Latour 1991, 103–132, 1993c, 50ff.; Latour et al. 1992, 33–57). This syntagmatic structure is the common property of all associations, and it has the same characteristics as the Latin conjunction *vel*, meaning at the same time both "and" and "or" (e.g. Latour 2001, 165). Applied to associations, *syntagm* implies that associations can assemble these actors "and" these others, or that they can separate them from each other (the meaning "or" of the *vel* conjunction). Seen over time, this means that associations combine the "and" and the "or", in other words they bind *new* elements together ("and"/"or"), or they change the bond between elements already connected to each other in order to produce new configurations. These new configurations can occur either immediately (combinations with "and", presupposing combinations with "or" as they rearrange the associations), or later (first the combinations with "and"/"or", then the rearrangement of associations). These configurations and modifications of configurations of associations are what Latour describes as the operations of "substitution" (Latour 1993c, 19, 2001, 165), where existing associations between humans and non-humans are replaced by other associations.

This syntagmatic structure of associations is at the heart of human and non-human work on the mediations of exchange, it is at the base of their alliances. But this structure does not exclude dissociation, and it does not guarantee that associations are being continuously produced. In other words, the syntagmatic structure of associations resolves the seeming contradiction in the concept of association, which flows from the dialectical logic that associations have to dissociate in order to associate again. But, in itself, it does not stabilise this concept, it does not explain how discontinuities are embedded in continuities, or how discontinuities produce continuities, and vice versa. Behind this instability of the concept of association, there is the more general dilemma with which Latour is confronted. Is it individual actors who, through their activities with and on mediations, guarantee the continuity of associations according to their own interests? Or, is it institutions which, in the name of their own interests, ensure the continuity of associations in place of individual actors?

To answer these questions, Latour uses the concept of "attachment" (Latour 1993c, 53). Attachment does not presuppose the labour of only individual actors on the mediations of exchange but that of all humans and non-humans who contribute to the associations, i.e. that of everyone and everything who is associated with it. From this viewpoint, the seeming discontinuity of associations with respect to micro-social events is an illusion. It is only a transition from one network of associations to another and we can observe this at its best when we take into account everyone and everything who/which has contributed to the first network of associations, and who/which will be redistributed into the next network of associations. Attachment becomes the only important thing

> that define[s] either the objects—through the likes and dislikes, the obligations and detachments, the passions and coldness they have aroused. This chart marks no difference between (superfluous) desires and (necessary) needs, no more than between so-called material goods and those that would be 'nonmaterial'...The only thing that counts here is the number of aliens that have to be multiplied along any given path, and whose presence is felt only in tests of innovation or privation. We now understand the importance of defining attachments as 'passionate interests': interest, as we have seen, is everything that lies between, everything through which an entity must pass to go somewhere; as for passion, it defines the degree of intensity of the attachment. (Latour 2013, 432; cf. also Latour and Stark 1999, 25)

Attachment also applies to humans as well as to non-humans. It can be understood in the sense of physical attachment, or in the sense of emotional attachment. It has several forms, depending on the fields of activities in society. For example, attachment to science is a particular form of attachment, characterised by an interest and a corresponding investment by the actors in specific mediations—measuring tools, bacteria, materials, authors. Attachment does not exclude detachment (Latour and Stark 1999, 27), however, Latour relativises this point in order to place more emphasis on the idea that there are degrees of attachment (ibid. 22). Degrees of attachment are experienced differently by different actors because their experience depends on their labour on current and further mediations, and therefore, on current and further associations, as well as on corresponding mobilisations of humans and non-humans. For example, "an article published in Nature or Science will elicit a greater degree of attachment than a preprint posted on a website" (Latour 2010, 224). Attachment therefore has a double function in Latour's sociology of associations.

On the one hand, it gives some stability to his concept of associations in the sense that attachment embeds detachment as a variation of the degree of attachment.

On the other hand, attachment recalls the importance of the actors' interests in specific associations, namely those attracting the interests of other actors who contribute to the extension of these associations, which can generate a mobilisation of other humans and non-humans. Therefore, attachment highlights best what Latour calls "passionate interests", which are compulsory points of passage for humans and non-humans in order for them to extend associations, as well as to ensure their continuity. This continuity of associations is important in the long run (in order to develop a network), as well as in the short run (in order to articulate the mobilisation of humans/non-humans and their labour on the mediations of exchange). Therefore, when Latour says, "The performative framework we are advocating, in effect, gives back to the word 'social' its original meaning of association" (Latour and Strum 1987, 794), he means that attachment—the cardinal property of any association—is social.

Latour's concept of attachment does not come out of nowhere, but from Gabriel Tarde's social psychology. According to Latour, Tarde sees society as associations. Quoting Tarde's *Monadologie* (Latour 2002, 121ff.), Latour adds that "Tarde's idea is simply that if there is something special in human society it is not be determined by any strong opposition with all the other types of aggregates and certainly not by some special sort of arbitrarily imposed symbolic order which will put it apart from 'mere matter'. To be a society of monads is a totally general phenomenon, it is the stuff out of which the world is made" (ibid. 120). Thus, Tarde would support Latour's argument that associations are associations of heterogeneous elements—elements which are themselves made of heterogeneous associations. This is why associations not only apply to one single society, but to *societies* (Latour points out that Tarde's concept of society not only applies to human but also to non-human societies). Therefore, how do we differentiate between a human society and a non-human one? Following Tarde, Latour indicates that it is above all a problem of quantity, in the sense that "In Tarde's general view of societies, human societies are typical because of the small number of agents they mobilize, contrary to biology or physics that deal with millions or billions of elements. So being particular is what encountering the social is all about" (Latour 2005, 137 note 194). However, is Latour right to say that Tarde distinguishes human and non-human societies in such a manner?

The Social

According to Tarde, one can indeed argue that a society of whatever kind (a society of plants, animals, cells, and of course, a human society) is based on associations. Nevertheless, all these societies do not share the same principle of association:

> the animals of La Fontaine's fables, the fox, the cricket, the cat, and the dog, live together in society, in spite of the difference in species which separates them, because they all speak the same language. We eat, drink, digest, walk, or cry without being taught. These acts are purely vital. But talking requires the hearing of conversation, as we know from the case of deaf mutes who are dumb because they are deaf. Consequently, I begin to feel a social kinship with everyone who talks, even if it be in a strange tongue, providing our two idioms appear to me to have some common source. This social tie may be weak and inadequate, but it gains in strength as other common traits, all originating in imitation, are added to it. (Tarde 1895b (1903), 67–68)

In human societies, these associations come from imitation because human beings are at the same time—in the sense of Latour—non-human. According to Tarde, this idea of "non-human" means above all that humans have a body that is under the influence of the external environment (ibid. 76ff.). Thanks to their body, human beings perceive their environment, they receive impulses to which their nervous system reacts, and which result in ideas, needs and expressions. In the framework of Tarde's social psychology, the body is very important. It contributes to the differentiation between human and other non-human societies because the influence of the environment does not only explain human psychic activity. It also contributes to the development of their social activities, which develop thanks to imitation, and this is why Tarde names these human activities "imitativités" (Tarde 1895a, 61, 76; also 108 where Tarde speaks of "imitativités instinctives"). These *imitativités* always come from "a first initiator" of an idea or an act, a brilliant inventor or a great invention (Tarde 1898 (2000), 23). They develop as a "kind of imitation of oneself by oneself" (Tarde 1881, 405) between the nerve cells of human individuals, which Tarde qualifies as "suggestion-imitation" (Tarde 1898 (2000), 23) and identifies with the concept of habit ("habitudes" in the French original; cf. Tarde 1898a, 36). These imitative activities transfer from one individual to another unilaterally, but this transition is not automatic—it involves the gathering of other humans. Humans must interact, they must notice their similarity, which they do by observing how others act, i.e. how they speak, behave and unite (Tarde 1901, 462). This attention to similarity generates, on the one hand, recognition of others as human beings, as well as feelings of responsibility toward these others (Tarde 1890b (1912), 4–5). On the other hand, it allows the repetition of actions, which in turn mobilises others—a mobilisation that is new in comparison to previous ones and that presupposes new actions. Similarity is what Tarde defines as a "medius terminus" (Tarde 1893, 630). It is a mediation that is not physical—like an object for example—and that will be differentiated in the course of actions and associations. It leads from one difference to another, i.e. from one individual actor to another, from one action to another, and from one association to another. Thus, differentiation of similarity ensures the multiplication of social activities between humans (Tarde 1874, 19) and, in the end, the constitution of a human society.

Tarde's observations are reminiscent of Latour's ternary explanation of the constitution of society. First, the environment—the non-humans—has a unilateral influence on humans. Second, this unilateral influence leads humans to act and recognise themselves as human beings and, third, leads them to constitute a society. According to Tarde, these three stages of differentiation of similarity correspond to the reciprocal action between bodies and minds at the level of each individual actor. This reciprocal action constitutes the root of Tarde's inter-psychology, which he uses in order to define society. "What is society? Society is not only the social spirit; it is the social spirit above all. The truth is that each of the peculiar social sciences—of which general social science is only the synthesis—cover at once a certain order of inter-spiritual actions, and a certain order of inter-bodily actions" (Tarde 1901, 470). Thus, we get a more complete picture of what Tarde conceives to be a human society. Tarde says that all societies are based on associations, but these associations must be differentiated depending on the type of society considered. Human societies are human societies because, in these societies, associations are rooted in the recognition of the resemblance between human beings.

Looking at Latour's interpretation of Tarde, we see two differences. The first is that, for Tarde, speaking of association in order to characterise human societies is not satisfactory because it is too general. The second difference results from the first. Tarde sees in the resemblance between human beings—and not in their attachment—the specific property of associations, which leads to human societies. These nuances do not fundamentally jeopardise Latour's interpretation of Tarde,[2] because in the end, Tarde speaks of associations when he talks about society. Nevertheless, the successive displacements that Latour alleges in his interpretation of Tarde have the function not to primarily support the *ANT* conceptual framework, but rather to strengthen Latour's position towards the history of sociology, particularly towards the founding father of French sociology, Émile Durkheim. Indeed, according to Latour,

> Tarde always complained that Durkheim had abandoned the task of explaining society by confusing cause and effect, replacing the understanding of the social link with a political project aimed at social engineering. Against his younger challenger, he vigorously maintained that the social was not a special domain of reality but a principle of connections...We don't need to accept all of Tarde's idiosyncrasies—and there are many—but in the gallery of portraits of eminent predecessors he is one of the very few, along with Harold Garfinkel, who believed sociology could be a science accounting for how society is held together, instead of using society to explain something else or to help solve one of the political questions of the time. (Latour 2005, 13)

We can question whether this observation—as well as others going in the same direction (e.g. Latour 2000, 113, 2002, 117–132, 2004, 264 note 30)—gives an adequate account of Durkheim's views on social behaviour. When Latour suggests that Durkheim reduces the social to "a special domain of reality", which domain are we talking of?

> For the last century during which social theories have been elaborated, it has been important to distinguish this domain of reality from other domains such as economics, geography, biology, psychology, law, science, and politics. A given trait was said to be 'social' or to 'pertain to society' when it could be defined as possessing specific properties, some negative—it must not be 'purely' biological, linguistic, economical, natural—and some positive—it must achieve, reinforce, express, maintain, reproduce, or subvert the social order. Once this domain had been defined, no matter how vaguely, it could then be used to shed some light on specifically social phenomena—the social could explain the social—and to provide a certain type of explanation for what the other domains could not account for—an appeal to 'social factors' could explain the 'social aspects' of non-social phenomena. (Latour 2005, 3)[3]

Such an interpretation does not prevent misunderstandings as it is too general and tends to sketch a strong opposition between Tarde and Durkheim that seems exaggerated in regard both to the relation between Tarde and Durkheim, and to the historical context in which Durkheim develops his sociology.

The dispute between Tarde and Durkheim is well known. It reached its strongest moments in 1895 and 1903, and it is discussed at length in the secondary literature on Durkheim, which presents results that are very much at odds with Latour's interpretation.[4] In this literature, there is consensus that the debate between Tarde and Durkheim was, above all and like several other similar debates of their time, about sociology as a very young scientific discipline, not about the social. Moreover, this debate was constantly kept alive by exchanges between Tarde and Durkheim in the form of either correspondence or public discussions. It shows that both authors were interested in the other's reasoning because they both wanted to provide a final answer to the question of what kind of sociology was wanted in France. Was it Durkheim's abstract sociology or, in Tarde's terms, Durkheim's "scholastic realism" (Durkheim 1903 (1975), 165),[5] in which social facts are seen as *sui generis*, i.e. as external and autonomous from individual consciousness? Or was it Tarde's sociology that analyses everyday activities and argues that social facts are the products of individual activities and, above all, of their psychological activities? Tarde and Durkheim never agreed on this point.

However, Tarde is not the only one with whom Durkheim did not agree, and the latter's critical attitude towards Tarde was not exceptional as is evident from the debates between Durkheim and some German thinkers. Durkheim frequently and to some, scandalously, used the work of German thinkers, as for example in *L'Année sociologique*.[6] From his early writings until 1895, Durkheim debated with German economists, particularly with leftist academics like Gustav Schmoller and Adolf Wagner.[7] Durkheim read Schmoller and Wagner because he was interested in the differences between economic and social sciences as he intended to exploit them in his struggle to gain a better position in the field of the social sciences in France, which, in turn, would enable him to institutionalise his sociology. His relationship with the German philosopher and sociologist Georg Simmel had the same purpose.

Secondary literature highlights how Durkheim and Simmel met, and how Durkheim invited Simmel to contribute to the first volume of *L'Année*.[8] Some authors have also commented on their misunderstanding, which reached a climax in 1900–1902, when Durkheim published an article on sociology in the Italian periodical *Rivista italiana di Sociologia*, going against Simmel (Durkheim 1900 (1975), 13–36). Yet, why did Durkheim criticise Simmel? Because Durkheim thought that Simmel's sociology was not scientific enough, if it is at all.[9] Paoletti concludes that Durkheim's criticism corresponds to the time at which Durkheim decided to strictly separate sociology from philosophy in order to distinguish himself from French and social philosophers like Henri Bergson, Xavier Léon and Elie Halévy (Paoletti 2012b, 81). Learning from what had happened to Tarde, Durkheim wanted to give his sociology an eminent place in France, i.e. a place separate and distinct from other social sciences, particularly from economy, psychology and philosophy. According to Durkheim, this was all the more important as everyone spoke of the social, and everyone conceived the social as something separate from the object of psychology or economics, even if no one was able to give an accurate definition of "what" the social was. Durkheim had the same difficulty when he prepared his articles about *The Rules of Sociological Method* between 1893 and 1894, which do not contain any accurate definition of the social.

Let us take, for example, his definition of social facts as "manners of acting or thinking, distinguishable through their special characteristic of being capable of exercising a coercive influence on the consciousness of individuals" (Durkheim 1895a (2013), 3). We now understand why such a definition is problematic. It either says too much—everything is social, and in this case, we do not know what distinguishes the social from the economic, the spiritual, the psychological, the political, etc.—or it says too little—only phenomena such as influence or collective constraint are social, but if this is so, we should make the origin of such a constraint clear. Does it come from the individual, from the group, or from elsewhere?[10] In order to avoid the first as well as the second criticism, Durkheim says: "We readily admit the charge that this definition does not express all aspects of the social fact and consequently that it is not the sole possible one. Indeed it is not at all inconceivable for it to be characterized in several different ways, for there is no reason why it should possess only the one distinctive property" (ibid.).

Following Durkheim in *The Rules*, what should remain of this definition is, above all, the idea that beliefs and practices have impacts on individuals that do not depend entirely on these individuals—a definition which is not far from the one that Tarde uses when he defines the social.

> For there to be a social fact and at the same time a social bound, a living being must act mentally on another living being...But is it enough that an action of a living being on another one would be a psychic action for there to be a social fact and a social bound? There is a psychic action of a human on another human when the former, by his gestures or his expressive signs which the latter understands or feels, or by his attitude and his look, or by his single presence modifies the mental state of the latter. (Tarde 1904, 539)

Certainly, this definition emphasises the individual, which is already enough to distinguish Tarde from Durkheim. But we also observe that, for Tarde as well as for Durkheim, the same idea of influence is mentioned. Moreover, both authors see this influence as based on an asymmetric relationship. Durkheim describes this situation as the constraint to coercion that determines individual consciousness. Tarde speaks of the modification of human mental states that presupposes first a unilateral act from one human to another, which then becomes a reciprocal action when it is repeated between humans. In both cases, we have two different ways to make the link between sociology and the social. With Tarde (imitation shows this link best), unilateral influence becomes reciprocal as imitation spreads into society until it forms a system of differences. With Durkheim, reciprocal relations are obligatory, and they are imposed on humans by specific non-humans, i.e. customs and social practices (this is the meaning of his discourse on coercion). The result is social order. This relation, which both Tarde and Durkheim understand as an asymmetric one, but which they otherwise define in a very different way, nevertheless remains for both of them the object of what they understand as sociology.

Thus, Latour is obviously not wrong in observing Tarde's and Durkheim's opposition but certainly exaggerates it. In his depiction, only Tarde is sensitive to associations or relations between humans and non-humans. But we find the same sensitivity in Durkheim's work as well. Yet, Latour's exaggeration has some advantages because it allows him to use Tarde to support his a-sociology, which, however, comes at a cost. Indeed, according to Tarde, what makes human associations unique is their foundation in unilateral acts, which rests, in the last instance, on the recognition of similarities between humans. This understanding of associations does not exactly correspond to Latour's concept of association. Latour instead picks up Tarde's general definition of associations as a functional relationship between humans, as well as between humans and non-humans. This general understanding of association certainly preserves a reference to Tarde's social psychology. But it does not solve the problem of Latour's concept of association, namely the problem of the closure of associations. Moreover, when Latour tries to find a solution to this problem by giving his concept of association a foundation in attachment, he is closer to Durkheim than to Tarde, because while the concept of attachment is very important to Durkheim and plays a key role in his notion of reciprocity, it does not find favour with Tarde.

Reciprocal Attachment

"Let us not forget that the social as association, invented by Tarde, bears no relation to the social of Durkheim" (Latour 2004, 264 note 30). When we look at Durkheim's concept of attachment, we have to relativise this sentence because Durkheim does not radically reject the ideas of association and resemblance. Rather the contrary, he is using them in order to make his understanding of the social more clear.[11] In *The Rules*, Durkheim says that "the determining condition for social phenomena consists, as we have demonstrated, in the very fact of association" (Durkheim 1895a (2013), 91).

With regard to the formation of professional groups, Durkheim combines association and resemblance.

> Within a political society, as soon as a certain number of individuals find they hold in common ideas, interests, sentiments and occupations which the rest of the population does not share in, it is inevitable that, under the influence of these similarities, they should be attracted to one another. They will seek one another out, enter into relationships and associate together. Thus a restricted group is gradually formed within society as a whole, with its own special features. (Durkheim 1893b (2013), 17)

What happens in professional groups is only a particular example of a more general trend, namely the building of a "solidarity sui generis which, deriving from resemblances, binds the individual directly to society" (ibid. 81). This solidarity by similarity between individuals rests on reciprocal sympathy, an attachment becoming more abstract as society becomes more complex.

> As soon as societies have increased in volume, the bond which has interconnected the individuals was not a personal one anymore. What has replaced this concrete sympathy is a more abstract attachment, which is no less powerful for the community itself to which we belong, i.e. for the material and ideal goods that we have in common, art, literature, science, morals, etc., etc. Therefore, the members of a same society have loved and assisted each other, not because they knew each other, and not to the extent to which they knew each other, but because they all were the basis of the collective consciousness. (Durkheim 1887 (1975), 309)

Tarde, like Durkheim, also refers to sympathy, and he also views it from the viewpoint of reciprocity. Nevertheless, describing his idea of the development of associations, Tarde does not see sympathy as the first concrete manifestation of reciprocal attachment between actors. On the contrary, for Tarde, sympathy is an achievement in the development of unilateral and asymmetrical associations. "The earliest societies are thus always formed by the unilateral tie of prestige before recognizing the reciprocal tie of sympathy" (Tarde 1890b (1912), 258, note 1).

Durkheim reverses this scheme. First, there is reciprocal attachment, and second, on this basis, the development of an asymmetry where individuals' interests move to the background—a "subordination of the particular to the general interest" in Durkheim's words (Durkheim 1893b (2013), 18). The idea of subordination is very important to Durkheim because it explains why individual actors do not attach themselves only to one another, but also to the unit they form, the union they represent (ibid.). Nevertheless, subordination is not spontaneous, and it cannot be imposed on the actors. As Durkheim puts it, "although the vanquished can for a while resign themselves to an enforced domination, they do not concur in it, and consequently such a state can provide no stable equilibrium. Truces imposed by violence are never anything other than temporary, and pacify no one. Men's passions are only stayed by a moral force they respect" (ibid. 9).[12] Therefore, "Why should we subordinate ourselves to such an extent in favor of a being so radically different from ourselves?" (Durkheim 1902–1903 (1973), 66).

Durkheim gives two answers: a general one based on his notion of individual consciousness, and a particular one resting on his views on secondary groups. Durkheim's general answer is already present in his book about the division of labour, and it regards the duality of individual consciousness. According to him:

> Two consciousnesses exist within us: the one comprises only states that are personal to each one of us, characteristic of us as individuals, whilst the other comprises states that are common to the whole of society. The former represents only our individual personality, which it constitutes: the latter represents the collective type and consequently the society without which it would not exist. (Durkheim 1893b (2013), 81)

This duality of individual consciousness makes Durkheim's concept of society unique. It is both a cognitive reality inside individual actors, and a public reality outside individual actors. This is what is known as Durkheim's sociologism: Durkheim sees society everywhere, and uses it both as *explanans* and as *explanandum*. Latour criticises Durkheim's sociologism, which, according to him, represents *par excellence* an "ostensive definition of the social link" (Latour 1986, 274). For Latour, this means that Durkheim does not take into account the role of objects in the mobilisation of the collective, or, to use Durkheim's terminology, the attachment of individual actors to social groups. However, Durkheim's sociologism is not really related to his (lack of) consideration of objects. It rather underlines Durkheim's difficulty in stabilising his view on reciprocal attachment. We shall return to this point later but, for now, let us briefly look at Latour's observations on the way in which Durkheim embeds, or rather does not embed, objects and, in general, non-humans in his sociological reasoning.

If we cannot be as affirmative as Latour when he says that Durkheim does not take non-humans into account, this is because Durkheim actually sees objects—material and immaterial things—as an integral part of his social morphology (Durkheim 1895 (1919) 138ff.). Incidentally, Latour briefly highlights this by using the example of *The Elementary Forms of Religious Life* (1912). He says that Durkheim shows how "material resources" keep members of clans together (Latour 1986, 274). Nevertheless, Latour regards Durkheim's understanding of objects in the formation of the clan as rather exceptional, at least in the *Forms*. "These are the only places in the whole book where the overarching society, used elsewhere as a cause to explain everything, is deemed insufficient" (ibid. 273). Given the importance of social morphology in Durkheim's work—the science of the physical forms of society, the basis of collective life—Latour's observation is not relevant.[13] Durkheim pays attention to objects and on how they contribute to the development of society. In other words, the material conditions of the existence of society are one of Durkheim's main interests, and he does not have much difficulty in explaining them. He has more difficulty, however, in describing the relation that can exist between humans and that particular non-human, which is society. By seeing society everywhere—and in this respect, Latour is right—Durkheim does not give a satisfactory explanation of the relation between humans and society, even if he sets the problem out in clear terms when he asks how individual actors can be subordinated to what is, for Durkheim, a reality of another nature, namely society. The explanation, resting on personal and social consciousness, does not provide a solution because Durkheim's question about the link between individual actors and society shows up again at the level of individual consciousness. Indeed, how do we explain that two elements as different as the social and the personal coexist in one individual consciousness? In *The Division of Labour in Society*, Durkheim simply provides a—quietly organicist—justification in principle, saying that "although distinct, these two consciousnesses are linked to each other, since in the end they constitute only one entity, for both have one and the same organic basis, thus they are interdependent" (Durkheim 1893b (2013), 81).

However, in his lectures on moral education, Durkheim proposes another explanation based on the expansion of his concept of attachment to the individual desire of society, meaning that individual actors spontaneously desire social consciousness in order to preserve themselves. Indeed, according to Durkheim, it is not true that the individual actor "can identify himself with society only at the risk of renouncing his own nature either wholly or in part" (Durkheim 1902–1903 (1973), 68). Rather, "the fact is that he is not truly himself, he does not fully realize his own nature, except on the condition that he is involved in society" (ibid.).[14] This expansion of attachment does certainly not solve the problem entirely. As mentioned in Chap. 2, the question of spontaneity remains problematic in Durkheim's work in general, as well as specifically here in relation to attachment. Nevertheless, it leads Durkheim to implement a circular causation in his concept of attachment, which he identifies as reciprocity in *The Rules*, saying that "the solid link which joins cause to effect is of a reciprocal character which has not been sufficiently recognized" (Durkheim 1895a (2013), 82).[15] In other words, if there is attachment between individual and society—as functional relation, or motivated by the individual desirability of collective consciousness—it is because of a reciprocity that operates the closure of their cycles of relation. Reciprocity makes this closure happen; it closes the configuration of the relation between individuals and society. Moreover, it preserves the individual, who fully corresponds to his own individual nature, according to Durkheim, if society is preserved, if it can develop continuously, i.e. if it also fully corresponds to its own social nature.

Nonetheless, there is a bit of rhetoric in Durkheim's argument, because the complementarity of these two apparently contradictory requirements applies to the level of the individual actor only. Indeed, only individual actors must conform to social rules and are attached to society in a disinterested way only—by desire (Durkheim 1902–1903 (1973), 122ff.). Thus, Durkheim can say without too much difficulty that these "two elements of morality are only two different aspects of the same reality. Their unity stems not from the fact that one is the corollary of the other or vice versa...Because society is beyond us, it commands us; on the other hand, being superior to everything in us, it permeates us. Because it constitutes part of us, it draws us with the special attraction that inspires us toward moral ends" (ibid. 98). However, why is there an asymmetry? Why does the individual actor only desire that part of himself that represents society? Why does society not desire individual actors? Because society "in a sense...constitutes what is best in us" (ibid. 71). In the conflict with Tarde, Durkheim's answer has advantages. Nevertheless, it also has its cost when it comes to his notion of reciprocal attachment.

First, by making reciprocity a circular link between individual actors and society, Durkheim definitively breaks with Tarde's idea that social life rests on a coercive influence by interindividual imitation. Social life does not depend on intermental actions between individuals, but on reciprocity between individuals and social groups/society. Reciprocity is not an abstract social contract. It closes the configuration of the relation between individuals and groups/society. Reciprocity is therefore not the original mould of all social relationships. In other words, the multitude of associations that we can observe in society are not necessarily reciprocal, even if they contribute to the existence of the configuration and beyond, of cycles of the relation. Thus, if reciprocity expresses a circular causation between individuals and groups/society, this causality changes according to the changes that may affect reciprocity in practice, in particular those regarding the material living conditions of individual actors, groups and societies. By saying that reciprocity is affected by the morphological conditions of life in society, Durkheim says that attachments between individuals and society do not remain identical over time or according to societies. Therefore, attachment is not a kind of universal imitative attachment, or from the viewpoint of imitation, imitation does not have the character of a social law as in Tarde. Thus, imitation is not the original mould of associations. Durkheim is then able to keep the idea of a multiplicity of social relations that Tarde's concept of association evokes, without assigning to this multiplicity a common universal origin, which, according to Tarde, is imitation. This can be seen even more clearly in the fact that Durkheim, finally, relativises his concept of reciprocity, which does not apply to all social relations, but represents a particular and concrete relation closing the configuration of the relation, preserving the identity of individuals and society.

However, according to Durkheim, this configuration and their cycles can be closed because there is an asymmetry between individual actors and the collective. And as we have seen, this closure depends on the assumption that only individual actors desire society, not the reverse. This desirability certainly contributes to reintroducing individuality into Durkheim's sociology, and to thinking about it in relation to the collective.[16] However, it does not consider the question of actors' resistance to this desirability and, beyond, to society. This is a point already noted in Chap. 2. The only resistance that Durkheim conceives of is the one coming from outside the individuals.

As he says when he describes the "sui generis" character of social facts, "if we notice that everything which has a determined nature, which is independent of the subjects who make it up is a thing, then we see that the social facts have this distinctive quality at the highest point. Indeed, what proves the existence of this nature is the resistance of the thing to us when we try to change it, since in this way, it asserts itself as distinct from us" (Durkheim 1895b (1975), 99). However, if individual actors can comprehend their individual identity and the existence of the social because of the resistance of social facts, how is it possible that this resistance does not influence their desire for the social, their attachment to society? By saying that the social resists the individual but the individual does not resist the social, Durkheim follows his general thesis, which rests in the duality of individual consciousness and postulates that society is imposed on individuals. This makes reciprocity useless, however—even as functional circularity of social causes and effects. Moreover, the expansion of attachment to desirability becomes superfluous, because even if we assume that this were the case, Durkheim's view on the individual actor is such that any actor cannot be thought as not to be attached to society. Durkheim's notion of individual consciousness damages his argument about reciprocity, which also weakens Durkheim's criticism of Tarde. Indeed, Durkheim gives the impression that he has replaced one automatism with another—imitation with attachment, in the narrow sense of a public functional relationship, as well as in the general sense of the private desirability of society. What remains of Durkheim's view on reciprocity is an element that refers to social cohesion and, specifically, to secondary groups.

For Durkheim, social cohesion takes place in the general framework of the transition from societies that are driven by mechanical solidarity to societies that are driven by organic solidarity, i.e. a transition from societies where the relations between individual actors depend on their similarities, to societies where these similarities are less present due to individualisation and an increasing specialisation of individual actors. This does not mean that there are no more similarities between individuals in contemporary societies. Actually:

> we all know that a social cohesion exists whose cause can be traced to a certain conformity of each individual consciousness to a common type, which is none other than the psychological type of society. Indeed under these conditions all members of the group are not only individually attracted to one another because they resemble one another, but they are also linked to what is the condition for the existence of this collective type, that is, to the society that they form by coming together...society insists upon its citizens displaying all these basic resemblances because it is a condition for its own cohesion. (Durkheim 1893b (2013), 81)

However, the reality of differences in the development of societies cannot be denied, neither can the changes that such a development brings about. These are mostly morphological changes, related to demographic, geographic and economic life conditions. The number of individual actors increases and, correspondingly, society extends geographically. The production of objects increases, as well as the activities related to these objects. Social diversity develops. This diversity goes hand in hand with social cohesion because—Durkheim refers here to Montesquieu—social cohesion means dealing with the diversity and inequality of actors (cf. for example Durkheim 1892b (1966), 65).[17] Therefore, how do societies driven by organic solidarity deal with the diversity and inequality of actors in order to preserve their social cohesion? The answer is, by promoting secondary groups, such as professional groups, for example, and more generally, by fostering the building of institutions that can have a "regulative influence" on associations between individual actors (Durkheim 1890–1900 (1958), 24).

If secondary groups are so important in societies driven by organic solidarity, it is above all because they foster the emancipation of individuals, giving them a structure based on the specific principles of their professional conditions. Nevertheless, in order to avoid individual actors to become subject to these secondary groups only, there must be a state whose:

> main function...is to liberate the individual personalities. It is solely because, in holding its constituent societies in check, it prevents them from exerting the repressive influences over the individual that they would otherwise exert. So there is nothing inherently tyrannical about State intervention in the different fields of collective life; on the contrary, it has the object and the effect of alleviating tyrannies that do exist. (ibid. 62–63)

Because the state regulates the power of secondary groups on their individual members, and because these secondary groups channel the interventions of the state, individual emancipation is guaranteed.

The same applies to the relation between individual actors and society.

> Individual personalities are formed and become conscious of themselves. Yet this growth in the psychological life of the individual does not weaken that of society, but merely transforms it. It becomes freer and more extensive, and since in the end it has no other substrata than the consciousnesses of individuals, these latter grow, becoming more complex and incidentally more flexible. (Durkheim 1893b (2013), 271)

We see here again a fragment of Durkheim's reasoning on reciprocity, and we can observe the changes that Durkheim brings to this concept. Society certainly remains superior to the individual, and the secondary groups as well as the state confirm this. But society vanishes if it does not expand to individual consciousness. Coercion or constraint as well as their empirical manifestations like violence or totalitarianism do not lead to this kind of expansion, and this is why Durkheim ultimately keeps reciprocity within the asymmetry between individual and society—against his sociologism. Because, as do individual actors, society is interested in its own preservation, the preservation of its identity as something that cannot be reduced to individual actors. Symmetrically to what happens to individual actors, society is preserved if it gains its legitimacy from the resistance of individual actors to itself. Only society can legitimate such resistance of individual actors, and this legitimization presupposes the existence of institutions in the social fields of activities that are in contact with these actors, and that regulate their resistance. This is why Durkheim says that societies "should attempt…to eliminate external inequalities as much as possible", because these inequalities prevent the expression of social diversity, which the individual actors represent either individually or as a social group (Durkheim 1893b (2013), 297). "[I]t is not only because the undertaking is a noble one, but because in solving this problem their very existence [of societies; CP] is at stake" (ibid.). If society or its institutions should fail to support reciprocity—even if the concrete social relationships remained asymmetric—we would have a society resting on constraint only, a constraint that Durkheim understands in the following way, "What constitutes real constraint is when even struggle becomes impossible, and one is not even allowed to fight" (ibid. 295). Thus, there is a strong link between reciprocity and secondary groups, which lead us to similarities between Durkheim and Latour on the consequences of this link between reciprocity, individual actors and institutions.

Consecration

In the previous section, we explored the problem of individual/society, which we used to reconstruct Durkheim's reasoning on reciprocity. His view on reciprocity applies to all fields of activity where individual actors are directly or indirectly in relation with multiple institutions regulating these activities. According to Durkheim, the most emblematic of these are the family, the school system, secondary groups and the state. We have seen that asymmetric reciprocity between individual actors and institutions can be understood similarly to the general case of asymmetric reciprocity between individual actors and society. According to Durkheim as well as to Latour, institutions have a positive role in society, as we mentioned briefly. For Durkheim, secondary groups and the state promote social diversity, and they thus contribute to the development and empowerment of individual actors.

As regards Latour, we have seen that he also attributes a positive meaning to institutions—in his case, mostly scientific institutions.[18] Institutions are good for everyone because they have a particular role that Latour clearly highlights in his discourse on the politics of nature, namely, they close the debates, i.e. the various associations that are produced in a given time (Latour 2004, 111). Yet, there certainly is a difference between Durkheim's and Latour's understanding of institutions. Indeed, according to Latour, institutions are not only public institutions—such as, for example, in the context of scientific institutions, research centres or professional publishers. Every institution is a form of power, the power to order associations so that what they put out cannot be put into question, even if it remains open to discussion (ibid. 109). Latour makes the institution out to be a form of the rational (ibid. 243) and makes it into the synonym for a form of life. Thus, an institution is, in contrast to Durkheim's view, more than a public institution that regulates society. Moreover, its key property is the usage of power, which is the power to close the cycles of associations and to constitute corresponding black boxes. Despite these differences, this operation of closure means for Latour, as for Durkheim, the legitimisation of an order—in the case of Latour, such an order should "prepare the re-collection of the collective as it goes through the next loop" (ibid.). Moreover, for both Latour and Durkheim, this order presupposes an initiation. In the context of the scientific laboratories that Latour and Woolgar analyse, scientists find it important to produce "hard facts" likely to convince other scientists (Latour and Woolgar 1986, 70). This production of "hard facts" mobilises the activity of these laboratories, and it leads to scientific articles where the scientists must demonstrate both their scientific skills (the product of an entire socialisation of work in science) and their rhetoric art in order to mobilise colleagues well beyond their own laboratory. In this context of never-ending initiation to science, scientific legitimacy is at stake. It is intimately linked to the alliances that can be built with colleagues, so that the question of scientific legitimacy appears all the more when the alliances have been made, i.e. when the cycle of associations which has led to these alliances can be closed.

Durkheim describes the same general pattern when he speaks of consecration.[19] For Durkheim, consecration means, above all, communication, similar to the communication which, in the context of his religious sociology, takes place between the sacred and the profane. This communication presupposes an initiation of which the "specific purpose...is to make, to fabricate, men" (Durkheim 1912 (1995), 297). As Latour says, Durkheim speaks of initiation almost exclusively in relation to the elementary forms of religious life. But initiation is not limited to the framework of religion. Durkheim regards it as a more general principle of education expressed in a multitude of societies at specific times in the actors' life and accompanied by, for instance, ritualistic ceremonies (Durkheim 1922, 122). The institution institutes. But it can only do this by initiating—by educating—actors, i.e. by communicating its principles, which are sacred things for the institution, to those actors and to everything that depends on them (particularly their mediations of exchange).[20] Without communication of the sacred to the actors and things, the actors and things cannot change qualitatively, and thus, they cannot go from one actor to another, from one mediation to another, and from one cycle of the relation to another. Consecration and the initiation that it presupposes are often unpleasant for the actor, "Many of those rites involve the systematic infliction of suffering on the neophyte, for the purpose of altering his state" (Durkheim 1912 (1995), 317). This suffering must ensure that the initiated actor acquires the sacred qualities corresponding to the principles of the institution, which the institution gives him during the initiation. For example, "Among the Arunta and the Kaitish, according to Eylmann, men and women make small wounds on their arms with red hot sticks so as to become skillful at making fire or gain the strength they need to carry heavy loads of wood" (ibid. 319).

"Communication of the sacred character very often brings about an appropriation. To consecrate is a way of appropriating" (Durkheim 1890–1900 (1958), 149). Appropriation gives the actors and their mediations of exchange an exclusiveness. It singles them out; it separates them from the collective as the law of property does by giving an inalienable character to the owner of a thing and to his thing. "It is here that the bond between the thing and the subject (or individual) who is the possessor reaches its maximum force and here too that the exclusion of the rest of the society is most strictly imposed" (ibid. 150). Consecration leads to a legitimisation of the actor and his social position, and it happens only if the actor has been discharged of the sacred character that he has obtained during the consecration. Translated into secular language, this means that the actor will be legitimated in using the principles received from the institution, and in applying them to his activities and to the mediations of exchange. Durkheim draws this reasoning from his work on the religious origins of private property and, more generally, of the appropriation of things.

In the family, these things are related to the land that the family cultivates, and that makes up the family itself. As Durkheim says, "The family means the individuals taken as a whole who lived in this insulated and sacred little island that made up the domain. It is the laws that bind them to the sacred soil they cultivated which therefore unite them amongst themselves" (ibid. 164). This is the case because the land is sacred. The soil "was far more a case of the sacredness of the holy thing being communicated to the family" (ibid.). Therefore, "How is it that individuals thus grouped together, attached to an identical group of things, came to acquire separate rights over separate things?...For as long as the things preserved this moral superiority over persons, as it were, it was impossible for the individual to become their owner and establish his own command over them" (ibid. 165). To explain this transfer of ownership from the family to individual actors, Durkheim recalls his concept of consecration.

To preserve itself, to avoid the domination of the land that makes up as well as dissolves the family, the family transmits a part of its sacredness to one of its members, who becomes the head of the family. As head of the family, this member gains a position of exclusiveness within the family in comparison to other family members. According to Durkheim, this explains how the patriarchal family was formed, because "The concentration of the family…which established patrimonial powers, causes all these sacred virtues (that were inherent in the patrimony and gave it an exceptional status), to issue from the person of the head of the family" (ibid. 168). The head of the patriarchal family becomes the one who exclusively possesses the patrimony, because as if it were sacred, everything the head touches becomes his property, and this property becomes taboo since, according to Durkheim, "To declare a thing taboo or to take possession of it are one and the same" (ibid. 144). However, if the head of the family has a certain legitimacy, it does not come from his sacred character only. He is also legitimated because, by owning the property of the family, he guarantees the preservation of the family by keeping that property inside the family. From there come the different rules of the cessation of the patrimonial property, particularly those that set the conditions of inheritance. The important point here is that the legitimacy that an institution (in this example, the family) gives to a particular actor (the head of the family) does not come at the same time as the consecration, but only after the consecration. The head of the family is legitimated because he preserves the family in applying the family's principles to all things likely to enter the framework of domestic activities. As Durkheim observes, this regards not only land. An important quantity of movable things gravitates around such land property and, because these things are not real estate property, they are less sacred than the land property. Therefore, they can be appropriated by other members of the family, provided the head allows it, i.e. that he does not appropriate them for himself, making them sacred and, therefore, taboo. If at the beginning, these movables are, for example, the tools used to work on the land, with the development of the division of labour, other movables become part of the family property, goods that have less and less direct link to the family property as time passes by. As Durkheim says:

> With time, however, and with the progress of trade and industry, the personal or movable property took on greater importance; it then cut away from this landed property of which it was only an adjunct; it played a social role of its own different from landed property, and became an autonomous factor in economic life. Thus, a fresh nucleus of property was made outside real estate, and so did not of course have its characteristic features. The things comprised in such a nucleus had in themselves nothing that put them beyond the reach of any trespass such as we discussed. They were only

> things, and the individual into whose hands they came was likely to find himself on an equal footing or even above them. He could therefore dispose of them more freely. Nothing tied them to any given point in space; nothing made them immovable. This meant that they depended direct only on the person of the one who acquired, or on some way in which he had acquired them. (ibid. 167)

Whatever we think about the evolutionary nature of Durkheim's division of labour, the main element of his explanation concerns the extension of appropriation from real estate property to movable property. Durkheim explains how the transformation of appropriation of property allows us to generalise the institutional principles of the family to other mediations of exchange, to other fields of activities, and to other actors. This process is not only bound to the family—other institutions act in the same way over the course of the division of labour, this all the more as property expands to objects that do not belong to one family or another, and are therefore less sacred, or less taboo. The question of the legitimacy of the social position depends on this expansion of institutions. This expansion is nothing more than the extension of the way in which an institution consecrates actors and mediations of exchange to all kinds of activities, i.e. the way in which the institution closes the cycles of the relation with the actors or, in other words, the way in which it contributes to establish a reciprocity that makes this closure manifest as a concrete configuration of the relation within society. We have discussed Durkheim's complete scheme explaining what consecration involves when we are going from societies driven by mechanical solidarity to those driven by organic solidarity. Now, we can look at the consequences for the relation.

On the one hand, consecration enables us to understand that the legitimisation of social positions happens in a top-down manner, from the institution to the actors and everything depending on them (activities and mediations of exchanges). On the other hand, if actors contribute to the legitimisation of institutions, they only do it indirectly. Durkheim gives some examples, particularly when he speaks of science, saying: "if it should happen that science resisted a very powerful current of public opinion, it would run the risk of seeing its credibility eroded" (Durkheim 1912 (1995), 210). However, Durkheim can say this because he applies his sociologism to the relationship between science and public opinion. Actually, speaking of public opinion, Durkheim speaks of nothing else than of society, which, as he says, "speaks through the mouths" of individuals (ibid.).

If we do not take such an explanation resting on Durkheim's sociologism into account but take his reasoning on secondary groups instead, then we observe that behind society speaking through the mouths of individuals, there are institutional principles that the individuals have taken up from several institutions during their socialisation. Or to put it in Latour's words, individuals appear as mediators of the exchanges between institutions—and not just as intermediaries. In Durkheim, this is the logical consequence of his reasoning on the relation between the state and secondary groups, particularly those professional groups that Durkheim considers as a counter-power to the state. By communicating the principles of a profession to individuals, professional groups give them the means to counter the arbitrary force of the state. These professional groups communicate their opposition to the state through their members, in the name of the principles of their profession.

This double legitimisation—which goes from institutions to individuals, and indirectly from individuals to institutions—leads us to two conclusions. First, Durkheim recalls the collective character of the relation. To maximise and rank a social position, to legitimise it in reciprocity with an institution, is a collective undertaking. Indeed, in order for reciprocity to be a concrete relation closing a configuration of the relation, and for legitimacy to be manifested in practice, the process that goes from the maximisation and ranking of a social position to its legitimisation in a special relation of reciprocity must embed directly or indirectly the collective that has been mobilised in order to support such a process, and not only one or a few actors of this collective. This does not mean that such a process aims for a more or less important change of social position for all the members of this collective. It means that this collective is necessary in order for such a change of social position to be possible for one or a few of these actors.

Second, Durkheim makes clear that institutions count on this leverage effect of reciprocity to single out their positions. This means that for an institution, reciprocity enables it to distinguish itself from other institutions, or even to substitute itself for other institutions in expanding, and therefore in generalising its principles to a greater number of actors, activities and mediations. Substitution is a word that describes how an institution becomes more powerful in society by becoming a more powerful provider of this special relation that we call reciprocity. This is why, *a priori*, every institution is open to each actor and each collective that an actor can mobilise. Everyone can access virtually every institution, an access that is regulated in practice by the contact from one institution to others, and by the actors evolving in fields of activity covered by these other institutions.

Nevertheless, Durkheim's argument has a weak point that originates from his reasoning on secondary groups. If Durkheim places such importance on secondary groups, it is because he believes in the emergence of new corporations that can assign each individual actor to a well-defined position in society[21]—a consequence of his functional view on the division of labour, social differentiation, and social inequalities. This reasoning rests on the idea that corporations are homogeneous professional groups, therefore well separated from each other because they pursue specific professional interests. Because corporations defend specific (professional) interests, they severely limit, if not completely remove, the risk of any conflict between them. Apparently, we are confronted here with what we have seen in our previous chapter about Latour and Bourdieu, namely a logic of alliance stimulated by reciprocity—and even by community—of interests, where the emphasis is on interests rather than on reciprocity. The advantage of Durkheim's concept of secondary groups is that it helps us to understand why reciprocity is subordinated to interests. It is because Durkheim fails to address the problem of what we would call inter-institutional space, and he is not the only one who has such a difficulty—this same difficulty can also be found in Latour's work.

Inter-Institutional Space

As observed in our Chap. 5, Durkheim speaks at length of the division of labour from an intra-professional point of view. In contrast, he says almost nothing about inter-professional relationships and, in general, about relations between different secondary groups. The idea that dominates Durkheim's discourse on secondary groups is one of their functional complementarity, which is based on the evolutionary scheme of the division of labour. As Durkheim says:

> the division of labour...consists in the sharing out of functions that up till then were common to all. But such an allocation cannot be effected according to any preconceived plan. We cannot say beforehand where the line of demarcation is drawn between tasks, once they have been separated. In the nature of things that line is not marked out so self-evidently, but on the contrary depends upon a great number of circumstances. The division must

> therefore come about of itself, and progressively. Consequently, in these conditions for a function to be capable of being shared out in two exactly complementary fractions, as the nature of the division of labour requires, it is indispensable that the two parties specializing should be in constant communication over the whole period that this dissociation is occurring. There is no other way for one part to take over from the other the whole operation that the latter is surrendering, and for them to adapt to each other. (Durkheim 1893b (2013), 216)

The scheme that prevails between institutions in societies driven by organic solidarity is therefore one of coordination between different secondary groups. They do not cease to communicate between one another, in order to ensure both their respective difference and their interdependence (Durkheim 1910 (1975), 285).

Durkheim's argument of the complementarity of functions is based on the idea that contemporary society must fight against the social evil that threatens it, of which one concrete expression is the anomie.[22] Therefore, the responsibility of secondary groups and, beyond, the state, is to regulate society as harmoniously as possible, so that social order is not threatened. However, this presupposes that institutions can clearly see what other institutions intend, which is, for Latour, an unbearable hypothesis.

Indeed, let us take the example of science. When we speak of scientists, we most often think of people with an academic qualification, involved in corresponding institutions that do not aim for economic profit (Latour 1987, 165). However, this representation is misleading. Using the example of scientific activity in the USA, Latour indicates that:

> only 34 per cent of all scientists and engineers in the US were engaged in R & D or managing it but more than 70 per cent of all the scientists and engineers engaged in R & D are working in industry. So, even the tip of the iceberg is not made of what is commonly called 'science'. If we wished to become closer to the cliché of pure disinterested science we would have to consider only doctorate holders employed by universities or other public institutions and doing research, that is limiting technoscience to academics. If we do so, the figures shrink still further. The number of people who most closely resemble what is commonly called 'scientist'—basic research in a non-profit institution—in the US amounts to something like 50,000 (full-time equivalent). This figure is obtained by rolling all the sciences into one. This is not the tip of an iceberg any more, it is the tip of a needle. (ibid.)

If scientific activity is so broadly distributed in society, there are chances that the products of these activities are not visible to all actors and institutions working in the field of science.

Yet, let us add that scientific institutions, scientists and the mediations that they use are all ranked—a feature that does not apply only to science, but to every institution, activity, mediation, and to the actors involved in any field of activity. Then, we understand that these asymmetries modify

> what is called the visibility of a scientist or of a claim. When discussing controversies and dissent, proof race and translations, I have always assumed that each claim and each counter-claim was highly visible and stimulated the debate. This was too favourable a presentation. The vast majority of the claims, of the papers, of the scientists, are simply invisible. No one is taking them up—no one even dissents. It seems that even the beginning of the process has not been triggered off in most cases. (ibid. 166)

In other words, it seems unlikely that even by constantly communicating, by assuming that all conditions are met to support coordination between institutions, these institutions could actually manage to control the development of the division of labour so that it would develop, as Durkheim hopes, as harmoniously as possible. We can even go further and say that the institutions or secondary groups Durkheim refers to do not compulsorily have to devote themselves to this task of coordinating with other institutions. The institution initiates, consecrates and legitimates. It does so in order to expand, and to increase its own legitimacy, i.e. the legitimacy of the hierarchical order that it represents, which is an order of actors, activities and corresponding mediations. To increase its legitimacy means for an institution to extend its principles to more actors, activities and mediations, and this is a process which is *a priori* limitless. In other words, the corollary of institutional legitimacy is the expansion of the institution. In a similar way, Latour says about science that "we should be as undecided as the various actors we follow as to what technoscience is made of; to do so, every time an inside/outside division is built, we should follow the two sides simultaneously, making up a list, no matter how long and heterogeneous, of all those who do the work" (ibid. 176). Here, Latour seems to understand this expansion to stem from the two conditions we have described, namely the mobilisation of actors and the mediations in which the actors invest. Therefore, in order to know to which limit an institution extends, it is sufficient to follow the actors bound to it, i.e. in the example of science, to follow the actors likely to support science in their activities at a given moment in scientific practice.

By following actors, we get a better understanding of their associations, and correspondingly, of institutional expansion. We can observe where and when the established associations break or, instead, why they persist, depending on whether actors support or leave "science". However, Latour's explanation is no more satisfying than Durkheim's views on the ideal coordination between institutions. Indeed, if we recall what Latour's general concept of association assumes, namely that associations develop unceasingly, then it is not possible to know where/when the institutional expansion stops, or where/when it (re)starts. Otherwise, we would have to accept that we can follow, as Latour suggests, all actors involved in the activities and the mediations of exchange that cover an institution. But as Latour himself says, this is actually not possible because it would mean that we are able to identify all actors, all mediations, and all activities involved in scientific practice. Following actors in order to understand institutional expansion remains attached to an ideal, too—namely an ideal understanding of a total network.

Therefore, for both Durkheim and Latour, the same question remains—how does inter-institutional space behave, how does it work? Let us suggest an answer based on our arguments for a sociology through relation. First, let us consider that both institutions and individual actors strive for their self-assertion and, therefore, the assertion of their social position in society. Second, let us consider that for an institution, its self-assertion is characterised by the generalisation of its principles to all possible actors and things that depend on them. Third, let us take into account that there are no well-defined institutional boundaries. In that case, we can say that what is at stake in the inter-institutional space is control, but not the control of this space's boundaries, or of these institutions. It is rather the control of the reciprocity, which institutions and actors establish together. If we remember that reciprocity takes place in an asymmetry between institutions and actors, then we can say that this control comes from the institutions and is subject to legitimisation by the individual actors who, by legitimising it, indirectly legitimise these institutions. Therefore, what is at stake in inter-institutional space is access to this reciprocity, which depends directly on the institutional principles and the forms of institutional control, and indirectly on their legitimisation by individual actors who manage (or don't manage) to appropriate these institutional principles and their related forms of control. This idea of control has not completely escaped either Durkheim's or Latour's attention.

Durkheim mentions the concept of control when he speaks of the role of secondary groups in societies driven by organic solidarity. This control is a form of social control that, according to Durkheim, means surveillance of individual actors in order to prevent anomie (cf. in particular Durkheim 1893b (2013), 233ff.). In these societies, social control can no longer be exerted by individuals because:

> society itself becomes generally more extensive. From then onwards, even the inhabitant of a small town lives less exclusively upon the life of the small group immediately around him...The centre of his life and concerns is no longer to be found wholly in the place where he lives. Thus he takes less interest in his neighbours, because they occupy a more minor place in his life...For all these reasons, the local public opinion weighs less heavily with each one of us, and as public opinion in society generally is not capable of replacing it, because it cannot supervise closely the behaviour of all its citizens, collective surveillance is irrevocably relaxed, the common consciousness loses its authority, and individual variability increases. In short, for social control to be rigorous and for the common consciousness to be maintained, society must be split up into moderately small compartments that completely enclose the individual. (ibid. 235–236)

For Latour, control is exerted when a group recruits actors in order to be sure that the recruited actors become allies who correspond to the expectations of those who enlist them (Latour 1987, 108). The goal of this control is not only to make sure that the new actors in the group follow the older ones. It is also performed in order to anticipate the actions of others, and therefore, to plan programs of action for a set of allies (ibid.). Although Durkheim and Latour have a general understanding of control, they highlight an important element at the heart of control, namely the access that institutions have to actors, activities, and mediations, as well as to everything that may depend on them. This is something that we can observe in Durkheim's work if we do not restrict his concept of control solely to surveillance, i.e. if we consider it in its diversity, such as when Durkheim speaks of initiation. Initiation does not only aim to put the neophyte to the test. It must also move him from one state to another, or in more concrete terms, it must give him access to the group of initiated actors. The ceremonies of consecration show how different operations of control exerted on members of a society at the time of their initiation aim at giving them access to new statutes, and consequently to corresponding new activities and new mediations.

If we relate this idea to what we have seen so far, we can say that control is more fundamentally a set of more or less formal operations intended to secure access to reciprocity as a special relation materialised through the contributions made by institutions and individual actors. Such operations mobilise a large amount of human resources (for example, the staff of an institution) or non-human ones (various instruments and techniques used to perform counselling tasks, planning tasks, to gather or spread information etc.), as Latour shows when he speaks of black boxes or, more generally, of the distribution of scientific activity in society. These resources are the means that an institution mobilises to measure itself, i.e. on the one hand to understand the hierarchy of actors, activities and mediations that it covers, and on the other hand, to be able to extract new prospects and strategies for its own expansion. It is this understanding of control that Latour refers to when he speaks of the effect of "totality" that any institution produces (cf. e.g. Latour 2004, 156). By "totality", Latour means that an institution exists in order to (re)assemble the collective, and this is the cardinal feature, that leads Latour to say that institutions have a positive meaning. Institutions do not exclude, and have no interest in excluding because, otherwise, they would be in danger of losing their position in society. Institutions include all possible actors likely to mobilise other actors working on various mediations of exchange. This extends the relational perspective to the collective and, therefore, increases the chance that there will be reciprocity between these institutions and all possible actors whom these institutions can include. This strategy of inclusion is, therefore, a facet complementary to institutional expansion. However, Latour points out a paradox, because "If others are enrolled they will transform the claims beyond recognition. Thus the very action of involving them is likely to make control more difficult" (Latour 1987, 108). According to Latour, this paradox can only be solved if there is a community of interests between institutions and individual actors. This community of interests can be established if institutional interests can be translated into personal interests, and vice versa. This translation is an operation that Latour calls "the interpretation given by the fact-builders of their interests and that of the people they enrol" (ibid.).

However, Latour's solution does not escape the problems posed by the network's undefined boundaries and by the fact that Latour's translation must be applied to each member of the set (actors, institutions). We illustrated this by using the example that Latour gives about science, which is not confined to actors working in non-profit academic and research institutions only. Therefore, the community of interests also depends on the understanding of a total network. Even if we allow that such a translation would be able to take, directly or indirectly, the interests of every human, non-human and activity related to an institution into account, this would be an extremely long and expensive process not only for the actors, but also for the institutions, and it would weaken their position in society. In order to have this community of interests, the translation of such interests not only requires various means, it also requires time—even if just to communicate on the basis of a more or less shared language. Furthermore, if we understand scientists as Latour does, their interests are likely to evolve rapidly in terms of scientific publications, and regardless of other structural difficulties related, for example, to the renewal of scientific collaborators or the quest for funding that ensures the continuity of the scientific activity etc., all of which make collaborations more or less volatile.

These are obstacles, which indirectly remind us that these translations, as well as the negotiations to which they might lead, collide more or less quickly with institutional constraints, as well as with individual resistance. Therefore, they do not represent the best way for an institution to solve the apparent paradox between inclusion and control that Latour points out. The opposite solution, resting on constraint where community of interests is obtained by social pressure or social control, is closer to Durkheim's understanding of institution-control and actually leads to the same result.

Yet, if we look at inter-institutional space from the perspective proposed so far—sociology through relation—there is no longer any paradox between inclusion and expansion. They represent two ways for an institution to control its own capacity to work out this particular relation of reciprocity at all levels of the hierarchy of actors, activities and mediations that it covers. In other words, inclusion-expansion as well as the forms of control of each institution are determined and transformed depending on the transformations affecting the inclusion-expansion of other institutions, thus, on inter-institutional space. Therefore, inter-institutional space has consequences for the reciprocity that institutions build with actors, as well as for the actors' maximisation and ranking of their social position, i.e. their social trajectory in society.[23] Let us illustrate these ideas of control and inter-institutional space, as well as their consequences for a sociology through relation.

If the institutional forms of control serve the purpose of inclusion of actors and expansion of institutions—if they are open to discussion or negotiation, and if they deliver access to reciprocity—this requires investments and causes corresponding costs on behalf of the institutions, and on behalf of the actors. For the institutions, this means that they, for example, develop recruitment policies, plan the procurement of equipment for performing the activities that the institution covers, adapt infrastructure to equipment and activities, and regulate and diversify their policies. In short, they mobilise a set of human and non-human resources likely to address each stratum of the hierarchy they cover. For the actors, we have seen that they also mobilise human and non-human resources in order to maximise and rank their position in the fields of activities covered by an institution.

Yet, let us recall the asymmetry between institutions and actors. This asymmetry is first due to the institutions providing these forms of control to the actors who have to deal with them in order to build a reciprocity with these institutions. Second, this asymmetry also means that these forms of control are subject to modifications depending on the changes that affect the inter-institutional space, i.e. other institutions, and how the institutions in this space address such changes regarding their current forms of control. Thus, we can conclude that even if these forms of control aim to include all possible actors, they also inevitably affect the way other actors are mobilised with an aim to rank their social position. Or, in other words, if institutions and actors equally contribute to reciprocity, the individual actors are likely to have a better ability to afford the costs related to this undertaking, no matter how successful they are in contributing to reciprocity with an institution. They pay these costs not only for the benefit of a single institution but also for the benefit of the inter-institutional space where the renewal of the institutional forms of control is at stake—and they do so to the detriment of other individual actors whom these actors have mobilised. In each particular configuration that the relation concretely represents, it is about reciprocity first, about closing this configuration to expand the cycles of the relation, to which particular interests are subsumed.

We remember Latour's sad story about Joao Dellacruz, a scientist in Brazil whom we briefly mentioned in the conclusions of Chap. 5 (cf. Latour 1987, 150–153). We want to give it special attention here, because it illustrates a typical case of this relation between inter-institutional space, single institutions and individual actors. At the industrial company where Joao first works with his boss on electronic MOS chips, they were given little attention from colleagues and collaborators of the company, because the chips did not pass industrial controls. These were controls based on industrial standards governing the costs of such chips, their quality, and the quantity of chips to produce for a given price. Thus, Joao leaves the company and joins the university to write a doctoral dissertation under the supervision of his boss. At university, there were other forms of control not subject to the requirements of economic profit, but involving the originality of a project, its reliability, or its robustness to peer testing. Joao is thus supposed to adapt to these new forms of control. But at his university and, more generally, in Brazil, no one is working on MOS chips, which could be regarded as an advantage because—one might think—Joao introduces new challenges and a new scientific field of activity to science. He hopes to mobilise colleagues around him to finally get legitimisation from the university, which would be recognition of his work and of his electronic chips.

However, innovation comes at a price. Since no one is working on these chips, Joao's university does not have the necessary equipment to perform the technical control that these chips require. It is a first hurdle that obstructs Joao's activity. In addition, his boss leaves Brazil and leaves him alone with his thesis. At the same time, his colleagues abroad, who are working on the same type of chip, are much more advanced than he is and therefore have other things to do than to check his work. Latour uses this example to draw two complementary conclusions, which, in our terms, regard the maximisation and the ranking of Joao's social position. Because Joao cannot manage to mobilise actors and mediations, he fails to maximise and rank his social position in the fields of activities regulated by the institutions at which he is successively working (industrial company, university). Exclusion threatens Joao because no one is interested in what he is doing.

If we take the perspective of institutional control, we see that the interest that an actor like Joao could generate has certainly something to do with his ideas, his work on his MOS chips, and his MOS chips themselves. But in the end, Joao has to deal with the forms of control provided by the institutions at which he works and, beyond that, with other activities, other human and non-human actors depending on these forms of control. Let us mention a reverse fictional scenario for making this point clearer,—what if Joao had been successful at his company?

If the company where Joao worked had developed activities in fields where these new MOS chips would have been of interest, then it is likely that Joao would have been able to mobilise a broader group of actors with him, and that he would have passed the industrial controls. Therefore, it is likely that Joao would not have had the idea of going to university in order to write a doctoral dissertation. He most probably would have remained at the company because these controls would have given him a guarantee of reciprocity with the company, and therefore, the possibility to renew a cycle of relation with other (human and non-human) actors, activities, mediations of exchange. Thus, Joao would have been able to reach other levels of the industrial hierarchy and to address other forms of control that would have led him to other challenges. He would have built a career, and his MOS chips would possibly have inspired other institutions—for example universities in Brazil—to invest in such a field. But, as we know, Latour's story does not end that way. Joao goes from one failure to another. Let us examine those failures from the point of view of institutional control in order to highlight the displacement and the related costs that accompany failures such as Joao's.

Joao's failure in the industry causes his displacement from his company to university, which is not only a physical displacement (from one place to another); it also involves Joao changing from one field of activities with known mediations of exchange and known forms of control, to another field of activity—the university—with other mediations of exchange and, correspondingly, new forms of control. This move makes clear that such a displacement presupposes a lot of labour for Joao to eventually get accustomed to these other forms of control, and this labour involves not only matching the costs that Joao has to meet, but also the actors that he was able to mobilise up to then. Do they follow him or not?

In the case of Joao, an important cost was the loss of his supervisor who first followed him, but then left him alone at the university. Despite initial state funding, which allowed Joao to travel to Belgium where the scientific instruments of control were available to Joao for improving his chips, Joao did not succeed in renewing his funding. Moreover, he did not succeed in providing his colleagues with arguments likely to mobilise them around him. His repeated failure led him to lose his own interest in a scientific activity that Joao progressively transforms into a kind of scientific journalism, writing papers no longer for scientific peers, but for the general public. This activity places Joao further away from the scientific forms of controls supported at the university, bringing him to the margin of academic life, thus forcing him to take on private teaching jobs in order to survive. Joao is now alone, trying to attract all possible actors in the hope of closing the successive configurations of the relation that have taken place, in this case, a cycle of repeated failure. Sometimes, Joao imagines closing them by again changing his field of activity, maybe by becoming an entrepreneur. This remains a dream, but if Joao had made it happen, then he would have had to start from the beginning again, with a new configuration of the relation to develop in a new state of inter-institutional space, i.e. within new institutional forms of control.

For the endocrinologist Pierre Kernowicz, another example used by Latour, and whom we have also mentioned in the previous chapter (Latour 1993a, 107–129), the story is quite different. Travelling from the USA to France, Pierre hopes to bring his knowledge to French scientific institutions. But he quickly understands that these institutions do not provide him with forms of control that are suitable for his activity. Pierre understands that the problem comes from inter-institutional space. The inter-institutional space in which French scientific institutions evolve is a more conservative one, where forms of control do not recur as quickly as in US inter-institutional space. This difference is reflected in the positions and roles assigned to the scientists and, more generally, in the strong hierarchy of French scientific institutions, the corresponding activities and mediations at each level of this hierarchy, etc. It makes it difficult to develop cycles of the relation at a relatively sustained pace. Compared to US research laboratories where Pierre has been educated, in France, Pierre would have to stay longer in positions in the institutional hierarchy in which he cannot imagine developing his scientific activity in a satisfactory way. Pierre can reflect on his position in France because he has the experience of another inter-institutional space whose principles he has internalised, and which he can compare with what he sees in France. This motivates him to leave France and to fly back to the USA. There, Pierre works at a scientific institution where it is less difficult to develop these cycles of the relation that increase his chances of successfully validating the original endocrinology solution he proposes, which eventually happens. Pierre becomes a famous scientist in his field of activities, he manages to mobilise many actors around him, and he takes advantage of the leverage effect of this mobilisation, which leads him to collaborate with further scientific institutions in the USA and in the world. Pierre builds a career, and this career depended on his transition from one inter-institutional space to another, as well as from one institution to another and, correspondingly, from one field of activities with its actors and mediations to other ones.

Yet, we have to make one last observation that we can make based on these examples of the relation between the forms of institutional control and inter-institutional space. This last observation concerns the role of the state that, as we have seen implicitly in the stories of Joao and Pierre, does not represent an exception to the rule of inclusion–expansion. Indeed, the state is not above, and does not behave differently than, other institutions. It is neither a coordinator of secondary groups, as Durkheim says, nor a special mobilising power that should strengthen the collective, as Latour thinks. The state is nothing more than another institution, which has its peculiarities and powers, its means of contributing to reciprocity with actors and, therefore, its own forms of control. This certainly does not mean that all states are the same. Depending on the country, the state can have more influence and power or less, because the inclusion–expansion of the economy, religion, organised crime, or foreign states is more powerful. Therefore, not all institutions are equally equipped to survive in inter-institutional space, all the more so as there are several inter-institutional spaces that are more or less interconnected. Paying attention to the inter-institutional space enables us to understand the general challenge related to the extension of a relational perspective to the collective from the view-point of an institution. Inter-institutional space gives institutions the power to shape society through the control they apply to actors, their activities and mediations of exchange. In the words of Latour, inter-institutional space represents for any institution the possibility of becoming the compulsory point of passage for any possible actors, activities or mediations. It represents an opportunity for each institution to include more actors, activities, mediations, to take up more space in inter-institutional space and to become, if not the unique vector of social tantalisation, at least the major provider of reciprocity in society. This is what is at stake inside inter-institutional space, and this is what should be taken into account when we want to understand the consequences of the configurations of the relation and their cyclic extension in society.

Conclusion

There are important differences between Durkheim and Latour, but their similarities are equally important. In this chapter, we first indirectly discussed both by examining Latour's use of Gabriel Tarde for his critique of Durkheim. We have underlined that for Latour, Durkheim's views on society and on the social have nothing to do with Tarde's views. However, we have also seen that the differences between Durkheim and Tarde are not as great as Latour suggests. One of our most important examples was that

Durkheim, like Tarde, uses a concept of association that allows him to develop an idea of attachment that is close to Latour's concept of attachment. The cardinal difference between Latour and Durkheim comes from the fact that, for Durkheim, attachment presupposes reciprocity, while according to Latour, attachment does not presuppose anything other than associations. However, because his concept of association remains general, Latour encounters difficulties at both a conceptual and a methodological level. Associations include attachments as well as detachments, which makes it difficult to know what we are talking about when we speak of association. To be more accurate, it would be necessary to know where associations stop, or what stops them. In Latour's sociology, this is a difficult task because it means that we must be able to take not one or two actors in a given association into account, but all actors likely to stand in the same associative spectrum, in the same network of associations.

If we take the example of science, we immediately understand—and Latour shows it well—that we are dealing with a very large quantity of actors, activities and mediations that largely exceed what can be commonly called science, i.e. the disinterested activities of researchers at non-profit academic and research institutions. By his view on reciprocal attachment, Durkheim offers a way to address this problem by making reciprocity the turning point of a cycle of the relation or, in the terms of Latour, the point where associations stop and can re-start. For Durkheim, as in the works of the other authors we have discussed in this book, reciprocity is not the mould of all social relations and it is not the framework of all possible associations. It is, instead, a special relation that makes closure of a cycle of the relation possible. It presupposes the consecration of the actors by institutions—in the case of Durkheim, these institutions are secondary groups, particularly professional groups. This reciprocity develops in the framework of an asymmetry—the institution consecrates individual actors directly, while individual actors can only indirectly legitimise an institution. We have seen that this reasoning does not appear in the foreground of Durkheim's analyses, which instead rest heavily on the theory of personal and social consciousness. It rather is an exploratory attempt to explain the relations between individuals and society based on the role of secondary groups, as well as on the state as a dominating type of group. Nevertheless, these secondary groups have a decisive importance in Durkheim's discourse on reciprocity, particularly when it comes to the examination of consecrations, which—beyond the question of the legitimisation between actors and institutions—enable Durkheim to underline a generalisation of the institutional principles towards actors, mediations, and activities in society. This is the root of what we have called institutional expansion, which for Durkheim remains subject to the ideal of a harmoniously coordinated society by the action of new corporations. These corporations do not exist in modern societies, but Durkheim hopes that they will be formed in order to offer each actor his rightful place in society. This process should be coordinated by the state, to which the corporation should represent a counter-power. This ideal tends to make Durkheim move the concept of reciprocity to the background of his reasoning, and to prefer the idea of shared common interests as the stabiliser of relations between actors and these new corporations—an argument shared by Latour. We have suggested that both authors do not come to the conclusion by accident but instead because their understanding of shared common interests presupposes a concept of control.

According to Latour, to control means to build a community of interests. Actors looking for alliances with other actors want guarantees that these alliances will hold, and that they will enable them to carry out their projects. According to Durkheim, control is the way in which secondary groups strengthen the coordination of their members and, further, their coordination with other secondary groups, which, in turn, strengthen their power against the state. In both cases, control should secure social cohesion. However, Latour's and Durkheim's views on control do not enable us to understand how control and legitimisation between institutions and actors work in the general framework of institutional expansion. Indeed, there seems to be a paradox. Latour mentions this when he says that the more an institution expands—i.e. the more it includes actors, mediations and activities—the less it keeps control over them and, therefore, over itself. Latour's solution to this paradox, i.e. to say that the interests of individual actors and institutions must be translated into one another, is not reliable because it assumes that we can mobilise both individual and corporate actors to get involved in this translation process. Durkheim's solution, drawn from his sociologism, does not provide a reliable solution either, because it assumes that the community of interests rests on the conformity of actors with institutional principles, or on the actors' subordination to these principles. Instead, if we focus on reciprocity rather than on these shared interests, the paradox disappears. This allows us to give a more precise definition of control as control of the access to reciprocity that institutions and actors contribute.

Control takes multiple forms, depending on the contexts of the legitimisation between institutions and individual actors. By using the examples that Latour provides in his work, we have explained and illustrated why these forms of control should not be examined in isolation but in relation to what we have called inter-institutional space—the space of expansion of institutions in which forms of control are renewed. Therefore, these forms of control have to be understood in relation to the changes affecting this space, which affect not only the expansion of the institutions in this space, but also actors' life courses. Taking the asymmetry between inter-institutional space-institutions and individual actors into account, we have said that individual actors pay the costs of their involvement in reciprocity with institutions always to the benefit of the institutions but, however, often to the detriment of many actors who had been mobilised in the process. However, this does not mean that institutional forms of control exclude those individual actors—on the contrary, they are open to them. This is consistent with the aim of institutions, which, in order to expand, have to include all possible actors in their fields of activities, and everyone/everything depending on them. Therefore, at the level of individual actors, such control may benefit them in the sense that it may give them the possibility to mobilise other actors for working out the maximisation and ranking of their social position.

We have seen this best in Latour's example of Pierre Kernowicz. However, as Latour demonstrates in his story about Joao Dellacruz, forms of control can also prevent actors from making progress in their social careers; they can even make them quit an institutional space, which puts them in a situation where they have to start a cycle of relation over again. If these examples provide illustrations that make us understand the consequences of institutional forms of control for individual actors, what about the institutions? We have said earlier that what is at stake in the renewal of forms of control and further in the renewal of the institutional logic of inclusion-expansion, is a dominating position in inter-institutional space. For an institution, domination means to include more actors, fields of activities and mediations than other institutions in order to become the major provider of reciprocity in society. In this regard, the state is not an exception—it is an institution like any other, contrary to Durkheim's view on the state as a super-authority dominating other institutions. Therefore, the state has to include and expand like other institutions in order to dominate in inter-institutional space, and to have a corresponding impact on the forms of control of other institutions, as well as on their renewal in inter-institutional space. We next turn to the conclusions that we can draw from our comparison of these French sociologists.

Notes

1. One might think that Latour bypasses the problem that we discussed in our previous chapter concerning legitimacy when he makes individual and corporate actors into collective actors. Indeed, in assimilating individual as well as corporate actors to collective actors, there is no way of knowing whether the distribution of legitimacy in the network rests on interpersonal relationships or, instead, on institutions. However, there is an ambiguity in Latour's discourse because he nevertheless distinguishes interpersonal relations from those between individual and corporate actors. He does not make this distinction by accident. The distinction rests in the principles of *ANT*, which postulates a gradual distinction between the micro-sociological level, where Latour sees little to no associations, and the macro-sociological level, where we find numerous associations.
2. This is not the opinion of Laurent Mucchielli's, who thinks that Latour misunderstands Tarde and that he takes the concept of association in order to give it a meaning that Tarde does not give it in his work (Mucchielli 2004, 53–60).
3. In this last quote, Latour refers to Durkheim by using the expression "the social could explain the social"—or, in the terms of Durkheim, "the social as such must be explained by the social" (Durkheim 1906 (1975), 57).
4. See e.g. Clark 1972, 152–186; Besnard 1987, 136ff.; Fournier 2007; Steiner 2011.
5. This quote refers to Durkheim's conference as well as to his public debate with Tarde after the conference, where Tarde used the expression to speak of Durkheim's sociology. We also find the expression in Tarde's *Logique sociale* (Tarde 1898b, VIII).
6. This has often been described as the "German crisis of the French thought" (cf. e.g. Digeon 1959; Lukes 1973, 41 note 15; Chamboredon 1984, 517 note 71; Feuerhahn 2014, 81). It is characterised by a controversy initiated by the Belgian philosopher Simon Deploige, debated in the *Revue Néo-Scholastique de Philosophie* from 1905 to 1909, later published as a book (Deploige 1911). According to Deploige, Durkheim's sociology is not original work because Durkheim takes everything from German intellectuals.
7. Durkheim writes reviews on them, and corresponds with them (Feuerhahn 2014, 79–98). Therefore, it is not exaggerated to speak of a debate between Durkheim and these authors. Regarding this debate, see Gane (1984, 305), Watts Miller (1996, 31–42) and Steiner (2011).
8. The text that Simmel published in the first volume of *L'Année sociologique* is entitled "Comment les formes sociales se maintiennent" (Simmel 2002, 66–106). On the conditions that led to the production of the text includ-

ing the roles of intermediaries played by Xavier Léon and Célestin Bouglé in the exchanges between Simmel and Durkheim, see Simmel (2002, 382–401).

9. For a contextualization of the relations and conflicts between Durkheim and Simmel, see, for example, Mestrovic (1994) and Rammstedt (1999, 139–162).
10. The abstract and general character of the definition of social facts has often been commented on in secondary literature (e.g. Borlandi 1995, 140–144; Besnard 2003, 66–69; Paoletti 2012b, 221 note 1).
11. Paoletti says that Durkheim's concept of association enabled him to stabilise his views on society as well as on the social, which Durkheim both understands as realities that are external to individuals (Paoletti 2012, 221; cf. also Alexander 1982, 470; Prendergast 1990, 316–333). Watts Miller also sees in Durkheim's concept of association Durkheim's hope to "find ways…to develop and renew the 'spirit of association' itself" (Watts Miller 1996, 153).
12. In the French original, Durkheim does not say "domination", but "subordination": "si le vaincu peut se résigner pour un temps à une subordination qu'il est contraint de subir, il ne la consent pas, et, par conséquent, elle ne saurait constituer un équilibre stable. Des trêves imposées par la violence ne sont jamais que provisoires et ne pacifient pas les esprits. Les passions humaines ne s'arrêtent que devant une puissance morale qu'elles respectent" (Durkheim 1893a (1922), III).
13. Cf. Lindemann (2011, 93–110) for a similar observation.
14. We quote from the French original again in order to underline Durkheim's usage of the semantic of attachment: "bien loin que l'individu ne puisse s'attacher à la société sans abdication totale ou partielle de sa nature propre, il n'est vraiment lui-même, il ne réalise pleinement sa nature qu'à condition de s'y attacher" (Durkheim 1902–1903 (1925), 77).
15. In the French original, Durkheim does not say "solid link", but instead "le lien de solidarité qui unit la cause à l'effet a un caractère de réciprocité qui n'a pas été assez reconnu" (Durkheim 1895 (1919) 118).
16. We see here the difference between Tarde's quantitative concept of desire, and Durkheim's relational one (cf. also Paoletti 2012, 258ff.).
17. Filloux has clearly highlighted the influence of Montesquieu on Durkheim's views regarding the relations between individuals, secondary groups and the state (Filloux 1977, 239ff.; cf. also Fournier 2007, 454–456).
18. For example, Latour says, "I belong to a field, science studies, which has been working hard to give a positive meaning to the term 'scientific institution'" (Latour 2013, 4; cf. also Latour 2004, 267 note 12).
19. Under the influence of his collaborators at *L'Année sociologique*, Durkheim begins in 1898 to progressively replace his concept of communion with the

concept of consecration (Fournier 2007, 396–397). This concept of consecration will evolve to the concept of communication that Mauss and Hubert use in their discourse on sacrifice (cf. Chap. 3).

20. As Durkheim says, "Just as society consecrates men, so it also consecrates things" (Durkheim 1912 (1995), 215).
21. On this point, see for example Spitz and Surkis (Spitz 2005, 339ff.; Surkis 2011, 142f.).
22. On Durkheim's views on social evil—the pathology of the social bond—see Paoletti (2008, 63–80).
23. In other words, control presupposes that we might not be able to control everything, and this is what makes institutional expansion, the corresponding inclusion of actors, their legitimacy, and their social positions vary. Latour underlines this point in his entire work, as does Durkheim (including in his *Suicide*).

CHAPTER 7

Conclusion: The Prospect of a Sociological Theory Through Relation

In order to draw a conclusion, we must first summarise the results of the comparisons between the French sociologists portrayed in this book. We then formulate six propositions, drawn from these results, which structure and synthetise the theoretical framework of the sociology through relation introduced in this book.

Having begun with questions of solidarity and social cohesion as seen in the work of Émile Durkheim and Gaston Richard, we did not choose these authors and topics by chance. We chose them because, in French sociology, the work of both authors probably illustrates the best first attempts of stimulating a debate within the Durkheim school about a sociological theory centred on relation. Their starting point was a macro-sociological perspective on old and new forms of corporations in society. According to Durkheim, corporations played a key role in history in the sense that they led to a society driven by organic solidarity. Corporations contributed massively to the functional progress of society. They delivered a scheme of organisation in which society should be organised along the actors' skills and their professional interests. Durkheim sees this type of organisation as the condition required to preserve the social cohesion of contemporary societies, solidarity, and in general, the relation between actors.

Richard, on the contrary, sees in corporations a traditional lifestyle that confines individuals and societies to inherited habits that should be criticised rather than be blindly adopted if one aims to develop new forms

C. Papilloud, *Sociology through Relation*, Palgrave Studies in Relational Sociology, https://doi.org/10.1007/978-3-319-65073-9_7

of social relations. The difference between the two authors is based in professional ethics. According to Durkheim, because corporations and, more generally, secondary groups distribute actors into corresponding professions according to their skills, they foster the harmonious coordination of actors in society. Richard regards this understanding of professions as idealistic. First, Durkheim's view on corporations implies that actors smoothly obey society, which is impossible for Richard. Second, no such harmonious coordination of corporations can be found in the professional world. Instead, there is fierce competition between corporations in the labour market, which threatens cooperation between professional groups and, more generally, secondary groups in society, as well as between the actors whom they include. Therefore, Richard asks, how do we obtain a better link between these groups and actors in society?

A social contract, as formulated by Rousseau, is not the solution—on this point, Richard and Durkheim agree. Nevertheless, the idea of the contract remains important for the question of relations in modern society, both for Richard and for Durkheim, if, however, for different reasons. In Durkheim, contracts foster agreements between individuals, and they contribute to reproducing them as social groups—as corporations in societies driven by mechanical solidarity do. For Richard, however, the contract is, above all, a formal and legal relation between actors. It gives them rights, obligations, and therefore, a specific status, i.e. an exclusivity that partially protects them from the influence of professional and secondary groups, as well as from the state.

This difference between Durkheim and Richard is reflected in the concept of obligation that provides the basis for any contract and cooperation between individual actors and professional/secondary groups. Durkheim understands obligation as an individual desire of society. For Richard, obligation presupposes reciprocity. It goes from individuals to secondary groups, state and society, as well as from society and its institutions to individuals. Both, individual actors and societies, take part in the development of one another because both of them want to materialise the ideal of a rational society. Does this mean that, for Richard, reciprocity makes individual actors and societies equal in their capacity to support the social bond? We have seen that this is not the case.

Indeed, despite his ideal of a rational society—a society entirely regulated by law—Richard does not think that reciprocity removes the asymmetry between individual actors, society and its institutions. The asymmetry remains, even if it is less compelling than the asymmetry that

Durkheim—referring to his sociologism—implies when he claims that individual actors are subjected to society. According to Richard, the asymmetry exists because there is resistance from individual actors to their society, as well as from society to its individual actors. Richard is not the only one to use this concept, rendering the question of what this resistance means even more prominent. Indeed, we also find the idea of resistance in the work of Durkheim's nephew, Marcel Mauss. Thus, in order to know more about resistance, we extended our comparison between Richard and Durkheim to that of Richard and Mauss.

The starting point of this second comparison was sacrifice and its link to the law. According to Richard and Mauss, these two topics go hand in hand, and they enable us to examine whether the law—particularly criminal law—has a religious origin. This would enable us to understand the relation between religion and society. To Mauss, this is the natural extension of the scientific program that Durkheim attempts to deliver to sociology. To Richard, it is the critical question at the foundation of his own views on solidarity and the relation. In their analyses of sacrifice, both Richard and Mauss show that it contains legal and religious elements, but that there are no strong relations between them. Legal elements even tend to be separated from religious ones while the objects of the sacrifice are transformed, as for example when they become symbols of something else—animals, human beings or gods. Subsequently, sacrifice as a religious practice is gradually distinguished from legal practices. The penalty, as one of the important legal elements of sacrifice, follows the same evolution, and Richard and Mauss use it to explain how the relations between sacrifice, contract and debt in the history of past and present societies evolved.

Like sacrifice, penalty expresses different types of contact between individuals and societies, which find their concrete manifestation in individual and collective expressions of pain. Pain is not only an individual reaction to the transgression of personal integrity. According to Richard and Mauss, pain warns individual actors and society that they are in danger of losing their contact. Richard and Mauss see this concept of pain as the manifestation of inhibition, a fundamental act of human conduct, the manifestations of which, such as waiting, withdrawal, modesty, disengagement, etc., are all reactions to the relation in its most elementary concrete form as contact between individual actors, as well as between individual actors and societies.

Contact can be described as this very moment at which the encoding of practices sets in, intended to develop the perspective of the relation in the collective, which for Richard and Mauss means to orientate social practices towards a possible reciprocity. This is a time at which individual actors are confronted with the conventions and social rules of institutions in society and, by extension, with society itself and its sanctioning power. Contact is the context in which resistance takes place, as both Richard and Mauss emphasise, but they do not give it the same meaning. Mauss speaks of resistance of collective habits on behalf of individual actors. Contrary to Mauss, Richard conceives of resistance as what causes individual actors never to be adjusted to social rules and conventions. Even if we assumed individual actors' unconditional obedience to social rules and their willingness to conform to society, the fundamental mismatch between individual actors and societies would remain. This mismatch has nothing to do with any substantial or functional incompatibility between individual actors and society, but with their incompatible positions in respect to contact. Position is of prior importance to the individual, which is reflected in a negative way by inhibition, suggesting that individual actors care about how they relate to a position in contact to other actors, and more generally, they care about the contact itself. Position is only of secondary importance for society and its institutions, whose priority challenge is their duration, to which their position in the contact as well as in the social space is subjected. Mauss is not completely insensitive to this argument, which leads him to relativise Durkheim's sociological framework and to take the resistance of individual actors to collective habits into account. We see this best in his essay, *The Gift* (1925), in which Mauss extends his reasoning on sacrifices and magic towards an approach of society through relation based on considerations of contact between actors and how they position themselves, in such contact, to other actors. His contribution inspired Pierre Bourdieu, who undertook a similar project, and who took advantage of Mauss' analysis of the gift in order to develop his own relational sociology.

According to Bourdieu, Mauss claims that gifts are gratuitous and disinterested exchanges. This is illusory, however. Gifts actually conceal the strategies and calculations of individual actors and, therefore, do not enable us to understand how they influence social practices. In his attempt to reanimate Mauss' views on the gift in current sociology, Alain Caillé criticises Bourdieu's interpretation of the gift, which he sees as nothing other than a sort of political economy of social practices. According to Caillé, Bourdieu sees social actors as egoistic and rational calculators seeking to maximise their profit in their own interest. Although individual interests are certainly part of social life for Caillé, Mauss enables us to understand (contrary to Bourdieu) that interests imply above all an interest in others and in the relation to others. The same idea can actually be found in Bourdieu's work as well, if, in the expression "profit maximisation", we emphasise maximisation rather than profit. In respect to maximisation, Bourdieu and Mauss are close to each other.

For both, maximisation refers to the assertion of actors' social position through the mobilisation of a large number of other actors and activities on mediations of exchange. Bourdieu speaks of the maximisation of habitus and the classification thereof in relation to other habitus. Similarly, Mauss observes in his *Gift* that maximisation means that actors move from the position in which they give presents, to that in which they receive them, and eventually to that in which they return presents. These three positions are the three moments of affirmation for actors and their classification in society. This classification always presupposes a hierarchy of social positions for both Bourdieu and Mauss. Nevertheless, there is an important difference between them at exactly this last point. While Bourdieu sees this hierarchical classification or ranking of social positions as driven by habitus, Mauss sees such ranking as driven by gift exchanges.

Gift exchanges produce the three social positions of the gift (to give, receive and return) that the actors adopt in the course of their mobilisation. Bourdieu's reasoning assumes that there is a power relationship between these habitus, a given dynamic of struggle present in all fields of activities in society. The institutions of each field rule those dynamics and impose them on the habitus in order to preserve the interests of the dominant classes in each field. Mauss' reasoning assumes a cycle of gift exchanges that actors extend to more actors, mediations of exchange and activities. Thus, the actors create alliances that benefit the renewal of social hierarchy and, consequently, the renewal of social positions in this hierarchy.

Thus, Bourdieu and Mauss present two different views of social hierarchy. For Bourdieu, social hierarchy can only be reproduced such as it is. It is a set of well-ordered social positions that do not change over time, and attract the same set of habitus and their corresponding social classes. Mauss, on the contrary, thinks that a social hierarchy can only be maintained if it—and all actors depending on it—commit to gift exchanges. At the same time, this collective commitment puts the collective itself into question, which contributes to its (more or less important) renewal. This renewal of social positions is the only way for a hierarchy to preserve its social cohesion over time. Therefore, if the mobilisation of actors is a necessary condition for social hierarchies to be renewed and preserved, it still needs the commitment of actors, i.e. their activity on and with material as well as immaterial mediations of exchange. However, this is the weak point in Mauss' *Gift*. Mauss certainly speaks of the importance of the mediations of exchange and of the labour of actors on and with them. But his reasoning on these matters remains only loosely connected to his views on gift exchanges. In French sociology, Mauss is not an exception. Indeed, there are only very few relational attempts that take this question of mediations seriously into account, the best known probably being Bruno Latour's sociology, which embeds a critique of Bourdieu's sociology. This extends the path of the debate about relation in French sociology from the comparison between Bourdieu and Mauss to the comparison between Bourdieu and Latour.

Both authors share the idea that social actors work on and with the mediations circulating in society, and that these activities include a technical dimension of actors' skills, as well as a symbolic dimension of actors' authority. Nevertheless, Bourdieu and Latour have a different understanding of these two dimensions. According to Bourdieu, the symbolic outweighs the technical dimension in actors' activities, and it strengthens the maximisation of their social position. In Latour, the symbolic only extends the technical dimension while both are needed in order for actors to maximise their social position, i.e. to gain credibility. This difference recalls the distinct way in which Bourdieu and Latour speak of the frame of reference of mediations, namely institutions.

If Bourdieu and Latour agree on the role of institutions that provide mediations of exchange in society, they differ as to the meaning of the link between mediations and institutions. For Bourdieu, institutions extend the dynamics of the fields in which they take place, and they must ensure that the symbolic dimension of the actors' labour with and on mediations outweighs its technical dimension. Therefore, the institution is the place *par excellence* of social control exerted on the actors' labour. For Latour, institutions guarantee the heterogeneity of social practices, preserving the emergence of potential novelties in society. Thus, these institutions drive the constant deployment of associations, the renewal of mediations in the areas of activities that they regulate, and their own duration and authority over time.

Despite this difference, Bourdieu and Latour come to the same conclusion—institutions create social inequality, no matter how they operate. Bourdieu describes this in clear terms, saying that because institutions exert social control on the actors' investments in the mediations of their exchanges, they develop principles of social division that favour some actors (those adapted to the forms of institutional control) to the detriment of others (those failing to adapt to these forms). Actors who successfully pass the institutional controls are those that invest the most in institutions. As institutions support the interests of the dominants classes, these actors are, unsurprisingly, the members of the dominant classes.

Bourdieu's theory of different forms of capital, which summarises his views on the mediations of exchange, underlines the strength of this logic. Actors can work on the volume and structure of the forms of capital inherited from their social class. But the conversions that they realise over the course of their lives remain dependent upon the logic of the field in which they behave, and its institutional controls. Therefore, actors' investments in mediations of exchange do not change the structure of social inequalities, and they do not influence the legitimisation of actors by institutions or, ultimately, by the state. We have observed that this asymmetrical understanding of relation as power relation leads to a difficulty.

Indeed, such an understanding assumes that actors' social careers have no chance to be structurally improved. Therefore, it is difficult to take for granted, as Bourdieu does, that social actors are constantly struggling in social fields, mobilising other actors and mediations in order to improve or, at least, preserve their social position. For Latour, social inequality is a by-product of the lifespan of institutions, passing from one cycle of associations to others, producing black boxes and closing them. These black boxes are forms of access to what it is and what it does that an institution provides. But at the same time, they are its best shields against any questions or doubts expressed by individual or other corporate actors.

As Latour shows, institutions are therefore in a difficult position. On the one hand, they have to preserve themselves, but in order to do so, they also have to remain attractive. They must constantly stimulate associations with heterogeneous elements, and they must therefore remain open to every possible question or doubt coming from actors who are internal or active in one of the domains of activities that they regulate, or else are external. For Latour, this makes it difficult to know where legitimisation of social positions maximised and ranked by actors comes from. Does it come from the institution, despite the actors' labour on and with non-humans? Does it come from the individual actors whose labour would then support or even improve the maximisation and ranking of their social position?

For Bourdieu, his unilateral understanding of legitimisation and power makes him answer the question in the same unilateral way. Legitimisation comes from institutions, and it goes to actors sharing the same interests as these institutions. For Latour, such an answer is unbearable because in society, even the strongest unilateral actions rest on associations. This is why legitimisation has to be understood from the point of view of associations between humans and non-humans. In other words, legitimisation means another form of association, which is the foundation of what Bourdieu calls the community of interests shared by humans and non-humans in such associations.

However, Latour's answer leads to another difficulty because everyone does associate—institutions, humans, non-humans and the state. Therefore, is the concept of association not too broad to provide a non-ambiguous answer to the question of legitimisation? Latour tries to address this difficulty by using another concept—attachment—for stabilising his concept of association and for making it more specific. In this context, Latour refers to Gabriel Tarde in order to clarify the link between association and attachment and to contrast his sociology with the French tradition, particularly the Durkheim School of sociology. In referring to Tarde, Latour makes clear that his own a-sociology has little, if anything, to do with the French sociological school, suggesting that his sociology of association breaks away from the path of the debate described in this book. But is this the case? This leads us to a comparison between Latour and Durkheim.

First, we wanted to know if there actually is such an immeasurable distance between them both. Second, we wanted to take a deeper look into the question of legitimisation between individual actors and institutions. For Latour, this question refers to the link between association and attachment and, further, to the way in which Latour uses and interprets Tarde in this context. We noticed that Latour favours Tarde's general definition of association—everyone and everything does associate—without taking the various meanings that association has in Tarde's work into account. Moreover, Latour uses this general understanding of association to propose an interpretation of the well-known conflict between Durkheim and Tarde, saying that this conflict has focused on the definition of the social and, by extension, of society. According to Latour, Tarde offers a flexible definition of society as a set of associations. Latour prefers this rather than what he refers to as Durkheim's ostensive definition of the social and society, i.e. Durkheim sociologism.

Nevertheless, Durkheim also provides a concept of association that builds the foundation of his general definition of the social. Moreover, Durkheim admits that this definition remains general, i.e. the social can be understood in other ways and is open to interpretation. This means that Durkheim's and Tarde's attempts to define association and the social are not so very different. This lack of difference enables us to understand what is at stake in the conflict between Durkheim and Tarde, which is less the definition of the social itself than it is sociology as a scientific discipline. In addition, we have observed that Tarde does not give the concept of attachment a major role in his social psychology of associations, while for Durkheim, attachment leads to the notion of reciprocal attachment between individual actors, social groups and society. Durkheim's concept of reciprocal attachment is at the centre of his discourse on the link between humans, non-humans—the elements of social morphology that make this reciprocal attachment vary—and institutions (the most important, for Durkheim, being family, secondary and professional groups, and the state). Durkheim even extends his concept of reciprocal attachment to the desirability of society. In conformity with his theory of the duality of individual consciousness, he first places this desire into individual actors. But his analysis of secondary groups leads Durkheim to move the anchor of desirability from individual consciousness to reciprocity.

Far from saying that reciprocity is the original mould of all social relations, Durkheim indicates that reciprocity is a special concrete relation taking place in the asymmetry between individual actors and institutions in society. As the name indicates, this reciprocal relation is not unilaterally imposed on individual actors by institutions, even if there is an asymmetry, i.e. even if institutions remain superior to the individual actors. This last point is particularly important for Durkheim because, despite his sociologism, Durkheim does not believe that individuals blindly obey their society. The institutions of society must be recognised and legitimised by individual actors in order to be valued as legitimate institutions. Consecration, as an operation by which the institution initiates individual actors to its principles, does not only apply to individual actors. It must also extend to the collective of humans and non-humans that these actors have mobilised to maximise and rank their social position, therefore to their mediations and activities. Otherwise, there is no reciprocity, and therefore neither a closure of the configuration that the relation concretely represents in practice, nor of its cycles in time, nor a diversification of the actors' activities on and with the mediations of their exchanges, nor a diversification of these mediations.

We find a similar observation in Latour, suggesting that Durkheim and Latour agree on the positive role of institutions in society. If institutions have a positive role, this is because they foster reciprocity, or a community of interests in society, either with other institutions, or with individual actors. This reciprocity, or community of interests, recalls the difficulties in relation to the concept of interest as seen in our comparison of Mauss and Bourdieu, and of Bourdieu and Latour. We summarised these difficulties by saying that the authors subordinate reciprocity to the interests of individuals and institutions. The comparison between Durkheim and Latour has given us a better understanding of the reason for such subordination, which fails to pay attention to inter-institutional space.

Indeed, Durkheim takes this kind of ideal view on institutions which harmoniously coordinate themselves and everything depending on them in order to guarantee a homogeneous division of social functions. Latour criticises this view because it would mean that institutions would be totally transparent and open to society. According to Latour, this hypothesis is open to being challenged. Institutions are no well-defined entities—it is difficult to understand how far they extend and, therefore, it is difficult to have an exhaustive representation of the actors, mediations and activities belonging to them. However, the same argument applies to Latour's own understating of the community of interests. Because if these institutions are not transparent—neither to other institutions, nor to the individual actors in society, nor to themselves, then there is little chance that they can succeed in building a community or a reciprocity of interests with actors or with other institutions. This does not only mean that an asymmetry between institutions and individual actors in society remains. It also means that more than the interests of the actors and institutions, reciprocity itself is at stake, access to which is subjected to forms of control defined and renewed in inter-institutional space. The question of legitimisation becomes more complex than it previously appeared. It presupposes inter-institutional space, which determines not only the definition of these forms of control, but also their modifications, as well as the liberty and flexibility that institutions have at their disposal to choose and to apply in order to legitimise individual actors. This process is, in turn, indirectly legitimised by these actors, depending on how successful they are in encoding their practices in these forms of control, and in applying these forms of control to the mediations and activities in their daily life.

This understanding of inter-institutional space enables us to answer the question of reciprocity. As Durkheim suggests—though without going into more depth—if reciprocity is a special relationship closing the cycles of the relation, this is because it takes place in the asymmetry between institutions and individual actors, and not between institutions, or between individual actors. This means that reciprocity and legitimisation go hand in hand in the cycles of relation, which explains why we only find them where and when the configuration of the relation comes to a closure.

Now that we have recalled the steps of our argument, let us come to the transverse results about relation as a perspective in sociology accumulated throughout the book. From the beginning to the end of this book, we have seen that we can describe what relation means by using a bottom-up approach, i.e. by reasoning from the viewpoint of the individual actors, and by observing the leverage effects of the cycles of relation for those actors and for that which depends on them (other actors, activities, mediations). Yet, each of our comparisons has enabled us to emphasise that such a bottom-up approach of relation only makes sense in a framework of a top-down approach of relation, i.e. an approach moving from institutions to actors. This should make us bear in mind that relation cannot be reduced to concrete social relationships only, a statement that we can break down into three rules.

First, relation is not "at hand", so to speak, everywhere and at every time. Second, even if there are concrete relationships, this does not mean that there is relation. And third, even if there is no concrete relationship, this does not mean that there is no relation. This, on the other hand, should also make clear that debates about relation as a structuring phenomenon in society do not lead to an either "yes", or a "no" answer. Rather, we should first understand which specific configuration and which transition from one configuration to other ones—i.e. which cycles of relation become structuring phenomena in society, and what consequences they happen to have in society.

In our comparisons, we have provided a way to address these questions by using reciprocity. Reciprocity as a special concrete relationship is not given in advance, but instead, it depends upon forms of control coming from inter-institutional space, taken up and applied by institutions to individual actors, their mediations and activities. These forms of control are used by actors, who indirectly determine the legitimisation of such forms of control, in many ways. Legitimisation extends to the corresponding institutions, their inclusion-expansion in inter-institutional space and to that which depends on it, namely future forms of control. This is what, in our view, makes relation a macro-sociological perspective in sociology, which should enable to understand sociological problems from the top to the bottom. Let us repeat this in clear terms in order to avoid misunderstandings, because it is an important point. We are not saying that bottom-up approaches to relation have to be thrown out of the sociological window in favour of an exclusively top-down approach to relation. On the contrary, we are saying that such bottom-up approaches are useful if their descriptions incorporate a top-down understanding of the asymmetrical context in which actors try to give their cycles of relation a structural strength in society.

We have to say a last word about the asymmetry between institutions and individual actors. In our comparisons, we have seen that we often deal with conflicting views on what asymmetry means. Sometimes, it is thought of as a subjection of individual actors to the sanctioning power of institutions. Sometimes it means the power of institutions to deliver every possible form of mediation and field of activities to individual actors. Actually, these are two complementary aspects of the same logic of inclusion–expansion that we have underlined as part of institutions, and that applies to inter-institutional space. But this alone is not enough to address the complexity of this asymmetry, which, in the framework of a sociology through relation, has to take what is going on with individual actors into account, namely the maximisation and ranking of their social position. According to a sociology through relation, this asymmetry takes its meaning from the difference between, on the one hand, the inclusion–expansion of institutions and, on the other, the maximisation-ranking of individual actors. Or to put it in other words, asymmetry implies asymmetry between what is at stake for institutions, namely their duration through inclusion–expansion, and what is at stake for individual actors, namely their place in social space through maximisation-ranking.

These main results can be synthetised in six proposals that define the theoretical framework of an approach to social phenomena through relation.

A Theoretical Framework Driven by Relation as an Analytical Perspective

The merit of relational approaches in sociology (and of affiliated work) is that they have relativised the concept of action, insisting on the productivity of reasoning which does not describe causal sequences of actions, but instead, reconstructs the contexts formed by the relation. We find a similar attempt in the work of Archer and Donati—both authors insist more on the relation than on action. We propose going beyond the reference to theories of action. We argue that relation, taken as an analytical perspective in sociology, is not a by-product of theories of action, but a specific separate attempt to analyse different activities of personal and non-personal actors. The comparisons between Durkheim and Richard and between Richard and Mauss highlight particularly that point by relativising the empiricist understanding of the relation in order to underline the productivity of relation as a way of looking at social phenomena. Indeed, sociology through relation is about how relation occurs, and can be described as a specific configuration of actors, actions, interactions, objects, symbols etc., the cycles of which can be observed in time. This is also why a sociology through relation is not a kind of compromise between holism and individualism, monism and dualism, or actor and structure. It is an approach of social phenomena fostering an understanding of the transverse character of such configurations and cycles of the relation as well as of their consequences.

The Importance of Numbers and Social Labour

This question is generally neglected in sociological theories focusing on relation, and the comparisons between Richard and Mauss, Mauss and Bourdieu, and Bourdieu and Latour have highlighted particularly that any sociology through relation has to pay attention to the number of actors, as well as to their labour on and with mediations of exchange. Indeed, to give a relational orientation to activities and mediations presupposes a mobilisation of numerous other actors, and of that which depends on them, namely other humans and non-humans, and their activities. This means that actors have to produce considerable social labour in order to acquire a concrete perspective out of this otherwise abstract relational perspective, supporting a cycle of the relation that they can extend to the collective. We summarised by saying that this rests on two conditions, namely the mobilisation of actors and of that which depends on them, and of the work on and with the mediations of exchange. These are conditions, which means that they vary in space and time as we have seen in the examples provided by the authors compared in this book. They can support or be substituted for one another—for example, a strong mobilisation of the collective can considerably reduce the work needed on the mediations of exchange but the extension of a mediation of exchange can make the mobilisation of humans and non-humans almost useless.

The Cycles of Relation

The comparison between Mauss and Bourdieu has enabled us to understand that the activities enabling the extension of a relational perspective to the collective and its concrete occurrence as a configuration of the relation are not linear, but are, instead cyclical. On an analytical level, these cycles describe what Emirbayer and Archer call agency. In our comparisons, we have seen that the cycles of relation do not presuppose one agency only, but two distinct agencies, namely the agency of individual actors driven by the maximisation-ranking of social position, and the agency of institutions driven by the inclusion of actors and by their own expansion in inter-institutional space. From this perspective, the interconnection between culture and relation never exists as such at the beginning of a cycle of the relation. Instead, it develops where and when individual actors encode their practices in the forms of institutional control and the forms of control in their practices. This is the interactive aspect in the forms of control which is decisive if reciprocity between individual actors and institutions is to occur.

Another important element found in the comparisons between Mauss and Bourdieu, between Bourdieu and Latour, and between Durkheim and Latour is that these cultural contexts refer to hierarchical contexts of social positions. Indeed, every cycle of the relation presupposes an asymmetry between individual actors and institutions, which is actually an asymmetry between the agency of individual actors and the agency of institutions. By this, we mean that what is at stake for individual actors in the cycles of relation is their place in a social order, from which they deal with the two other dimensions attached to the cycle of relation, namely the time it takes to begin and extend the cycle, and reciprocity with the institutions. For institutions, what is at stake in the cycles of relation is their duration in inter-institutional space, from which they take their place in society, and enter into reciprocity with individual actors. The cycles of relation contribute toward relativising the formal views on social and cultural contexts which rule domains of activities, as, for example, in Bourdieu's fields theory. However, unlike Latour's views on the cycles of associations, the cycles of the relation enable us not to give up on the idea that there are broad contexts of activities that can be clearly identified, and which we therefore name "configuration of the relation". Such configuration depends on reciprocity built between individual actors and institutions and, therefore, on the forms of control between both agencies, individual actors, and institutions. Hence, we do not have to follow the (personal and non personal) actors in order to understand how far an institution, a domain of activities or a group of actors extends. We have to reconstruct the cycle of the relation, i.e. the consecutiveness of its configurations.

Institutions and Control

As stated in the introduction, we understand the notion of institution in a broad sense, meaning not only public institutions, but also organisations of every kind, i.e. enterprises, firms, the state and so on. We can shorten this description by saying that institutions are providers of legitimacy through a specific relation of reciprocity. Thus, distinction between individual and corporate actors or institutions is important to us because it enables us to understand the question of legitimisation in society, particularly its reciprocal component—a component that we find again in the forms of control. Legitimisation, like control, involves both institutional and individual actors, even if their involvement is not the same, as we have seen when we said that institutions directly legitimise and control individual actors, and the latter only indirectly legitimise and control institutions. This is an observation that is close to Archer's and Donati's arguments even if, in our case, it has made us insist on the importance of inter-institutional space. As we particularly emphasised in our comparison between Durkheim and Latour, the investigation of inter-institutional space has been neglected in sociologies focusing on relation. It requires more analysis because it enables us to understand how institutions manage or do not manage to include actors and expand in this space, i.e. how they become or do not become strong providers of reciprocity and legitimacy in society on which they build their power. In order to facilitate such an investigation, we have suggested that attention should be paid to the forms of control developed and changed in this inter-institutional space. These forms of control are often understood as forms of surveillance, or (old or new) forms of social control. We suggested to view them instead through reciprocity, and to take them as indicators for the extension of reciprocity and its consequences for institutions and individual actors.

Reciprocity

Reciprocity is an issue in all the comparisons made in this book. If we want to briefly summarise the work on this concept, we would say that we have strongly polarised views on reciprocity—it is either everywhere or nowhere, it is either the mould of our concrete relations or nothing more than an abstract idea forcing the interpretation of social phenomena. We propose another understanding of reciprocity, saying on the one hand that there can be cycles of relation without reciprocity; therefore, reciprocity is not the mould of our relationships in real life. But on the other hand, relation cannot be a structuring phenomenon in society without reciprocity. Therefore, we cannot give up on the idea of reciprocity when we are doing any kind of relational sociology. We can fuse both proposals into one statement, saying that reciprocity is a concrete and specific social relation. It is needed in order to close the configurations and cycles of relation. It may or may not occur in the asymmetry between institutions and individual actors, and this has consequences not only for individual actors but also for institutions, inter-institutional space and the forms of control that have to be examined. The aspect complementary to this view on reciprocity is that reciprocity is the product of a collective commitment in an asymmetry between individual actors and institutions. Therefore, it can neither be identified with single bilateral exchanges between individual actors, nor with the same kind of exchanges between institutions. In these last examples, what we would call "reciprocity" is rather a somewhat distorted echo of past closed configurations of relation that are referred to in interpersonal or inter-institutional relationships. This is where the historicity of individual and corporate actors in society occurs.

Cultural Forms of Resistance

The comparisons between Durkheim and Richard and between Mauss and Richard enable us to understand the asymmetry between personal and non-personal actors—not in terms of a power relation, but in terms of a resistance by these actors to each other, which has no other justification than the independence of their agency. On a basic empirical level, resistance recalls the dimension of historicity that we find in reciprocity on behalf of individual actors and institutions. At the same time, such historicity is derived from the configurations of relation which actors inherit—a heritage that is not simply taken up by the actors, but that depends on these actors' agency in the contact of everything coming about in these configurations of relation, namely other (individual or corporate) actors, mediations and activities. This is precisely what we have called contact in our comparison of Richard and Mauss, where past configurations of relation are positioning and influencing actors, not in the exclusive sense of conformity with this heritage, but in the sense of a relation to it. As contact is part of every configuration of relation, we propose to see the forms of resistance as cultural forms of resistance. In our view, contact and the related cultural forms of resistance enable us to get rid of Durkheim's idea of spontaneity, which sociologists more or less always rely on today when they say that concrete social relations are phenomena emergent within society.

* * *

The motivation for this book was driven by the belief that, in sociology, we currently have no satisfactory theoretical framework with which to investigate society through relation. We have suggested that French sociological tradition delivers fragmented elements of an ongoing debate about a kind of relational sociology around the heritage of the Durkheim school. We have systematically reconstructed this debate by comparing its most typical contributors. We have summarised our results in six propositions structuring what could be a sociological theory centred on relation better adapted to the complexity of the problem, and devoted to this problem only. These propositions enable to understand how it comes to a configuration of the relation and, ultimately, to cycles of the relation. This theory contains two specific points.

The first should foster a discussion on the history of the discipline that looks at its contribution to this kind of theory. As we suggested, relation is no ubiquitous perspective that structures sociology. Even if it shows up everywhere as a concept, it hardly remains at the centre of sociological theory—unlike action, for example. Therefore, this book represents an attempt to reconsider the history of the discipline from the viewpoint of relation, and it aims at making that history productive for sociological theory.

The second point is related to the methods and techniques of investigation which we did not cover in this book, and which deserve special attention in future work. Network sociologists have particularly encouraged the usage of new research methods and techniques in order to understand what the concept of context means once seen from a relational perspective. In this book, we have made some propositions in order to bind this notion of context to what we have called the configuration and the cycles of the relation. It would be interesting to further discuss this part of the problem in terms of the evolution of these new methods, as Emirbayer and Mische have already suggested. This suggestion remains relevant today, not only to amend the empiricist views on relations as concrete social relations or inter-personal networks, but especially in order to promote empirical investigations on the configurations and cycles of the relation themselves. This would enable us to understand the variations of the transverse characters of relational objects in society, as well as their consequences for the life course of actors, the expansion of institutions, and any mediations and activities depending on both.

Bibliography

Abbott, Andrew. 1988. *The System of Professions. An Essay on the Division of Expert Labor*. Chicago: The University of Chicago Press.

———. 1997. Of Time and Space: The Contemporary Relevance of the Chicago School. *Social Forces* 75: 1149–1182.

———. 2001. *Chaos of Disciplines*. Chicago: University of Chicago Press.

———. 2016. *Processual Sociology*. Chicago: University of Chicago Press.

Adkins, Lisa. 2003. Reflexivity: Freedom or Habit of Gender. *Theory Culture and Society* 20: 21–42.

Alexander, Jeffrey C. 1982. *Theoretical Logic in Sociology. II. The Antinomies of Classical Thought: Marx and Durkheim*. Los Angeles: University of California Press Berkeley.

Alpert, Harry. 1939. *Emile Durkheim and His Sociology Sciences*. London: P. S. King & So.v.

Archer, Margaret S. 1995. *Realist Social Theory: The Morphogenetic Approach*. Cambridge: Cambridge University Press.

———. 2010. Critical Realism and Relational Sociology. *Journal of Critical Realism* 9: 199–207.

Archer, Margaret S., and Pierpaulo Donati. 2015. *The Relational Subject*. Cambridge: Cambridge University Press.

Aron, Raymond. 1938. Richard, Gaston – La conscience morale et l'expérience morale; Richard, Gaston – La loi morale. Les lois naturelles et les lois socials. *Zeitschrift für Sozialforschung* 7: 412–414.

Bataille, Georges. 1991. *The Accursed Share 1: Consumption*. New York: Zone Books.

C. Papilloud, *Sociology through Relation*, Palgrave Studies in Relational Sociology, https://doi.org/10.1007/978-3-319-65073-9

Beaulavon, Georges. 1937. Richard – La critique de l'hypothèse du contrat social avant J. J. Rousseau. *Annales de la Société Jean-Jacques Rousseau* 26: 335–337.

Becher, Heribert J. 1971. *Georg Simmel. Die Grundlagen seiner Soziologie.* Stuttgart: Ferdinand Enke.

Besnard, Philippe. 1987. *L'Anomie, ses usages et ses fonctions dans la discipline sociologique depuis Durkheim.* Paris: PUF.

———. 2003. *Etudes durkheimiennes.* Genève-Paris: Droz.

Best, Elsdon. 1900. Spiritual Concepts of the Maori. *The Journal of the Polynesian Society* 9: 173–199.

Bidart, Claire, Alain Degenne, and Michel Grossetti. 2011. *La vie en réseau. Dynamique des relations sociales.* Paris: PUF.

Boltanski, Luc, and Laurent Thévenot. 1987. *Les économies de la grandeur.* Paris: PUF.

Borlandi, Massimo. 1995. Les faits sociaux comme produits de l'association des individus. Le fil conducteur des Règles. In *La Sociologie et sa méthode: les "Règles" de Durkheim un siècle après*, ed. Massimo Borlandi and Laurent Mucchielli, 139–164. Paris: PUF.

Bothner, Matthew, Toby Stuart, and Harrison White. 2004. Status Differentiation and the Cohesion of Social Networks. *Journal of Mathematical Sociology* 28: 261–295.

Bourdieu, Pierre. 1975. L'ontologie politique de Martin Heidegger. *Actes de la recherche en sciences sociales* 1: 109–156.

———. 1976. Le champ scientifique. *Actes de la recherche en sciences sociales* 2: 88–104.

———. 1977. *Outline of a Theory of Practice.* Cambridge: Cambridge University Press.

———. 1980a. The Production of Belief: Contribution to an Economy of Symbolic Goods. *Media, Culture and Society* 2: 1–93.

———. 1980b. Le mort saisit le vif. *Actes de la recherche en sciences socials* 32–33: 3–14.

———. 1981a. Epreuve scolaire et consécration sociale. *Actes de la recherche en sciences sociales* 39: 3–70.

———. 1981b. La représentation politique. *Actes de la recherche en sciences sociales* 36–37: 3–24.

———. 1982. Les rites comme actes d'institution. *Actes de la recherche en sciences sociales* 43: 58–63.

———. 1983. Erving Goffman, Discoverer of the Infinitely Small. *Theory, Culture and Society* 2: 112–113.

———. 1984. *Distinction. A Social Critique of the Judgement of Taste.* Harvard: Harvard University Press.

———. 1985a. The Social Space and the Genesis of Groups. *Theory and Society* 14: 723–744.

———. 1985b. Effet de champ et effet de corps. *Actes de la recherche en sciences sociales* 59: 73.
———. 1986. La force du droit. *Actes de la recherche en sciences sociales* 64: 3–19.
———. 1988. *Homo Academicus.* Stanford: Stanford University Press.
———. 1990a. *The Logic of Practice.* Stanford: Stanford University Press.
———. 1990b. *In Other Words.* Stanford: Stanford University Press.
———. 1991a. *Language and Symbolic Power.* Cambridge: Polity Press.
———. 1991b. The Peculiar History of Scientific Reason. *Sociological Forum* 6: 3–26.
———. 1991c. Le champ littéraire. *Actes de la recherche en sciences sociales* 89: 3–46.
———. 1993. *The Field of Cultural Production. Essays on Art and Literature.* Cambridge: Polity Press.
———. 1995. *The Rules of Art. Genesis and Structure of the Literary Field.* Stanford: Stanford University Press.
———. 1998. *The State Nobility. Elite Schools in the Field of Power.* Cambridge: Polity.
———. 2001. *Masculine Domination.* Stanford: Stanford University Press.
———. 2005. *The Social Structures of the Economy.* Cambridge: Polity.
———. 2008. *Political Interventions. Social Science and Political Action.* London: Verso.
Bourdieu, Pierre, and Jean-Claude Passeron. 1979. *Inheritors.* Chicago: The University of Chicago Press.
Bourdieu, Pierre, and Luc Boltanski. 1976. La production de l'idéologie dominante. *Actes de la recherche en sciences sociales* 2: 3–73.
Bourdieu, Pierre, Alain Darbel, and Dominique Schnapper. 1997. *The Love of Art. European Art Museums and Their Public.* Cambridge: Polity.
Bourdieu, Pierre, and Yvette Delsaut. 1975. Le couturier et sa griffe: contribution à une théorie de la magie. *Actes de la recherche en sciences sociales* 1: 7–36.
Bourdieu, Pierre, and Jean-Claude Passeron. 1979. *Inheritors.* Chicago: The University of Chicago Press.
———. 1990. *Reproduction in Education, Society and Culture.* London: Sage.
Bourdieu, Pierre, Loic Wacquant, and Samar Farage. 1994. Rethinking the State: Genesis and Structure of the Bureaucratic Field. *Sociological Theory* 12: 1–18.
Breiger, Ronald L. 1990. Social Control and Social Networks: A Model from Georg Simmel. In *Structures of Power and Constraint: Essays in Honor of Peter M. Blau*, ed. Craig Calhoun, Marshall W. Meyer, and W. Richard Scott, 453–476. Cambridge: Cambridge University Press.
Breslau, Daniel. 2000. Sociology After Humanism: A Lesson from Contemporary Science Studies. *Sociological Theory 18*: 289–307.
Burt, Ronald S. 1982. *Toward a Structural Theory of Action.* New York: Academic Press.

Caillé, Alain. 1982. Socialité primaire et socialité secondaire. (Réflexion à partir d'un ouvrage de Hervé Le Bras et Emmanuel Todd). *Bulletin du MAUSS* 2: 51–76.

———. 1991. Une soirée à 'l'Ambroisie'. Rudiments d'une analyse structurale du don. *Revue du MAUSS* 11: 106–113.

———. 1994. *Don, intérêt et désintéressement*. Paris: La Découverte.

———. 1996. Ni holisme, ni individualisme méthodologiques. Marcel Mauss et le paradigme du don. *Revue du MAUSS* 8: 12–59.

———. 2010. *Anthropologie der Gabe*. Frankfurt am Main: Campus.

Callon, Michel, and Bruno Latour. 1981. Unscrewing the Big Leviathan; or How Actors Macrostructure Reality and How Sociologists Help Them to Do So? In *Advances in Social Theory and Methodology*, ed. Karin Knorr and Aaron Cicourel, 277–303. London: Routledge.

Cefaï, Daniel, and Alain Mahé. 1998. Echanges rituels de dons, obligation et contrat. Mauss, Davy, Maunier: trois perspectives de sociologie juridique. *L'Année Sociologique* 48: 209–228.

Chamboredon, Jean Claude. 1984. Émile Durkheim: le social, objet de science. *Critique* 445–446: 461–531.

Charriaut, Henri. 1902. Auguste Comte et ses nouveaux disciples. *Le Siècle* 67: 2–3.

Christian, Petra. 1978. *Einheit und Zwiespalt. Zum hegelianisierenden Denken in der Philosophie und Soziologie Georg Simmels*. Berlin: Duncker und Humbolt.

Clark, Terry N. 1971. Le patron et son cercle: clef de l'Université française. *Revue Française de Sociologie* 12: 19–39.

———. 1972. Emile Durkheim and the French University: The Institutionalization of Sociology. In *The Establishment of Empirical Sociology: Studies in Continuity, Discontinuity, and Institutionalization*, ed. Anthony Oberschall, 152–186. New York: Harper & Row.

Coliot-Thélène, Catherine. 2005. Die deutschen Wurzeln der Theorie Bourdieus. In *Pierre Bourdieu. Deutsch-französische Perspektiven*, ed. Catherine Coliot-Thélène, 106–136. Frankfurt am Main: Suhrkamp.

Crick, Malcom R. 1982. Anthropology of Knowledge. *Annual Review of Anthropology* 11: 287–313.

Crossley, Nick. 2010. *Towards Relational Sociology*. London: Routledge.

Dahme, Heinz-Jürgen. 1988. *Georg Simmel und der Darwinismus*. Bielefeld: Universität Bielefeld.

Degenne, Alain, and Michel Forsé. 1999. *Introducing Social Networks*. London: Sage.

Dépelteau, François. 2008. Relational Thinking: A Critique of Co-Deterministic Theories of Structure and Agency. *Sociological Theory* 26: 51–73.

Deploige, Simon. 1911. *Le conflit de la morale et de la sociologie*. Paris: Alcan.

Dewey, John, and Arthur Bentely. 1948. *Knowing and the Known*. Great Barrington: Behavioral Research Council.

Dianteill, Erwan. 2003. Pierre Bourdieu and the Sociology of Religion: A Central and Peripheral Concern. *Theory and Society* 32: 529–549.

Digeon, Claude. 1959. *La crise allemande de la pensée française*. Paris: PUF.

Donati, Pierpaolo. 1991. *Teoria relazionale della società*. Milan: Angeli.

———. 2003. Giving and Social Relations: The Culture of Free Giving and Its Differentiation Today. *International Review of Sociology* 13: 243–272.

———. 2011. *Relational Sociology. A New Paradigm for the Social Sciences*. London: Routledge.

Dumont, Louis. 1999. Bourdieu and the Logic of Practice: Is All Giving Indian-Giving or Is 'Generalized Materialism' Not Enough? *Sociological Theory* 17: 3–31.

Durkheim, Émile. 1895 (1919). *Les règles de la méthode sociologique*. Paris: Alcan.

Durkheim, Émile. 1885a. Schaeffle, A., Bau und Leben des sozialen Körpers: Erster Band. *Revue Philosophique* 19: 84–101.

———. 1885b. Gumplowicz, Ludwig, Grundriss der Soziologie. *Revue Philosophique* 20: 627–634.

———. 1886 (1975). La science sociale selon De Greef. *Textes I. Eléments ďune théorie sociale*. Paris: Minuit, 37–43.

———. 1887 (1975). La science positive de la morale en Allemagne. *Textes I. Eléments ďune théorie sociale*. Paris: Minuit, 267–343.

———. 1890–1900 (1958). *Professional Ethics and Civic Morals*. Glencoe: The Free Press.

———. 1892a. Montesquieu: sa part dans la fondation des sciences politiques et de la science des sociétés. *Revue d'histoire politique et constitutionnelle* 1: 405–463.

———. 1892b (1966). *Montesquieu et Rousseau précurseurs de la sociologie*. Paris: Marcel Rivière et Cie.

———. 1893a (1922). *De la division du travail social*. Paris: Alcan.

———. 1893b (2013). *The Division of Labour in Society*. New York: Palgrave Macmillan.

———. 1893c (1975). Définition du fait moral. *Textes II. Religion, morale, anomie*. Paris: Minuit, 257–312.

———. 1895a (2013). *The Rules of Sociological Method and Selected Texts on Sociology and Its Method*. New York: Palgrave Macmillan.

———. 1895b (1975). L'état actuel des études sociologiques en France. *Textes I. Eléments ďune théorie sociale*. Paris: Minuit, 73–108.

———. 1897. *Le suicide. Etude de sociologie*. Paris: Alcan.

———. 1900 (1975). La sociologie et son domaine scientifique. *Textes I. Eléments ďune théorie sociale*. Paris: Minuit, 13–36.

———. 1902–1903 (1973). *Moral Education. A Study in the Theory and Application of the Sociology of Education.* New York, London: The Free Press.

———. 1903 (1975). La sociologie et les sciences sociales. *Textes I. Eléments ďune théorie sociale.* Paris: Minuit, 160–165.

———. 1906 (1975). Remarques sur le problème de l'individu et de la société. *Textes I. Eléments ďune théorie sociale.* Paris: Minuit, 56–57.

———. 8.11.1907 (1975). Deux lettres sur l'influence allemande dans la sociologie française. Réponse à Simon Déploige. *Textes I. Eléments ďune théorie sociale.* Paris: Minuit, 401–405.

———. 1907a (1975). Les lois de la solidarité morale. *Textes II. Religion, morale, anomie.* Paris: Minuit, 339–340.

———. 1907b (1975). Cours sur les origines de la vie religieuse. *Textes II. Religion, morale, anomie.* Paris: Minuit, 65–122.

———. 1909 (1975). Morale professionnelle et corporation. *Textes III. Fonctions sociales et institutions.* Paris: Minuit, 217–220.

———. 1910 (1975). Formation des sociétés germaniques. *Textes III. Fonctions sociales et institutions.* Paris: Minuit, 282–292.

———. 1912 (1995). *The Elementary Forms of Religious Life.* New York: The Free Press.

———. 1913. La sociologie générale et les lois sociologiques. *L'Année Sociologique* 10: 1–3.

———. 1922. *Education et sociologie.* Paris: Alcan.

———. 1998. *Lettres à Marcel Mauss.* Paris: Presses Universitaires de France.

Durkheim, Émile, and Marcel Mauss. 1903a (1974). De quelques formes de classification. Contribution à l'étude des représentations collectives. *Œuvres 2. Représentations collectives et diversité des civilisations.* Paris: Minuit, 13–89.

———. 1903b (2009). *Primitive Classification.* London: Cohen & West.

Emirbayer, Mustafa. 1996. Useful Durkheim. *Sociological Theory* 14: 109–130.

———. 1997. Manifesto for a Relational Sociology. *The American Journal of Sociology* 103: 281–317.

Emirbayer, Mustafa, and John Goodwin. 1994. Network Analysis, Culture, and the Problem of Agency. *The American Journal of Sociology* 99: 1411–1454.

Emirbayer, Mustafa, and Ann Mische. 1998. What Is Agency? *The American Journal of Sociology* 103: 962–1023.

Essertier, Daniel. 1930a. *Philosophes et Savants français du XX° siècle. Extraits et notices – V – La Sociologie.* Paris: Alcan.

———. 1930b. La sociologie française contemporaine – M. Gaston Richard. *Foi & Vie* 6: 364–375.

Fauconnet, Paul, and Marcel Mauss. 1901 (1969). Sociologie. *Œuvres 3. Cohésion sociale et division de la sociologie.* Paris: Minuit, 139–177.

Favereau, Olivier. 2001. L'économie du sociologue ou penser (l'orthodoxie) à partir de Pierre Bourdieu. In *Le travail sociologique de Pierre Bourdieu*, ed. Bernard Lahire, 255–314. Paris: La Découverte.

Feuerhahn, Wolf. 2014. Zwischen Individualismus und Sozialismus: Durkheims Soziologie und ihr deutsches Pantheon. In *Europäische Wissenschaftskulturen und politische Ordnungen in der Moderne (1890–1970)*, ed. Gangolf Hübinger, 79–98. Munich: R. Oldenbourg Verlag.

Filloux, Jean-Claude. 1977. *Durkheim et le socialisme*. Genève, Paris: Droz.

Fournier, Marcel. 1994. *Marcel Mauss*. Paris: Fayard.

———. 2007. *Émile Durkheim (1858–1917)*. Paris: Fayard.

Fuhse, Jan. 2006. Gruppe und Netzwerk – eine begriffsgeschichtliche Rekonstruktion. *Berliner Journal für Soziologie* 2: 245–263.

Fuhse, Jan, and Sophie Mützel. 2011. Tackling Connections, Structure, and Meaning in Networks: Quantitative and Qualitative Methods in Sociological Network Research. *Quality & Quantity* 45: 1067–1089.

Gane, Mike. 1984. Institutional Socialism and the Sociological Critique of Communism (Introduction to Durkheim and Mauss). *Economy and Society 13*: 304–330.

Gephart, Werner. 1990. *Strafe und Verbrechen. Die Theorie Emile Durkheims*. Opladen: VS-Verlag.

Girard, René. 1986. *The Scapegoat*. Baltimore and London: Johns Hopkins University Press.

Gooday, Graeme. 2008. Placing or Replacing the Laboratory in the History of Science? *Isis* 99: 783–795.

Gouldner, Alvin. 1960. The Norm of Reciprocity: A Preliminary Statement. *American Sociological Review* 25: 161–178.

Grenfell, Michael, and Cheryl Hardy. 2007. *Art Rules. Pierre Bourdieu and the Visual Arts*. Oxford: Berg.

Guggenheim, Michael, and Jörg Potthast. 2012. Symmetrical Twins: On the Relationship Between Actor-Network Theory and the Sociology of Critical Capacities. *European Journal of Social Theory* 15: 157–178.

Gurvitch, Georges. 1952a. Réponse à une Critique. Lettre ouverte au Professeur Leopold von Wiese. *Cahiers Internationaux de Sociologie* XIII: 94–104.

———. 1952b/1953. Réponse à une Critique. Lettre ouverte au Professeur Leopold von Wiese. *Kölner Zeitschrift für Soziologie* 5: 98–105.

Hénaff, Marcel. 2010. *The Price of Truth: Gift, Money, and Philosophy*. Stanford: Stanford University Press.

Honneth, Axel. 1986. The Fragmented World of Symbolic Forms: Reflections on Pierre Bourdieu's Sociology of Culture. *Theory, Culture & Society* 3: 55–66.

Hubert, Henri, and Marcel Mauss. 1899 (1964). *Sacrifice. Its Nature and Functions*. Chicago: The University of Chicago Press.

———. 1904 (1974). L'origine des pouvoirs magiques dans les sociétés australiennes. *Œuvres 2. Représentations collectives et diversité des civilisations.* Paris: Minuit, 319–369.

———. 1905 (1929). *Mélanges d'histoire des religions.* Paris: Alcan.

Isambert, Francois-A. 1976. L'élaboration de la notion de sacré dans l'«école» durkheimienne. *Archives de Sciences Sociales des Religions* 42: 35–57.

James, Wendy, and N.J. Allen. 1998. *Marcel Mauss. A Centenary Tribute.* New York: Berghahn Books.

Jones, Robert Alun. 1994. The Positive Science of Ethics in France: German Influences on 'De la division du travail social'. *Sociological Forum* 9: 37–57.

Kale-Lostuvali, Elif. 2016. Two Sociologies of Science in Search of Truth: Bourdieu Versus Latour. *Social Epistemology* 30: 273–296.

Karsenti, Bruno. 1997. *L'homme total. Sociologie, anthropologie et philosophie chez Marcel Mauss.* Paris: PUF.

———. 2011. From Marx to Bourdieu: The Limits of the Structuralism. In *The Legacy of Pierre Bourdieu*, ed. Simon Susen and Bryan S. Turner, 59–90. London: Anthem Press.

Käsler, Dirk. 1985. *Soziologische Abenteuer. Earle Edward Eubank besucht europäische Soziologen im Sommer 1934.* Opladen: Westdeutscher Verlag.

Knorr, Karin. 1979. Tinkering Toward Success: Prelude to a Theory of Scientific Practice. *Theory and Society* 8: 347–376.

Kögler, Hans-Herbert. 2011. Overcoming Semiotic Structuralism: Language and Habitus in Bourdieu. In *The Legacy of Pierre Bourdieu*, ed. Simon Susen and Bryan S. Turner, 271–300. London: Anthem Press.

König, René. 1972. Marcel Mauss (1872–1972). *Kölner Zeitschrift für Soziologie und Sozialpsychologie* 24: 633–657.

———. 1978. *Émile Durkheim zur Diskussion. Jenseits von Dogmatismus und Skepsis.* München: Hanser Verlag.

Lahire, Bernard. 1998. *L'homme pluriel. Les ressorts de l'action.* Paris: Nathan.

Lamont, Michèle. 2010. Looking Back at Bourdieu. In *Cultural Analysis and Bourdieu's Legacy. Settling Accounts and Developing Alternatives*, ed. Elizabeth Silva and Alan Warde, 128–141. New York: Routledge.

Landmann, Michael. 1987. Einleitung des Herausgebers. In *Das individuelle Gesetz. Philosophische Exkurse*, ed. Michael Landmann, 7–30. Frankfurt am Main: Suhrkamp.

Lane, Jeremy. 2006. *Bourdieu's Politics.* New York: Routledge.

Lapie, Paul. 1903–1904. G. Richard – Notions élémentaires de sociologie. *L'Année Sociologique* 8: 171–175.

Latour, Bruno. 1986. The Powers of Association. In *Power, Action and Belief. A New Sociology of Knowledge?* ed. John Law, 264–280. London: Routledge & Kegan Paul.

———. 1987. *Science in Action.* Cambridge: Harvard University Press.

———. 1988a. A Relativistic Account of Einstein's Relativity. *Social Studies of Science* 18: 3–44.
———. 1988b. How to Write 'The Prince' for Machines as Well as for Machinations? In *Technology and Social Change*, ed. Brian Elliott, 20–43. Edinburgh: Edinburgh University Press.
———. 1991. Technology Is Society Made Durable. In *A Sociology of Monsters: Essays on Power, Technology and Domination*, ed. John Law, 103–132. London: Routledge.
———. 1993a. *Petites Leçons de sociologie des sciences.* Paris: La Découverte.
———. 1993b. *The Pasteurization of France.* Cambridge: Harvard University Press.
———. 1993c. *We Have Never Been Modern.* Cambridge: Harvard University Press.
———. 1994a. On Technical Mediation – Philosophy, Sociology, Genealogy. *Common Knowledge* 3: 29–64.
———. 1994b. Pragmatogonies. A Mythical Account of How Humans and Nonhumans Swap Properties. *American Behavioral Scientist* 37: 791–808.
———. 1996. *Aramis, or the Love of Technology.* Cambridge: Harvard University Press.
———. 2000. When Things Strike Back: A Possible Contribution of 'Science Studies' to the Social Sciences. *British Journal of Sociology* 51: 107–123.
———. 2001. *L'espoir de Pandore. Pour une version réaliste de l'activité scientifique.* Paris: La Découverte.
———. 2002. Gabriel Tarde and the End of the Social. In *The Social in Question. New Bearings in History and the Social Sciences*, ed. Patrick Joyce, 117–132. London: Routledge.
———. 2004. *Politics of Nature. How to Bring the Sciences into Democracy.* Cambridge: Harvard University Press.
———. 2005. *Reassembling the Social. An Introduction to Actor-Network-Theory.* Oxford: Oxford University Press.
———. 2010. *The Making of Law. An Ethnography of the Conseil d'Etat.* Cambridge: Polity.
———. 2011. Politics of Nature: East and West Perspectives. *Ethics & Global Politics* 4: 1–10.
———. 2013. *An Inquiry into Modes of Existence. An Anthropology of the Moderns.* Cambridge: Harvard University Press.
Latour, Bruno, and Paolo Fabbri. 1977. La rhétorique du discours scientifique. *Actes de la recherche en sciences sociales* 13: 81–96.
Latour, Bruno, Philippe Mauguin, and Geneviève Teil. 1992. A Note on Socio-Technical Graphs. *Social Studies of Science* 22: 33–57.

Latour, Bruno, and Monique Girard Stark. 1999. Factures/Fractures: From the Concept of Network to the Concept of Attachment. *RES: Anthropology and Aesthetics* 36: 20–31.

Latour, Bruno, and Shirley Strum. 1986. Human Social Origins: Oh Please, Tell Us Another Story. *Journal of Social and Biological Structures* 9: 169–187.

———. 1987. Redefining the Social Link: From Baboons to Humans. *Social Science Information* 26: 783–802.

Latour, Bruno, and Steve Woolgar. 1986. *Laboratory Life. The Construction of Scientific Facts*. Princeton: Princeton University Press.

Law, John. 1992. Notes on the Theory of the Actor-Network: Ordering, Strategy, and Heterogeneity. *Systemic Practice and Action Research* 5: 379–393.

Leach, Edmund Ronald. 1983. The Kula: An Alternative View. In *The Kula. New Perspectives on Massim Exchange*, ed. Jerry W. Leach and Edmund Leach, 529–539. Cambridge: Cambridge University Press.

Lefort, Claude. 1951. L'échange et la lutte des homes. *Les Temps Modernes* 6: 1400–1417.

Levine, Donald N., Ellwood B. Carter, and Eleanor Miller Gorman. 1976. Simmel's Influence on American Sociology. I. *American Journal of Sociology* 81: 813–845.

Lévi-Strauss, Claude. 1967. *Les structures élémentaires de la parenté*. Paris: Mouton.

———. 1987. *Introduction to the Work of Marcel Mauss*. London: Routledge & Kegan Paul.

Lévi-Strauss, Claude. 1989. Introduction à l'oeuvre de Marcel Mauss. In *Sociologie et anthropologie*, ed. Marcel Mauss, IX–LII. Paris: PUF.

Liebersohn, Harry. 1982. Leopold von Wiese and the Ambivalence of Functionalist Sociology. *Archives européennes de sociologie* 23: 123–149.

Lindemann, Gesa. 2011. On Latour's Social Theory and Theory of Society, and His Contribution to Saving the World. *Human Studies* 34: 93–110.

Lock, Margaret. 1993. Cultivating the Body: Anthropology and Epistemologies of Bodily Practice and Knowledge. *Annual Review of Anthropology* 22: 133–155.

Lukes, Steven. 1973. *Emile Durkheim. His Life and Work*. London: Allen Lane Press.

Mahé, Alain. 1996. Un disciple méconnu de Marcel Mauss: René Maunier. *Revues européennes des sciences sociales* 34 (105): 237–264.

Marica, George E. 1932. *Emile Durkheim. Soziologie und Soziologismus*. Jena: Verlag von Gustav Fischer.

Martelli, Stephano. 1993. Mauss et Durkheim: un désaccord sur la question du sacré et une perspective relationnelle sur Simmel et la société post-moderne. *Social Compass* 40: 375–387.

———. 1996. Mana ou sacré: La contribution de Marcel Mauss à la fondation de la sociologie religieuse. *Revue européenne des sciences sociales* 34: 51–66.

Mauss, Marcel. 1896 (1974). La religion et les origines du droit pénal d'après un livre recent. *Œuvres 2. Représentations collectives et diversité des civilisations.* Paris: Minuit, 651–698.

———. 1902–1903 (2001). *A General Theory of Magic.* London and New York: Routledge.

———. 1902–1905 (1974). Leçons sur la magie. *Œuvres 2. Représentations collectives et diversité des civilisations.* Paris: Minuit, 390–391.

———. 1904–1905 (2004). *Seasonal Variations of the Eskimo. A Study in Social Morphology.* London and New York: Routledge.

———. 1921 (1969). Une forme ancienne de contrat chez les Thraces. *Œuvres 3. Cohésion sociale et division de la sociologie.* Paris: Minuit, 35–43.

———. 1924 (1989). Rapports réels et pratiques de la psychologie et de la sociologie. In *Sociologie et anthropologie*, ed. Marcel Mauss, 285–310. Paris: PUF.

———. 1925 (2002). *The Gift. The Form and Reason for Exchange in Archaic Societies.* London, New York: Routledge.

———. 1927 (1969). Divisions et proportions des divisions de la sociologie. *Œuvres 3. Cohésion sociale et division de la sociologie.* Paris: Minuit, 178–245.

———. 1929 (1974). Les civilisations. Éléments et formes. *Œuvres 2. Représentations collectives et diversité des civilisations.* Paris: Minuit, 456–479.

———. 1934 (1989). Les techniques du corps. In *Sociologie et anthropologie*, ed. Marcel Mauss, 365–386. Paris: PUF.

———. 1938 (1989). Une catégorie de l'esprit humain: la notion de personne celle de 'moi'. In *Sociologie et anthropologie*, ed. Marcel Mauss, 333–362. Paris: PUF.

———. 1947 (2007). *Manual of Ethnography.* New York, Oxford: Durkheim Press/Berghahn Books.

———. 1973. The Techniques of the Body. *Economy and Society* 2: 70–88.

Mauss, Marcel, Paul Fauconnet, Dominique Parodi, and Lapie Paul. 1979. Correspondance reçue par Célestin Bouglé. *Revue Française de Sociologie* 20: 32–48.

Mestrovic, Stjepan C. 1994. *The Balkanization of the West: The Confluence of Postmodernism and Postcommunism.* London: Routledge.

Mische, Ann. 2007. *Partisan Publics: Contention and Mediation Across Brazilian Youth Activist Networks.* Princeton: Princeton University Press.

———. 2011. Relational Sociology, Culture, and Agency. In *Social Network Analysis*, ed. John Scott and Peter Carington, 80–97. London: Sage.

Mooney, Kathleen. 1976. Social Distance and Exchange: The Coast Salish Case. *Ethnology* 15: 323–347.

Morchón, Gregorio Robles. 2005. *La Influencia del Pensamiento Alemán en la Sociología de Emile Durkheim.* Garrigues: Editorial Aranzadi, SA.

Moreau, Joseph. 1944. Chronique. Gaston Richard. *Revue des études anciennes* 46: 375–376.

Mucchielli, Laurent. 2004. *Mythes et histoire des sciences humaines.* Paris: La Découverte.

Mürmel, Heinz. 1997. Marcel Mauss (1872–1950). In *Klassiker der Religionswissenschaft. Von Friedrich Schleiermacher bis Mircea Eliade*, ed. Alexander Michaels, 211–221. München: C.H. Beck.

N.N. 1946. Nécrologie – Gaston Richard. *Revue de Métaphysique et de Morale* LVI: 96.

Nau, Heino Heinrich, and Philippe Steiner. 2002. Schmoller, Durkheim, and Old European Institutionalist Economics. *Journal of Economic Issues* XXXVI: 1005–1024.

Nielsen, Donald A. 1987. Auguste Sabatier and the Durkheimians on the Scientific Study of Religion. *Sociological Analysis* 47: 283–301.

Ouy, Achille. 1926. Un sociologue indépendant: Gaston Richard. *Revue Internationale de Sociologie* 34: 229–233.

Paoletti, Giovanni. 2008. Some Concepts of 'Evil' in Durkheims' Thought. In *Suffering and Evil. The Durkheimian Legacy*, ed. William S.F. Pickering and Massimo Rosati, 63–80. New York: Berghahn.

———. 2012a. Les deux tournants ou la religion dans l'œuvre de Durkheim avant Les Formes élémentaires. *L'Année Sociologique* 62: 289–312.

———. 2012b. *Durkheim et la philosophie. Représentation, réalité et lien social.* Paris: Garnier.

Parodi, Dominique. 1902–1903. G. Richard– L'idée d'évolution dans la nature et l'histoire. *L'Année Sociologique* 7: 161–166.

Pattison, Pip. 1993. *Algebraic Models for Social Networks.* New York: Cambridge University Press.

Pickering, William S.F. 1975. *Durkheim on Religion. A Selection of Readings with Bibliographies.* London, Boston: Routledge & Kegan Paul.

———. 1979. Gaston Richard: collaborateur et adversaire. *Revue Française de Sociologie* 20: 163–182.

———. 1984. *Durkheim's Sociology of Religion: Themes and Theories.* London: Routledge and Kegan Paul.

Prendergast, Christopher. 1990. The Impact of Fustel de Coulanges' La Cité Antique on Durkheim's Theories of Social Morphology and Social Solidarity. In *Emile Durkheim. Critical Assesments*, ed. Peter Hamilton, 316–333. London: Routledge.

Price, Sally. 1978. Reciprocity and Social Distance: A Reconsideration. *Ethnology* 17: 339–351.

Pyyhtinen, Olli. 2010. *Simmel and 'the Social'.* New York: Palgrave Macmillan.

Rammstedt, Otthein. 1999. Les relations entre Durkheim et Simmel dans le contexte de l'affaire Dreyfus. *L'Année Sociologique* 48: 139–162.

Rawls, Anne Warfields. 1996. Durkheim's Epistemology: The Neglected Argument. *The American Journal of Sociology* 102: 430–482.

Richard, Gaston. 1892. *L'origine de l'idée de droit.* Neufchâteau: Gontier-Kienné.

———. 1894a. La discussion judiciaire et l'État de droit. *Revue Philosophique* 38: 478–500.

———. 1894b. Paul Aubry – La contagion du meurtre. *Revue Philosophique* 38: 197–202.

———. 1895a. La sociologie ethnographique et l'histoire: leur opposition et leur conciliation. *Revue Philosophique* 40: 476–508.

———. 1895b. Theodor Elsenhans – Wesen und Entstehung des Gewissens: Eine Psychologie der Ethik, Leipzig, Wilhelm Engelmann. *Revue Philosophique* 40: 85–97.

———. 1897. *Le socialisme et la science sociale*. Paris: Alcan.

———. 1898a. Avertissement. *L'Année Sociologique* 1: 392–394.

———. 1898b. Émile Durkheim, Le suicide. Étude de sociologie, 1 vol. in.-8 de la Bibliothèque de philosophie contemporaine, 402 pages, Paris, Félix Alcan, 1897. *L'Année Sociologique* 1: 397–406.

———. 1899. La responsabilité et les équivalents de la peine. *Revue Philosophique* 48: 475–494.

———. 1900. Les droits de la critique en matière sociologique [réponse à Vaccaro]. *Revue Philosophique* 49: 517–521.

———. 18.05.1902. Correspondance - Auguste Comte [Réponse à Henri Charriaut]. *Le Siècle* 67: 3.

———. 1902a. Sociologie et science politique. *Revue Philosophique* 53: 300–317.

———. 1902b. La notion de l'arrêt de développement en psychologie sociale. *Revue de synthèse historique* 5: 1–16.

———. 1903a. *Manuel de morale, suivi de notions de sociologie*. Paris: C. Delagrave.

———. 1903b. *Notions élémentaires de sociologie*. Paris: C. Delagrave.

———. 1903c. *L'idée d'évolution dans la nature et l'histoire*. Paris: Alcan.

———. 1905. Sur les lois de la solidarité morale. *Revue Philosophique* 60: 441–471.

———. 1908. Encyclopédie scientifique – Bibliothèque de sociologie. In *Géographie sociale – La mer*, ed. Camille Vallaux, iii–iiv. Paris: Doin.

———. 1909a. *La femme dans l'histoire: étude sur l'évolution de la condition sociale de la femme*. Paris: O. Doin et Fils.

———. 1909b. Philosophie du droit. La contrainte sociale et la valeur du droit subjectif. *Revue Philosophique* 67: 285–318.

———. 1910a. G.-L. Duprat – La solidarité sociale. Ses causes, son évolution, ses consequences. *Revue Philosophique* 69: 103–106.

———. 1910b. La solidarité au point de vue démographique. *Revue de la solidarité sociale* 7: 49–51.

———. 1911a. Sociologie et métaphysique (1). La distinction du bien et du mal chez Durkheim. *Foi et vie* 14: 395–399.

———. 1911b. *Pédagogie Expérimentale*. Paris: Octave Doin et Fils.

———. 1911c. Sociologie et métaphysique. A propos de M. Durkheim. *Foi et vie* 14: 331–332.

———. 1911d. Sociologie et métaphysique. Brève histoire des variations de M. Durkheim. *Foi et vie* 14: 356–359.

———. 1911e. Sociologie et métaphysique. La sociologie religieuse de M. Durkheim et le problème des valeurs. *Foi et vie* 14: 431–436.

———. 1912a. *La sociologie générale et les lois sociologiques*. Paris: Octave Doin et Fils.

———. 1912b. La sociologie juridique et la défense du droit subjectif. *Revue Philosophique* 73: 225–247.

———. 1915. La morale sociologique et la crise du droit international. *Revue Philosophique* 80: 385–411.

———. 1925a. Sociologie religieuse et morale sociologique. La théorie solidariste de l'obligation. *Revue d'histoire et de philosophie religieuses* 5: 244–261.

———. 1925b. *L'évolution des moeurs*. Paris: Octave Doin et Cie.

———. 1926. La psychologie de la conversion chez les peuples non civilisés. *Revue de Métaphysique et de Morale* 33: 493–508.

———. 1929. *L'Enseignement de la Sociologie à l'École Normale Primaire*. Neuilly: La Cause.

———. 1930. La pathologie sociale d'Emile Durkheim. *Revue Internationale de Sociologie* 38: 113–126.

———. 1932. Auguste Comte et Émile Durkheim selon M. G.-L. Duprat. *Revue Internationale de Sociologie* 40: 603–612.

———. 1934. Le droit naturel et la philosophie des valeurs. *Archives de philosophie du droit et de sociologie juridique* 1–2: 7–24.

———. 1935. Avant-propos inédit. *Revue Internationale de Sociologie* 43: 11–33.

———. 1943a. *De la présomption scientifique à la foi chrétienne*. Carrières sous Poissy et Cahors: La Cause.

———. 1943b. *Sociologie et théodicée: leur conflit et leur accord*. Paris: Les Presses continentales.

Riis, Søren. 2008. The Symmetry Between Bruno Latour and Martin Heidegger: The Technique of Turning a Police Officer into a Speed Bump. *Social Studies of Science* 38: 285–301.

Sahlins, Marshall. 1972. *Stone Age Economics*. New York: Aldin de Gruyter.

Sapiro, Giseèle. 2003. Forms of Politicization in the French Literary Field. *Theory and Society* 32: 633–652.

Schinkel, Willam. 2007. Sociological Discourse of the Relational: The Case of Bourdieu and Latour. *The Sociological Review* 55: 707–729.

Schmitt, Marco. 2009. *Trennen und Verbinden. Soziologische Untersuchungen zur Theorie des Gedächtnisses*. Wiesbaden: VS-Verlag.

Schmitt, Marco, and Jan Fuhse. 2015. *Zur Aktualität von Harrison White. Einführung in sein Werk*. Wiesbaden: VS-Verlag.

Schubert, J. Daniel. 2008. Suffering. In *Pierre Bourdieu. Key Concepts*, ed. Michael Grenfell, 183–198. Stocksfield: Acumen.

Schütz, Alfred. 1932 (2004). *Der sinnhafte Aufbau der sozialen Welt. Eine Einleitung in die verstehende Soziologie. ASW Band II.* Konstanz: UVK.

Simmel, Georg. 1908 (1992). *Soziologie. Untersuchung über die Formen der Vergesellschaftung. GSG 11.* Frankfurt am Main: Suhrkamp.

———. 1989. Über sociale Differenzierung. In *Aufsätze 1887–1890. Über sociale Differenzierung. die Probleme der Geschichtsphilosophie (1892). GSG 2*, ed. Georg Simmel, 109–296. Frankfurt am Main: Suhrkamp.

———. 1992. Skizze einer Willenstheorie. In *Aufsätze und Abhandlungen 1894–1900. GSG 5*, ed. Georg Simmel, 130–144. Frankfurt am Main: Suhrkamp.

———. 1995. Die Religion. In *Philosophie der Mode. Die Religion. Kant und Goethe. Schopenhauer und Nietzsche. GSG 10*, ed. Georg Simmel, 39–118. Frankfurt am Main: Suhrkamp.

———. 2002. *Französisch- und italienischsprachige Veröffentlichungen. Mélanges de philosophie relativiste. GSG 19.* Frankfurt am Main: Suhrkamp.

Spitz, Jean-Fabien. 2005. *Le moment républicain en France.* Paris: Gallimard.

Steiner, Philippe. 2011. *Durkheim and the Birth of Economic Sociology.* Princeton: Princeton University Press.

Strenski, Ivan. 1997. *Durkheim and the Jews of France.* Chicago: University of Chicago Press.

Surkis, Judith. 2011. *Sexing the Citizen.* In *Morality and Masculinity in France, 1870–1920.* Cornell: Cornell University Press.

Swartz, David. 1997. *The Sociology of Pierre Bourdieu.* Chicago: University of Chicago Press.

Tarde, Gabriel. 1874. *Les possibles.* Bibliothèque de la ville de Lyon: Fonds Lacassagne.

———. 1881. La psychologie en économie politique. *Revue Philosophique de la France et de l'étranger* 6: 232–249; 401–418.

———. 1890a (1903). *La philosophie pénale.* Paris: A. Storck & Cie.

———. 1890b (1912). *Penal Philosophy.* Boston: Little Brown, and Company.

———. 1893. Questions sociales. *Revue Philosophique de la France et de l'étranger* 18: 618–638.

———. 1895a. *Les lois de l'imitation.* Paris: Alcan.

———. 1895b (1903). *The Laws of Imitation.* New York: Henry Holt and Company.

———. 1898 (2000). *Social Laws: An Outline of Sociology.* Kitchener: Batoche Books.

———. 1898a. *Les lois sociales. Esquisse d'une sociologie.* Paris: Alcan.

———. 1898b. *La logique sociale.* Paris: Alcan.

———. 1901. La réalité sociale. *Revue Philosophique de la France et de l'étranger* 26: 455–477.

———. 1904. L'inter-psychologie. *Archives d'anthropologie criminelle, de criminologie et de psychologie normale et pathologique* XIX: 537–564.

Utz, Richard, and Urs-Peter Krämer. 1994. Die Intrige: Der geheime Streit in der Triade. *Simmel Newsletter* 4: 20–41.

Veyne, Paul. 1983. *Les Grecs ont-ils cru à leurs mythes? Essai sur l'imagination constituante*. Paris: Seuil.

Vogt, W. Paul. 1976. The Uses of Studying Primitives: A Note on the Durkheimians, 1890–1940. *History and Theory* 15: 33–44.

Wacquant, Loic J.D. 1989. Towards a Reflexive Sociology: A Workshop with Pierre Bourdieu. *Sociological Theory* 7: 26–63.

Waszek, Norbert. 2002. La 'tendance à la sociabilité' (Trieb der Geselligkeit) chez Christian Garve. *Revue Germanique Internationale* 18: 71–85.

Watts Miller, William. 1996. *Durkheim, Morals and Modernity*. Bristol: UCL Press.

Weber, Max. 1922. *Wirtschaft und Gesellschaft*. Tübingen: J.C.B. Mohr (Paul Siebeck).

Weiner, Annette B. 1980. Reproduction: A Replacement for Reciprocity. *American Ethnologist* 7: 71–86.

———. 1985. Inalienable Wealth. *American Ethnologist* 12: 210–228.

White, Harrison C. 1970. *Chains of Opportunity. System Models of Mobility in Organizations*. Cambridge: Harvard University Press.

———. 1992 (2008). *Identity and Control. How Social Formations Emerge*. Princeton: Princeton University Press.

———. 1995. Passages réticulaires, acteurs et grammaire de la domination. *Revue Française de Sociologie* 36: 705–724.

White, Harrison C., Scott A. Boorman, and Ronald Breiger. 1976. Social Structure from Multiple Networks. I. Blockmodels of Roles and Positions. *The American Journal of Sociology* 81: 730–780.

Wiese, Leopold von. 1910. Neuere soziologische Literatur. *Archiv für Sozialwissenschaft und Sozialpolitik* 31: 882–907.

———. 1951/1952. Gurvitch' Beruf der Soziologie. *Kölner Zeitschrift für Soziologie* 4: 365–374.

Index[1]

A

[1] Note: Page number followed by 'n' refers to notes.

C. Papilloud, *Sociology through Relation*, Palgrave Studies in Relational Sociology, https://doi.org/10.1007/978-3-319-65073-9

G

H

I

R

S

Zeitfracht Medien GmbH
Ferdinand-Jühlke-Straße 7
99095 Erfurt, Deutschland
produktsicherheit@kolibri360.de